Learning from Experience

Learning from Experience

Minority Identities,
Multicultural Struggles

Paula M. L. Moya

UNIVERSITY OF CALIFORNIA PRESS
Berkeley · *Los Angeles* · *London*

Chapter 1 appeared previously in *Feminist Genealogies, Colonial Legacies, Democratic Futures,* edited by Jacqui Alexander and Chandra Talpade Mohanty (New York: Routledge, 1996). Chapter 2 appeared previously as "Chicana Feminism and Postmodernist Theory," *Signs* 26(2): 441–83. © 2001 by the University of Chicago. All rights reserved. An earlier version of chapter 3 appeared in *Hispanics/Latinos in the United States: Ethnicity, Race, and Gender,* edited by Jorge J. E. Garcia and Pablo de Greiff (New York: Routledge, 2000).

University of California Press
Berkeley and Los Angeles, California

University of California Press, Ltd.
London, England

Library of Congress Cataloging-in-Publication Data
Moya, Paula M. L.
    Learning from experience : minority identities, multicultural struggles / Paula M. L. Moya.
        p.   cm.
    Includes bibliographical references and index.
    ISBN 0–520-23013-2 (cloth : acid-free paper) —
ISBN 0–520-23014-0 (paper : acid-free paper)
    1. American literature — Mexican American authors — History and criticism — Theory, etc.
2. American literature — Women authors — History and criticism — Theory, etc.   3. American literature — 20th century — History and criticism — Theory, etc.   4. Feminism and literature — United States — History — 20th century.   5. Women and literature — United States — History — 20th century.
6. Mexican American women — Intellectual life.
7. Postmodernism (Literature) — United States.
8. Multiculturalism — United States.   9. Feminist theory — United States.   10. Minorities — United States.   I. Title.
PS153.M4 M69   2001
810.9'9287'0896872 — dc21   2001003857

Manufactured in the United States of America

10 09 08 07 06 05 04 03 02 01
10 9 8 7 6 5 4 3 2 1

The paper used in this publication meets the minimum requirements of ANSI/NISO Z39.48–1992 (RBB 1997) (*Permanence of Paper*).

For Halina Victoria and Eva María Lourdes

¿Arte por el arte? No, nunca. Arte para la vida, arte para el entendimiento, arte para la acción, arte para elegir entre los senderos en que continuamente se bifurca nuestra historia.

Este es mi credo. Y en las circunstancias por las que actualmente atraviesan nuestros países subdesarrollados, convulsos, urgidos de encontrar su nombre y su camino, la mayor parte de los intelectuales sustentan un credo semejante. . . . En los últimos tiempos se nos ha mostrado con una evidencia indudable que también estamos obligados a examinar aquello que se nos propone como dogma, a revisar nuestros mitos, a ejercitar nuestro sentido crítico.

(Art for art's sake? No, never. Art for life, art for understanding, art for action, art for choosing between those paths into which our history continually bifurcates.

This is my creed. And given the circumstances through which our underdeveloped countries are now passing — convulsed, pushed to find their name and their way — most intellectuals defend a similar creed. . . . Lately, it has become incontrovertibly evident that we also have an obligation to examine what has been presented to us as our dogma, to revise our myths, and to exercise our critical sense.)

Rosario Castellanos, "Rosario Castellanos
habla de Rosario Castellanos"

Contents

Acknowledgments

I have benefited greatly from the many friends and mentors who have stimulated my thinking and guided me through the process of writing this book. I am especially indebted to Satya Mohanty, Linda Martín Alcoff, and Michael Hames-García, all of whom have profoundly influenced the trajectory of my work. Indeed, were it not for Satya's original theorizing and his meticulous criticisms, Michael's insightful commentary and his steadfast friendship, and Linda's scholarly example and her affirmation of my ideas about identity, this book would not exist.

I have been fortunate to have found in my colleagues at Stanford a tremendous resource. The Feminist Studies Program and the Center for Comparative Studies in Race and Ethnicity (CCSRE) have provided supportive contexts for pursuing the kind of interdisciplinary work I am interested in. I am particularly grateful for the many conversations I have had with Al Camarillo, Estelle Freedman, Stephanie Fryberg, Hazel Markus, Rob Reich, and the other members of the Inequalities and Identities Workshop here at Stanford.

My colleagues and students in the English Department have been equally generous with their time and expertise. I am beholden to John Bender, David Halliburton, Shirley Brice Heath, Lora Romero, Ramón Saldívar, and Robert Warrior for commenting on various chapters of this book and providing me with much-needed mentoring. Sharon Holland has supported and influenced me in immeasurable ways. I hold her close to my heart. A casual conversation with Alex Woloch proved immensely valuable for my thinking about chapter five. Marcial Gonzalez, Ernesto Martinez, and Inger Pettersson have been extraordinarily generous students and friends: all commented on parts this manuscript and provided excellent research assistance. Erik Kruger, another valued student, provided much-appreciated help during the preparation of the index. I am grateful to Alyce Boster, Dagmar Logie, and the other members of the departmental staff for making the office a humane and enjoyable place to work.

I would also like to thank my colleagues from across the country who commented on parts of this manuscript or helped me in crucially important ways. These wonderful people include Jacqui Alexander, Bernadette Andrea, Martin Bernal, Junot Díaz, Charlene Gima, Jorge Gracia, Mickie Grover, Shuchi Kapila, Josephine Mendez-Negrete, Eduardo Mendieta, Chandra Talpade Mohanty, Ben Olguín, José David Saldívar, Rosaura Sánchez, and William Wilkerson. I am deeply obliged to Helena María Viramontes for writing such a wonderful novel. Also, I want to thank Ted Estess, Lois Parkinson Zamora, and Robert Zaretsky for their friendship, and for what they taught me while I was an undergraduate at the University of Houston.

I also value the enthusiasm and professionalism of the team at the University of California Press who shepherded this book into existence. Special thanks are due to Linda Norton, whose continuing faith in my work is deeply appreciated, and to Erika Büky, who did more than she needed to do to accommodate my schedule. I extend my heartfelt esteem to Susan Carter, Estrella Fichter, Nicole Hayward, Randy Heyman, Leslie Larson, and Lynn Meinhardt.

I would like to give special thanks to my family. My parents and my brother and sisters have always supported me and shown a keen interest in my work. My daughters, to whom this book is dedicated, provide me with love and motivation to keep doing the work I set out to do. I hope they find this work to be worthy of them.

My greatest debt is to my husband, Tim Young. A partner in the true sense of the word, he has read and commented on every chapter in this book. His editorial advice has been tremendously valuable; his emotional support, however, is priceless.

Identity in the Academy and Beyond

When I was a candidate on the academic job market in 1996, I had an interview with the dean at a leading university in the South. During that interview, the dean asked me whether I would be comfortable teaching in the English department. On one level, his question made no sense. After all, my first language is English, and I express myself most articulately in that language. Additionally, I received my Ph.D. training in an English department at a major research university (a fact of which he would have been aware), and the literature I write about is composed primarily in English. Also, the job for which I was interviewing had been posted by the English department at his university. Why, then, wouldn't I be comfortable teaching in the English department? On another level, however, I understood exactly why he asked me that question. I am, after all, Chicana. Moreover, since this dean had already mentioned that he was a transplanted Texan, I understood that whatever else he knew, he would have known that some Chicana/os speak Spanish as a first language. Add to this the fact that he would have been aware that the literature I work on is primarily written by Chicana/o and Latina/o authors, and one can begin to reconstruct the reasoning behind his question. He may have presumed that my first language was Spanish and that the literature I work on is written in Spanish. If this were the case, wouldn't the kind of work I do more properly belong in a Spanish department, or, perhaps, an ethnic studies program?

The dean's question about my comfort was thus really a question of belonging and legitimacy. It may have been a question not only about *where* in the academy work like mine belonged, but more profoundly, about *whether* it belonged in the academy at all. Although it was clear to me during that campus visit that the English department very much wanted to make an appointment in U.S. Latina/o literature, it also became evident during my meeting with the dean that he was not as enthusiastic about the appointment as the department was. Apparently, the dean needed to be convinced that the kind of scholarship I was doing was worth the dedication of a faculty billet. He needed to know that the kind of work I do is important.

This experience was just one of many that has revealed to me the complex nexus of identity, experience, knowledge, and belonging that has concerned generations of Chicana/o writers and scholars before me. Some thirty years after the founding of the first Chicana/o studies programs, the cultural productions of Chicana/os still do not occupy a secure place within academia. It is a predicament that mirrors the situation of Americans of Mexican descent who, some 150 years after the signing of the Treaty of Guadalupe Hidalgo, still do not occupy a secure place within the imagined community of the United States. It occurs to me now that the range of responses I might have given to the dean would have invoked at least one of the various strategies of cultural negotiation engaged in by writers such as Juan Seguín, Mariano Vallejo, Maria Amparo Ruíz de Burton, Cleofas Jaramillo, Fray Angelico Chávez, Jovita González, Américo Paredes, and more contemporary Chicana/o writers.[1] Like my *antepasados,* I found myself in the midst of a negotiation where the terms were not ones I had agreed to. Yet, also like them, I was at a disadvantage; because the dean was in a position of power, he could keep me from taking for granted my existence within the proverbial ivory tower. The experience thus affirmed for me the continuing necessity of justifying a scholarly focus on the lives and experiences of Americans of Mexican descent. My need to justify my interest in the literature of Chicana/os and other marginalized people has surely provided much of the motivation for this scholarly project.

One of my goals in this book is to provide a reconstructed universalist justification for the kind of work being done by myself and other ethnic studies scholars. In the course of making an extended theoretical

---

1. Over the last fifteen years a number of scholars, some of whom have been supported by the Recovering the U.S. Hispanic Literary Heritage Project, have done valuable work in revealing and theorizing the complex negotiations such figures undertook. See esp. Gutiérrez and Padilla; Limón; Padilla, *My History, Not Yours;* Padilla, Introduction; Rosaura Sánchez, *Telling Identities;* Rosaura Sánchez and Pita.

argument for the epistemic significance of identity, I demonstrate that studying the texts and lived experiences of Chicana/os (and other marginalized people) is necessary to construct a more objective understanding of the (social and economic) world we live in. I show that while the experiences of Chicana/os are admittedly subjective and particular, the knowledge that is gained from a focused study of their lives can have general implications for all Americans. The texts and lived experiences of Chicana/os and other marginalized people are rich sources of frequently overlooked information about our shared world.

I approach my task by elaborating and further specifying the details of a postpositivist realist theory of identity that takes seriously the epistemic consequences of identities.[2] This theoretical approach, which is only now emerging in the field of literary criticism, theorizes the concepts of identity, experience, and knowledge in ways that go beyond understandings of those concepts widely accepted within the humanities today. It makes pointed departures from academic postmodernist conceptions of identity even as it explicitly identifies and elaborates the epistemological presuppositions that many ethnic and lesbian, gay, and bisexual studies scholars already work with. My aim is thus to provide a theoretical clarification that affirms the work of some minority studies scholars even as it provokes others to rethink the usefulness of postmodernist theory.[3] As I show in chapter two, some ethnic studies scholars engage postmodernist theoretical frameworks even though they rely on assumptions that are recognizably realist. While their deployment of postmodernist precepts has had the positive effect of garnering for them a certain amount of academic recognition, it has ultimately undermined the cogency of their scholarly projects. Meanwhile, those ethnic studies scholars who avoid postmodernism in favor of realist or materialist approaches have been frequently marginalized and their theoretical insights ignored or misin-

2. The postpositivist realist theory of identity emerged from a collective of scholars working together in and around Cornell University during the 1990s. The scholars who initially came together did so partly in response to the excesses of the widespread skepticism and constructivism in literary theory and cultural studies, and partly because we were interested in formulating a complex and rigorous theory of identity that could be put to work in the service of progressive politics. I provide a fuller account of the theory later in this introduction, as well as throughout the chapters of this book. See also Moya and Hames-García; Mohanty, *Literary Theory*, esp. chap. 7.

3. Some books on ethnic identity that have a generally realist orientation toward identity, but that do not label themselves as such, include Flores, *Divided Borders;* Gracia; Oboler; and Rosaura Sánchez, *Telling Identities*. Books in lesbian, gay, and bisexual studies that similarly resonate with a realist epistemology are D'Emilio and Freedman; Bulkin, Pratt, and Smith.

terpreted. At best, such work is considered by postmodernist critics who serve as academic gatekeepers to be theoretically naive; at worst, it is labeled essentialist and summarily dismissed.[4] Through my work, I hope to contribute to a situation in which advocates of ethnic studies can reverse this marginalizing trend, and argue successfully for the general epistemic significance of their particular scholarly projects.

THE POLITICS OF IDENTITY

At stake in debates about identity is the legitimacy (political and intellectual) of a range of identity-based initiatives that have the potential to materially affect the lives of marginalized people in the United States. Political issues like affirmative action and bilingual ballots, educational issues such as multicultural education and textbook selection, and intellectual projects in the areas of ethnic, women's, and gay, lesbian, and bisexual studies, are all justified by a logic of identity. For example, if there were no sociologically distinct and identifiable groups of people such as "African Americans" who can be shown to have been systematically denied access over a long period of time to economic and educational opportunities, there would be little reason to institute a government-sponsored program to redress those historical exclusions. Similarly, if it were impossible to identify relatively distinct groups of people who differ from each other in culturally significant ways, there would be no logic behind multicultural education. And finally, if there did not exist entire groups of people such as "Chicana/os" or "women" whose histories and accomplishments have been systematically ignored or distorted by previous generations of scholars, then there would be no reason for present-day scholars to devote themselves to a focused study of the histories, socioeconomic situations, political movements, or literary and cultural productions of those groups.[5] The concept of identity is at the heart of each such educational and political project.

Recently, such projects have come under increased scrutiny in the

---

4. My own work has provoked this reaction. For example, one anonymous reviewer of my article in *Signs* (reprinted as chapter two in this book) declared that my work follows "a strategy that echoes the moves of Chicano nationalists" and that my discussions "lack sophistication and demonstrate that the author is out-of-touch with current lines of inquiry being developed in the field of Chicana and women of color feminist theory." Fortunately, two other readers (one of whom, I later found out, is a Chicana feminist) and the editorial board of *Signs* disagreed with this assessment.

5. Whenever a scholar undertakes to study something, she must have a conception of what her object of study is. In the case of the ethnic studies scholar, who takes as her object

political sphere and are being attacked precisely because they are identity-based initiatives. For example, conservative political pundits, like the neoconservative minorities whose writings I discuss in chapter three, argue that racial identity is becoming less important as a factor in determining life chances, and that government-sponsored redress movements premised on the salience of racial or gender identities have the negative effect of obscuring what is common to all Americans. Several have advocated the abandonment of the whole enterprise of determining who belongs to what racial group or what that belonging might mean to the lives of group members; they argue that paying attention to racial identities will unnecessarily balkanize our society and obscure the ways in which we are all universally human. Neoconservative minorities like Richard Rodriguez and Shelby Steele further argue against multicultural educational reform efforts on the grounds that cultural difference is not epistemically or morally significant and should be eradicated through cultural assimilation. Finally, as detractors of ethnic studies programs, they consider scholarly projects that focus on the lives and cultural productions of racialized minority groups in the United States to be excessively narrow in scope and, as a result, virtually useless for helping us to understand the world we live in. What politically conservative opponents of identity-based initiatives generally share is a notion that "difference" is overrated and that what Americans really need to do is work toward a common identity.

Such critiques of identity-based initiatives coming from the political right raise some serious questions. Does a focus on particular lives preclude the production of a more general knowledge? Does paying attention to racial identities always obscure our universal humanity? Or is it

---

of inquiry groups of people such as "Chicana/os," the concept of identity provides the organizing principle that justifies her scholarly focus. Unless "Chicana/os" exist as a sociologically distinct group with identifiable characteristics that can be specified and described, and unless studying them will help the scholar understand something important about them and the world in which they are constituted as "Chicana/os," it makes little sense to engage in studying them as "Chicana/os." What would be the purpose of studying their conditions of existence, their cultural practices, or their literary productions unless doing so might yield information that contributes to the scholar's understanding of herself, the others with whom she interacts, or the world in which she lives? And how can she study that group without a good conception of who they are and where they fit into existing social structures? The need to have a good conception of her object of study thus brings her right back to the question of identity, and makes urgent the necessity of having an adequate theory guiding her as she goes about determining both who "Chicana/os" are and what aspects of their lives are most crucial to her study.

possible to understand the concept of identity in a complex enough way so that an understanding of our particularity contributes to an understanding of the way in which we are all universally human? For the ethnic studies scholar, the necessity of answering these questions is made more urgent by recent developments in the academy that further undermine the concept of identity from a somewhat different angle. Especially within the humanities, the prevalence of postmodernist thought has created an intellectual atmosphere in which invocations of identity, appeals to experience, and claims to truth have been judged to be both theoretically naive and ideologically suspect. For example, in her essay " 'Experience,' " feminist historian Joan Scott maintains that appeals to experience serve to weaken "the critical thrust of histories of difference" because they "take as self-evident the identities of those whose experience is being documented" (24–25). According to Scott, the evidence of experience precludes, rather than enables, a critical analysis of the constitutive workings of the discursive systems through which identities (and experiences) are produced (25). Given its ideological function, Scott is tempted to abandon the word *experience* altogether (37). Since she cannot do this, she opts to put it in scare quotes in order to render its historically contingent and linguistically constructed nature more visible. She concludes by suggesting that what is needed is "not the reproduction and transmission of knowledge said to be arrived at through experience, but the analysis of the production of that knowledge itself. . . . Experience is, in this approach, not the origin of our explanation, but that which we want to explain" (37–38). Thus, in her efforts to establish the correct causal (and historical) relationship between discourse, experience, subjectivity, and identity, Scott effectively delegitimizes experience as an authoritative source for knowledge.[6] Critics holding views like Scott's have managed to dominate academic discussions of identity insofar as they have found theoretical support for their position in French poststructuralism.[7]

The significance of French poststructuralism for the concept of iden-

6. For critiques of Scott's position see Alcoff, "Politics of Postmodern Feminism"; Stone-Mediatore; Wilkerson; Zammito. For an account of experience that responds to the challenges posed by Scott's essay, see Mohanty, *Literary Theory*, esp. 202–16.

7. Poststructuralism is a philosophical movement that emerged in France in the late 1960s as a critique of phenomenology and structuralism. It is primarily associated with theorists (who were themselves trained by phenomenologists and structuralists) like Jacques Derrida, Julia Kristeva, Jacques Lacan, Michel Foucault, and Roland Barthes. Although poststructuralism includes a variety of perspectives deriving from the different theories of its principal thinkers, it is characterized by an opposition to structuralist principles (condemned as "totalizing" and "deterministic") and a focus on (sometimes a celebration of)

tity is exemplified by the way deconstruction has been applied within social and cultural theory.[8] Postmodernist critics inspired by deconstruction, for example, have tended to analogize and thus understand social relations with reference to linguistic structures. The deconstructionist thesis about the indeterminacy and indeed arbitrariness of linguistic reference leads many U.S. literary theorists and cultural critics to understand concepts like experience and identity (which are fundamentally about social relations) as similarly indeterminate and hence epistemically unreliable. Such critics argue that inasmuch as meaning is constituted by systems of differences purely internal to the languages through which humans interpret the world, meaning is inescapably relative. Meaning is never fully present because it is constituted by the endless possibilities of what it is not, and is therefore always at least partially deferred. Because meaning exists only in a shifting and unstable relationship to the webs of signification through which it comes into being, and because humans have no access to anything meaningful outside these sometimes disparate webs, there can be no "objective" truth. The desire for "truth" or "objective" knowledge is therefore seen as resting on a naively representational theory of language that relies on the following mistaken assumptions: first, that there is a one-to-one correspondence between signs and their extralinguistic real-world referents; and second, that some kind of intrinsic meaning dwells in those real-world referents, independent of human thought or action. Knowledge, insofar as it is mediated by language, cannot be said to be objective.

As a result of the influence of poststructuralism, the terms of the debate in the academy regarding selves and cultural identities have shifted considerably. Broadly speaking, postmodernist scholars in the United States who have been influenced by poststructuralist theory have undermined conventional understandings of identity by discounting the possibility of objective knowledge. Instead of asking how we know who we are, poststructuralist-inspired critics are inclined to suggest that we

---

difference and multiplicity. It has been credited with the textualizing of the social world, the critique of subject-centered thought, and the demise of grand narratives and general truth claims. It is distinguishable from postmodernism insofar as it is an "essentially theoretical shift, not a claim that anything in the external world had changed to necessitate a new theory" (Calhoun 114). The significance of poststructuralism for my discussion is that postmodernism, as a theoretical and/or critical position, derives substantially from poststructuralism (Calhoun 100).

8. Several paragraphs in this introduction (including the following two) have been adapted from my introduction to Moya and Hames-García, *Reclaiming Identity*.

cannot know; rather than investigating the nature of the self, they are likely to suggest that it has no nature. The self, the argument goes, can have no nature because subjectivity does not exist outside the grammatical structures that govern our thought; rather, it is *produced by* those structures. Because subjects exist only in relation to ever evolving webs of signification, and because they constantly differ from themselves as time passes and meanings change, the self — as a unified, stable, and knowable entity existing prior to or outside language — is merely a fiction of thought. Social and cultural identities, it is argued, are similarly fictitious because the selves they claim to designate cannot be pinned down, fixed, or definitively identified. Moreover, identities are not simply fictitious — they are dangerous. They are dangerous precisely because they treat fictions as facts and cover over the fissures, contradictions, and differences internal to the social construct we call a "self." Inasmuch as the desire to identify ourselves and others remains complicit with idealist assumptions about a fully knowable world — a world that can be described, hierarchized, named, and mastered — identity as a concept will serve oppressive and reductive ideological functions. Under this view, to speak of identities as "real" is to naturalize them and to disguise the structures of power involved in their production and maintenance.

Cultural critics drawn to postmodernism have thus seen themselves as articulating the conditions of possibility for a new kind of political practice, one based on the impossibility of objective knowledge.[9] Although

---

9. Postmodernism is a more diffuse, and so harder to define, cultural phenomenon than poststructuralism. Most critics agree that it can be characterized in at least three (analytically separable) ways: (1) as an aesthetic practice; (2) as a historical stage in the development of late capitalism; and (3) as a theoretical and/or critical position. In this volume, I am not concerned with postmodernism as either a historical period or an aesthetic movement. While I will describe the (often implicit) epistemological underpinnings of "postmodernist" theoretical conceptions of identity, I am aware that postmodernist theory does not constitute a unified intellectual movement. Rather, it embodies a range of theoretical and political practices that emphasize the unstable and contingent nature of discursively produced meaning. Moreover, the arguments of many prominent figures in contemporary feminist, postcolonial, antiracist, and queer theory (some of whom reject the terms I am using to describe them) share important commonalities; they are characterized by a strong epistemological skepticism, a valorization of flux and mobility, and a general suspicion of, or hostility toward, all normative and/or universalist claims. It is this theoretical bias, recognizable in much of the work done in the humanities today, that I am pointing to with the use of the adjective *postmodernist*. Readers interested in learning more about postmodernist theory and the critiques to which it has been subjected should consult Calhoun, esp. chap. 4.; Eagleton; McGowan; Nicholson, esp. the introduction; Nicholson and Seidman, esp. the introduction. Readers interested in learning more about postmodernism as a historical or cultural phenomenon should see Anderson; Best and Kellner; Harvey; Jameson; Waugh.

they employ a variety of methodological approaches, they unite in their efforts to expose the lie of universalizing systems that, in the process of categorizing, normalize some people and practices while rendering others abnormal or deviant. Such critics have seen the epistemological and political dangers of essentialist conceptions of identity; in the absence of attractive alternatives, postmodernist deconstructions of identity seem to be the safest, most progressive way to go.[10] For example, French philosopher Michel Foucault, whose genealogies have influenced the work of generations of postmodernist scholars, explores "the history of the relations between thought and truth" in order to weaken the hegemonic power of our present-day truths by revealing them as discursively constructed and historically contingent ("Concern for Truth" 256).[11] According to his interpreters, Foucault's refusal of the possibility of a truth that can transcend a particular discursive formation is motivated by liberatory as well as epistemological concerns.[12] The idea is that when we can see our present-day truths as socially constructed and historically contingent we will be free to imagine new, less repressive social practices and ways of interacting.

The postmodernist approach to identity should thus be understood partially as a corrective to a prior social and intellectual tendency toward essentialism.[13] By refusing to privilege any one viewpoint or valorize any one identity, postmodernist theorists hold open the possibility that previously subjugated knowledges can become manifest; previously subordinated identities can become intelligible. For instance, in her influential essay "A Manifesto for Cyborgs," feminist theorist Donna Haraway heralds the arrival of a "cyborg world" in which "people are not afraid . . .

10. It would be an impossible task to determine the true motives of all critics who attack identity. A generous reading demands that we take postmodernist critics at their word, and that we accept the idea that they believe that all but the most strategic claims to identity are essentialist and therefore politically pernicious. A less generous reading, but one that also deserves consideration, is that the charge of essentialism might also result from a racist counterstance to the agency of newly politicized minorities.

11. See also Foucault, "Truth and Power"; "Two Lectures"; *Archaeology of Knowledge*.

12. For a discussion of how Foucault has influenced debates about epistemology, see Alcoff, *Real Knowing*, chaps. 4 and 5.

13. When I refer to essentialism, I am referring to the notion that individuals or groups have an immutable and discoverable "essence" — a basic, invariable, and presocial nature. As a theoretical concept, essentialism expresses itself through the tendency to see *one* social category (class, gender, race, sexuality, etc.) as determinate in the last instance for the cultural identity of the individual or group in question. As a political strategy, essentialism has had both liberatory and reactionary effects.

of permanently partial identities and contradictory standpoints" (196). Haraway's contention is that by disrupting mythic unities (like women and nature) through mechanisms involving irony, blasphemy, and the refusal of a privileged perspective from which to view the world, critics maximize their ability to unmask the repressive social practices that contribute to the construction and domination of those beings produced as "women." According to Haraway, "the political struggle is to see from both perspectives at once because each reveals both dominations and possibilities unimaginable from the other vantage point" (196).[14] From this perspective, the postmodernist denial of objectivity seems profoundly liberating: it appears to offer a way of apprehending the world that acknowledges the existence and validity of alternative perspectives, practices, identities, and knowledges.

The success of postmodernist theories of identity is perhaps best exemplified by the tremendous intellectual influence of scholars such as Judith Butler, a postmodernist feminist philosopher who bases her critique of identity on the poststructuralist deconstruction of the subject. In *Gender Trouble,* the book through which she has had the most influence upon academic theorizations of identity, Butler understands selves (and the subjectivities through which they come into being) as having no existence apart from the discourses that produce them. She recognizes the existence of subjects, but portrays them as existing only as a result of the grammar through which they are mobilized. She admits of no aspects of the self that are prior or external to discourse, and acknowledges no "doer behind the deed" in the sense of an intentional agent who exercises effective choices and displays discernible intentions (25). According to the line of reasoning she follows in *Gender Trouble,* the subject is not an authorial agent, a conscious intender, or the bearer of natural attributes. Rather, the subject is the site of a complex and contingent network of discourses and social practices that are seen as constructing it. Furthermore, in characteristic postmodernist fashion, Butler extends the deconstruction of the subject to call into question the very possibility of identities based on the social categories of gender and race. Because the subject has been

14. Analogously, influential feminist philosopher Judith Butler implies in her book *Gender Trouble* that previously unintelligible identities will be revealed when we dislodge current constellations of identity by exposing, through parody, their constructed and contingent constitution. She writes: "The task here is not to celebrate each and every new possibility qua possibility, but to redescribe those possibilities that *already exist,* but which exist within cultural domains designated as culturally unintelligible and impossible" (148–49, emphasis added).

exposed as an effect of discourse or a mask for social practices, gender and racial identities are no longer taken to be essential or foundational, but are now revealed to be "arbitrary," "fictive," and even politically "dangerous." As a result, identity has been denaturalized, put under erasure, or — as the subtitle of Butler's book announces — subverted.[15]

Thinkers like Butler assume that the problem lies not only in the way we have conceived of identity, but in the very existence of categories that are seen as logically prior to and constitutive of identity. Their critiques focus on these categories because access to sociopolitical power and material resources has historically been conditioned by our social identities and by how well we have been able to trade on them. Thus, identities have been central to the oppression of entire groups of people as well as to individual and group efforts to shift their status relative to others in the same society. The political force of arguments like Butler's thus derives from the presumption that if we can do away with categories of identity — that is, if we can "subvert" them — we will no longer benefit, or be denied benefits, on the basis of the identities we used to have.[16]

This is the political and theoretical context within which my entry into the debate about identity must be located. And, although the general

15. See especially the last chapter of *Gender Trouble*, where Butler argues in favor of denaturalizing identities: "The critical task for feminism is not to establish a point of view outside of constructed identities; that conceit is the construction of an epistemological model that would disavow its own cultural location and, hence, promote itself as a global subject, a position that deploys precisely the imperialist strategies that feminism ought to criticize. The critical task is, rather, to affirm the local possibilities of intervention through participating in precisely those practices of repetition that constitute identity and, therefore, present the immanent possibility of contesting them. . . . The task is not whether to repeat, but how to repeat or, indeed, to repeat and, through a radical proliferation of gender, to *displace* the very gender norms that enable the repetition itself" (147, 148).

16. For support of this claim, see Butler's analysis of the New Bedford rape case at the end of "Contingent Foundations." In her deconstruction of a question the defense attorney asked the rape victim, Butler concludes that the real culprit of the crime is the "category of sex." She writes: "Here sex is a category, but not merely a representation; it is a principle of production, intelligibility, and regulation which enforces a violence and rationalizes it after the fact. The very terms by which the violation is explained enact the violation, and concede that the violation was under way before it takes the empirical form of a criminal act. . . . As a category that effectively produces the political meaning of what it describes, 'sex' here works its silent 'violence' in regulating what is and is not designatable" (19). I see two problems with Butler's analysis. The first is that by focusing on the relationship between the rape and discourse ("The very terms by which the violation is explained enact the violation, . . ."), Butler misrepresents the causal nature of the crime. She presumes, but never shows, that the categories she excoriates (sex and identity) determine that such violations will inevitably occur. It is this unsupported presumption that underlies her claim that "the violation was under way before it takes the empirical form of a criminal act." Meanwhile, the agency (not

political aims of postmodernist critics diverge from those of neoconservative minorities, the theoretical framework postmodernists employ dove-
tails with the neoconservative minority critique of the epistemic value of
identity. The necessity of affirming the significance of identity is thus a
project that confronts any cultural critic attempting to work within the
area of ethnic studies. Over the course of this book, I put pressure on various neoconservative minority and postmodernist theorists' claims in an
effort to test the political and epistemological adequacy of the assumptions they employ. Contra neoconservative minorities, I show that while
they are justified in their efforts to identify a core of humanity which is
universal to all people, they make a serious mistake when they identify
that core with a historically and culturally particular model of humanity.
Against postmodernist theorists, I show that the extreme linguistic constructivism informing postmodernist conceptions of identity impedes
rather than enables the achievement of the liberatory political goals they
claim as their own. Through an elaboration of the postpositivist realist
theory of identity, I demonstrate that effective political agency is best
located in the project of examining and explaining, rather than dismissing or subverting, identity.

THE POSTPOSITIVIST REALIST THEORY OF IDENTITY

The postpositivist realist theory of identity I elaborate in this book is an
adaptation and extension of the epistemological framework known as
philosophical realism. The postpositivist version of realism I defend in this
book emerges partly from within the philosophy of science and from ana-
lytic philosophy more generally, and is particularly indebted to the work
of Charles Peirce, W. V. O. Quine, Donald Davidson, Hilary Putnam, and
Richard Boyd. While disagreement exists among those who would call
themselves realists, the most sophisticated versions of realism today entail
a postpositivist conception of objectivity, together with the anti-idealist
thesis that the world exceeds humans' mental conceptions of it.[17] In using

---

to mention responsibility) of the men involved is erased; she represents them as mere
"effects" of discourse, as subjects mobilized through the grammar of the discourse that has
"produced" them. The second problem is that by focusing on the words spoken by the
defense attorney, Butler unwittingly silences the victim and ignores her experience of the
rape.

    17. For an exceptionally clear exposition on what makes a theory realist, see Collier,
esp. 6–7. See also R. N. Boyd, "How to Be a Moral Realist"; Alcoff, "Who's Afraid of
Identity Politics?"

realism to illuminate the theoretical and political significance of identity, I develop and extend the work of the literary theorist Satya Mohanty, who was the first to bring an explicitly realist approach to bear on the consideration of cultural identities ("Epistemic Status").

First and foremost, realism about identity involves a commitment to the idea that identities refer outward — albeit in partial and occasionally inaccurate ways — to the social world within which they emerge. Contra postmodernist theorists, who argue that the relationship between identities and the "real" or "material realm" is arbitrary, I argue that the "real" is causally relevant to our epistemic endeavors (including the formation of our identities) because it shapes and limits our knowledge-generating experiences. It is on the basis of this precept that I argue that humans, working from within their particular social locations, *can* develop reliable knowledge about the world. But simply because I look to the "evidence of experience" does not mean that I am a naive empiricist; I do not hope to simply flip the poststructuralist critique on its head and return to an uncritical belief in the possibility of theoretically unmediated knowledge. Rather, consistent with a generally postpositivist realist orientation, I refuse the terms through which postmodernists have defined concepts such as "identity" and "experience." I understand identities to be socially significant and context-specific ideological constructs that nevertheless refer in non-arbitrary (if partial) ways to verifiable aspects of the social world. Moreover, I contend that it is precisely because identities have a referential relationship to the world that they are politically and epistemically important: indeed, identities instantiate the links between individuals and groups and central organizing principles of our society. Consequently, an examination of individual identities can provide important insights about fundamental aspects of U.S. society.

An important feature of the postpositivist realism I defend in this book is a rethinking of the idea of objectivity. Just as the postmodernist dismissal of identity is based on a denial of the possibility of objectivity, so my realist reclaiming of identity is based on a reaffirmation of the possibility of (postpositivist) objectivity. The reason postmodernists deny the possibility of objectivity is that they have an impoverished view of what can count as objective. For postmodernists (as for positivists), objective knowledge is knowledge that is completely free of theoretically mediated bias. And since postmodernists rightly conclude that there is no such thing as a context-transcendent, subject-independent, and theoretically unmediated knowledge, they therefore conclude that there can be no such thing as objective knowledge. Postmodernist literary critic

Barbara Herrnstein Smith, for example, employs a positivist conception of objectivity in her response to feminist legal scholar Robin West. In that response, Smith understands the "rhetoric of objectivism" as involving "the invocation of self-evident truth and objective fact, of intrinsic value and absolute right, of that which is universal, total, and transcendent" (*Belief and Resistance* 5). Smith later defends a standard for evaluating theories that is similar, in some crucial ways, to a postpositivist conception of objectivity, suggesting that theories can be "found better or worse than others in relation to measures such as applicability, coherence, connectibility, and so forth." Crucially, however, she notes that these "measures are not objective in the classic sense, since they depend on matters of perspective, interpretation, and judgment, and will vary under different circumstances." Like the positivist, Smith assumes that any standard for deciding between competing theories or positions that involves matters of perspective, interpretation, and judgment must be, by definition, "non-'objective'" (77–78).[18]

Defenders of a *post*positivist conception of objectivity, by contrast, stake out a less absolutist and more theoretically productive position. As a realist, I conceive of objectivity as an ideal of inquiry necessarily involving theoretical bias and interest, rather than as a condition of absolute and achieved certainty that is context transcendent, subject independent, and free of theoretical bias. I can thus assert (without contradiction) both that (1) all observation and knowledge is theory mediated (that is, mediated by language, bias, or theoretical presuppositions — as, indeed, postmodernists argue) *and* that (2) a theory-mediated objective knowledge is both possible and desirable. Because I have given up the dream of transcendence, I understand objective knowledge as an ongoing process involving the careful analysis of the different kinds of subjective or theoretical bias and interest through which humans apprehend the world. Rather than trying to free my inquiry from bias, I work to bring into view the presuppositions I am working with, as well as to distinguish "those biases that are limiting or counterproductive from those that are in fact necessary for knowledge, that are epistemically productive and

18. Unfortunately, because Herrnstein Smith lacks a complex theory of reference, she is unable to fully exploit the implications of her insight regarding the epistemically normative significance of "applicability, coherence, and connectibility." After all, in order for a theory to be "applicable" or "connectible" it must be applicable or connectible *to* — that is, *with reference to* — something outside. As long as Smith retains her extreme and limited notions of objectivity and reference, she will be limited to the defensive posture she adopts in *Belief and Resistance* and will be unable to develop further even the contingent standards she thinks are necessary for deciding between different theories or political or ethical positions.

useful" (S. P. Mohanty, "Can Our Values Be Objective?").[19] Moreover, by conceiving of objectivity as an ideal of inquiry rather than an achieved condition, I am able to avoid one of the more familiar traps of postmodernist epistemologies. Unlike postmodernist critics, who are so concerned about rejecting a (positivist) notion of objectivity that they are hardpressed to justify their theoretical and normative commitments, I justify my commitments with reference to a normative conception of the human good — one that I am willing to interrogate, and if necessary, revise.[20]

Realists can be further distinguished from postmodernists in that they replace a simple correspondence theory of truth with a more dialectical causal theory of reference in which linguistic terms (and identities) both shape our perceptions of and refer (in more or less partial and accurate ways) to causal features of a real world.[21] Because, for instance, I am willing to test my hypotheses and truth claims against the world, I can modify my beliefs in the light of new or more convincing evidence. I do not shy away from making truth claims, but (following C. S. Peirce) I understand those claims to be "fallibilistic" — that is, like even the best discoveries of the natural sciences, open to revision on the basis of new or relevant information. In fact, it is my realist willingness to admit the (in principle, endless) possibility of error in the quest for objective knowledge that enables me to avoid positivist assumptions about certainty and unrevisability that inform the (postmodernist) skeptic's doubts about the possibility of arriving at a more accurate account of the world. Just as it is possible to be wrong about one's experience, I contend, so it is possible to arrive at more accurate interpretations of it.[22] The result is a theoretically productive approach that enables a richer analysis of the different kinds of subjective or theoretical bias or interest involved in projects of knowledge production.

19. For a fuller discussion of postpositivist objectivity, see Mohanty, *Literary Theory,* esp. chap. 6.

20. When postmodernists do attempt to justify their theoretical and political commitments, they generally end up appealing to some kind of strategic essentialism or contingent foundation. However, as critics have shown, the problems with strategic essentialisms are manifold: they lack persuasive force; they frequently presume a system of values that has not been thoroughly interrogated; and they set up a "pernicious elitism and even vanguardism when [they operate] to divide the 'knowing' theorists who deploy identity strategically and the 'unknowing' activists who continue to believe in identity" (Alcoff, "Who's Afraid of Identity Politics?" 323). See also chapter two of this book.

21. For more on causal theories of reference, see R. N. Boyd, "Metaphor and Theory Change"; Devitt and Sterelny, esp. part 2; Field; Mohanty, *Literary Theory,* esp. 66–72; Putnam, "The Meaning of 'Meaning' "; Putnam, "Explanation and Reference."

22. For a fuller discussion of the relationship between error and objectivity, see Hau.

Another feature of my realist understanding of objectivity is a rejection of the positivist idea that objective knowledge should be sought by attempting to separate the realm of hard facts from the realm of values.[23] Because I understand that *all* knowledge is the product of particular kinds of social practice, I recognize the causal constraints placed by the social and natural world on what humans *can* know. Moreover, because humans' biologically and temporally limited bodies enable and constrain what we are able to think, feel, and believe and because our bodies are themselves subject to the (more or less regular) laws of the natural and social world, I know that what humans are able to think of as "good" is intimately related to (although not monocausally determined by) the social and natural "facts" of the world.[24] Consequently, humans' subjective and evaluative judgments are neither fundamentally "arbitrary" nor merely "conventional." Rather, they are based on structures of belief that can be justified (or not) with reference to their own and others' well-being. These judgments and beliefs have the potential to contribute to objective knowledge about the world.[25]

Postpositivist realism therefore provides an interpretive approach that resolves the dilemmas that attend absolutist conceptions of identity, objectivity, and knowledge, going beyond both dogmatic certainty and unyielding skepticism. Moreover, the postpositivist realist theory of identity is able to do what other theories of identity cannot. It can account for

23. For more on the realist position regarding the necessary interdependence of facts and values, see Collier, esp. chap. 6; Mohanty, *Literary Theory,* esp. chap. 7; Nguyen; Putnam, *Realism with a Human Face,* esp. chaps. 9–12; Putnam, *Reason, Truth, and History,* esp. chap. 6. See also my discussion of linguistic reference in chapter five.

24. Calhoun, whose epistemological approach is substantially similar to the postpositivist realist approach I advocate, provides a pithy example of how knowledge is tied to social practice when he says that "it is not imaginable that Marx would have developed his theory of capitalism had he lived in the ninth and not the nineteenth century" (86).

25. Some of my students, all of whom have been educated in a postmodernist academic climate, have occasionally objected to what they perceive as the judgmental or moralistic aspects of realism. When faced with this kind of objection, I remind them that the salient question is not *whether* to evaluate, but *how* to evaluate. Every moment of every day involves countless conscious and unconscious acts of evaluation: what to wear, what to eat, who to smile at, who to fear, who to associate with, who to avoid, who to date, who to hire, who to fire. For scholars, the daily judgments we make also involve who to read, who to cite, who to emulate, what claims to accept, what claims to reject, who to engage with, and who to ignore. By insisting on a reconsideration of our processes of critical evaluation, postpositivist realists are not asking cultural and literary critics to do anything that they do not already do. We are not even asking them to do something that they can avoid. Rather, we are striving to develop a theoretical and political practice that draws attention in a methodological way to the often-uninterrogated assumptions about other people's identities that structure all critics' scholarly and political choices.

the causal influence that categories of identity like race, sex, and socioeconomic status have on the formation of identity, even as it accounts for
how identities can adapt to changing historical circumstances. It is, I
argue, the sophisticated and nuanced theory of identity needed by ethnic
studies scholars who are moving into the twenty-first century.

THE ARGUMENT

I begin my extended theoretical argument in chapter one, "Postmodernism, Realism, and the Politics of Identity: Cherríe Moraga and
Chicana Feminism." I start by calling into question postmodernist theorists' ability to create the conditions necessary for the emergence of alternative perspectives and new voices. My reading of the work of influential
postmodernist feminists Judith Butler and Donna Haraway suggests that
the voices of so-called "others" — in this case, Chicana feminist Cherríe
Moraga — are as silenced by postmodernist theory as they have been by
an abstract individualist ideology that judges their views as "subjective"
and therefore epistemically unreliable. To the extent that these "others"
speak of being women, of being racialized, of seeking to understand (in
order to change) the world, postmodernist theorists tend to misinterpret,
ignore, or dismiss their ideas as theoretically naive. In the second section
of the chapter, I elaborate the details of a postpositivist realist theory of
identity that goes beyond essentialism by disclosing how identities are
grounded in the social categories of race, class, gender, and sexuality,
without being determined by them. I establish the link between identity
and social location as mediated through experience and argue that there
is an epistemic component to identity that enables us to read the world in
particular ways. Finally, I provide my own realist reading of Moraga, one
that is consistent with her "theory in the flesh." By resituating her work
within the cultural and historical conditions from which it emerged, I
show that Moraga's elaboration of a "theory in the flesh" gestures
toward a realist theory of identity. A realist reading of Moraga's work
presents a strong case for how and why the theoretical insights of women
of color are necessary for understanding fundamental aspects of United
States society.

In chapter two, "Chicana Feminism and Postmodernist Theory," I
deepen my critique of prevailing postmodernist theoretical tendencies by
examining their influence on theorizations of Chicana identity and subjectivity. I focus on the attempts of the Chicana theorists Norma Alarcón
and Chela Sandoval to rework an identity-based politics by incorporat-

ing and revising postmodernist deconstructions of the subject. I have found that these Chicana theorists demonstrate an ambivalent relationship to postmodernist theory even though they accept many of its presuppositions and claims. I argue that the presupposition of a fragmented subjectivity seriously limits these thinkers' efforts to theorize the agency of women of color. Norma Alarcón, for example, proposes a theory of subjectivity without attending to the question of identity. Consequently, while her theory of multiple subjectivities can account for the demonstrable fact that identities are not essential, self-evident, or fixed, it finally cannot account for the process of identity formation. The failure to attend to the question of identity formation is a characteristic weakness of postmodernist theories of subjectivity: they are unable to explain the persistent correlation between certain kinds of bodies and certain kinds of identities. My reading of Chela Sandoval focuses primarily on the inconsistencies in her argument generated by her postmodernist-inspired epistemological denial. Although I acknowledge the value of Sandoval's theoretical typology, and appreciate her political vision, I demonstrate that her attempts to refigure an identity-based agency would be better served by a realist theoretical framework. In order to propose a more appropriate theoretical trajectory for the critic concerned with representing the cultural productions and experiences of women of color, I recast *la facultad* — the "survival skill" described by Gloria Anzaldúa and theorized by Sandoval — as a realist concept in order to interrogate its epistemic value. I conclude by arguing that Chicana identity should be seen not as a principle of abstract oppositionality, but as a historically and materially grounded perspective from which we can work to disclose the complicated workings of ideology and oppression.

In chapter three, "Cultural Particularity vs. Universal Humanity: The Value of Being *Asimilao*," I work forward from this premise to argue that even those identities that do not work well as explanations of the social world are worth examining. To the extent that an identity fails to refer adequately to the central organizing principles of the society from which it emerges, it can help reveal the contradictions and mystifications within which members of that society live. Taking the writer Richard Rodriguez as exemplary, I examine the writings of neoconservative minorities to trace the contours of a neoconservative minority identity politics. Prompting my inquiry into their politics is the conviction that the outcomes of the debates in which neoconservative minorities engage (about bilingualism, affirmative action, multicultural education) have significant cultural, material, and epistemic consequences for all those who reside within the borders of the United States. The conclusions Americans come to regarding these hotly contested political issues have serious implications both for what we think our future society should be like and for how we will try to educate the ideal citizens of that future society. At stake is nothing less than the definition of American identity and the future well-being of our already culturally diverse society.

I begin my analysis by looking at the centerpiece of neoconservative minority identity politics: the insistence that minorities be required to assimilate to mainstream American culture. As part of my evaluative project, I examine the central claim of Rodriguez's intellectual autobiography — that he has been successfully assimilated. After demonstrating the role of interpretive error in the formation of Rodriguez's neoconservative minority identity, I show that neoconservative minorities' erroneous conception of what is "universal" to all humans causes them to make policy recommendations that hinder, rather than facilitate, the development of productive cross-cultural interaction. I then turn to the postpositivist realist theory of identity elaborated in chapters one and two to posit one way in which progressive intellectuals might go about fostering the conditions conducive to working toward a better society. I argue that when we pay the right kind of attention to our own and others' particularity, we position ourselves to develop a more productive understanding of our universal humanity. Working with a reconstructed notion of the human universal, I end by defending the value of cultural diversity on the basis of an understanding of multiculturalism as epistemic cooperation.

In chapter four, "Learning How to Learn from Others: Realist Proposals for Multicultural Education," I extend the realist theory of identity into the realm of multicultural education. I begin by reviewing the central debates surrounding multicultural education and by discussing the implicit claims about the nature of culture and the value of cultural diversity held by key opponents and proponents of multiculturalism. Working with accounts written by educational researchers who have studied the implementation of multicultural educational initiatives in primary and secondary public schools in the United States, I demonstrate that the postpositivist realist theory of identity can account for the complex intercultural dynamics these researchers have observed in educational settings. In response to some of the dilemmas identified by multicultural educational researchers, I propose eight postpositivist realist principles that I believe should be central to the pedagogical practice of educators and researchers who are interested in promoting a truly democratic and culturally diverse society. I conclude by showing that the realist conception of multiculturalism as cooperative cross-cultural inquiry into the nature of human welfare provides the strongest justification for multicultural education yet proposed — even as it helps us to understand how and why some initiatives that rely on a model of multiculturalism as cultural pluralism have failed.

In chapter five, I bring the various strains of my argument together in a reading of Helena María Viramontes's remarkable novel *Under the Feet of Jesus*. By examining the expanded notion of literacy that Viramontes develops in her novel, I show that the novel dramatizes what I describe elsewhere in this book as a postpositivist realist approach to understanding and knowledge. On a metaphorical level, Viramontes analogizes words to tools to figure the act of interpretation as a materialist engagement with the world. On a structural level, she employs the narrative strategy of focalization to emphasize the epistemic status of identity. Finally, on a thematic level, the novel documents the young protagonist's transformation of consciousness and her personal empowerment by tracing the process through which she becomes a better reader of her social world. I show that it is in part by guiding her readers' processes of identification through the narrative technique of focalization that Viramontes powerfully contests the outsider status typically accorded to migrant farmworkers. By encouraging her readers to enter into a relationship of empathetic identification with Estrella and her family and by exposing them to the moral and epistemic blindness of those Americans who would view migrant farmworkers as outsiders to American society, Viramontes implicitly invites her readers to transcend their own particular perspectives, to complicate their own previous understandings of the world, and to reach for a less partial, more objective understanding of our shared world. Viramontes's expanded notion of literacy is thus more than a pious statement about the importance of learning to read; rather, it is an implicitly postpositivist realist vision of social justice. Her vision of how humans can become better "readers" is intimately wedded to her moral vision of how humans most effectively interact with one another.

However well I have argued my case, I do not imagine that the publication of this book will suddenly or substantially change the conditions within which I and other minority scholars live and work. Nevertheless, I do believe that ideas can be very powerful. I also believe that humans are agential beings with the (admittedly constrained) capacity to employ ideas in the service of transforming the conditions of their existence. Thus, it was with a certain amount of faith in my fellow human beings that I began this scholarly project. It is in the same spirit that I offer my analysis of the ideas, insights, and visions of the artists and intellectuals whose writings have inspired this book.

CHAPTER I

Postmodernism, Realism, and the Politics of Identity

Cherríe Moraga and Chicana Feminism

If we are interested in building a movement that will not constantly be subverted by internal differences, then we must build from the insideout, not the other way around. Coming to terms with the suffering of others has never meant looking away from our own.

Cherríe Moraga, *This Bridge Called My Back*

In her foreword to the second edition of *This Bridge Called My Back*, co-editor Cherríe Moraga admits to feeling discouraged about the prospects for a third world feminism. The three years intervening between the first and second editions of *Bridge* have confirmed her insight that "Third World feminism does not provide the kind of easy political framework that women of color" run to in droves. Time has strengthened her awareness that women of color are not a " 'natural' affinity group" but are people who, across sometimes painful differences, "come together out of political necessity." However, if Moraga has abandoned an easy optimism, she has not forsaken her dream of building a "broad-based U.S. women of color movement capable of spanning borders of nation and ethnicity." Urging us to "look deeply" within ourselves, Moraga encourages us to come to terms with our own suffering in order to challenge and, if necessary, "change ourselves, even sometimes our most cherished block-hard convictions." In calling for us to look within ourselves, Moraga demonstrates her comprehension that coalitions across difference require a thorough understanding of how we are different from others, as well as how they are different from us. Because differences are relational, our ability to understand an "other" depends largely on our willingness to examine our "self." For Moraga, in the service of a larger project, "difference" is something to be deliberately and respectfully engaged.

In another context, we see a quite contrary treatment of the concept of difference. Within the field of U.S. literary and cultural studies, the institutionalization of a discourse of postmodernism has spawned an approach to difference that ironically erases the distinctiveness and relationality of difference itself. Typically, postmodernist theorists either internalize difference so that the individual is herself seen as "fragmented" and "contradictory" (thus displacing attention from the distinctions that exist between different kinds of people), or they attempt to "subvert" difference by showing that "difference" is merely a discursive illusion (thus leaving no way to contend with the fact that people experience themselves as different from each other). In either case, postmodernists reinscribe, albeit unintentionally, a kind of universalizing sameness (we are all marginal now!) that their celebration of "difference" had tried so hard to avoid.[1] Under the hegemonic influence of postmodernism within U.S. literary and cultural studies, the feminist scholar concerned with engaging difference in the way Moraga suggests will be bound by certain theoretical and methodological constraints. She will be justifiably wary of using categories of analysis (such as "race" or "gender") or invoking concepts (like "experience" or "identity") that have been displaced or "deconstructed" by postmodernist theorists. If, as Judith Butler and Joan Scott claim in their introduction to *Feminists Theorize the Political*, concepts like "experience" and "identity" enact a "silent violence . . . as they have operated not merely to marginalize certain groups, but to erase and exclude them from the notion of 'community' altogether," then any invocation of these "foundational" concepts will be seen as always already tainted with exclusionary and totalizing forms of power (xiv). In the current theoretical climate within U.S. literary and cultural studies, the feminist scholar who persists in using categories such as race or gender can be presumptively charged with

---

1. For useful overviews of what theorists generally mean when they refer to "postmodern theory," see Nicholson, esp. the introduction; Nicholson and Seidman, esp. the introduction; Rosaura Sánchez, "Postmodernism and Chicano Literature," esp. 1–6. The term *postmodernism*, like many others, is contested, and not all critics who can be described as "postmodernist" under the definition I provide in the introduction to this book would identify themselves as such.

essentialism, while her appeals to "experience" or "identity" may cause her to be dismissed as either dangerously reactionary or hopelessly naive. If, on the contrary, she accepts the strictures placed on her by postmodernism, the concerned feminist scholar may well find it difficult to explain why some people experience feelings of racial self-hatred while others feel a sense of racial superiority, some people live in poverty while others live in comfort, and some people have to worry about getting pregnant while others do not.

Feminist scholars have begun to note the legislative effect of postmodernism on feminist theorizing. Linda Singer, for example, points to what she sees as an "impulse" within contemporary feminist discourse "to establish some privileged relationship with postmodern discourse which is intended to have regulative impact on the conduct of feminist theory and practice."

> Both from within and from outside feminist discourse, there re-emerges with regularity these days a cautionary invective with respect to the appropriation of the language concepts and rhetoric — like that of the subject or personal identity — which has been placed in a problematized epistemic suspension by postmodern tactics of deconstruction. While such cautionary considerations are not without merit (and many, at least to my mind, are truly compelling), it is both presumptuous and pre-emptive to assume that such considerations must occupy some privileged position with respect to the development of feminist theory in the range and breadth of its concerns and approaches. (468)

Similarly, Linda Martín Alcoff notes that "the rising influence of postmodernism has had a noticeably debilitating effect on [the project of empowering women as knowledge producers], producing a flurry of critical attacks on unproblematized accounts of experience and on identity politics" ("Elimination of Experience" 4). Such critical attacks have served, in conventional theoretical wisdom, to delegitimize *all* accounts of experience and to undermine *all* forms of identity politics — unproblematized or not.

The problem posed by postmodernism is particularly acute for U.S. feminist scholars and activists of color, for whom "experience" and "identity" continue to be primary organizing principles around which they theorize and mobilize. Even women of color who readily acknowledge the nonessential nature of their political or theoretical commitments persist in referring to themselves as, for instance, "Chicana" or "black" feminists, and continue to join organizations, such as Mujeres Activas en Letras y Cambio Social (MALCS), that are organized around principles of identity. For example, Moraga acknowledges that women of color are not a " 'natural' affinity group" even as she works to build a movement around and for people who identify as women of color. She can do this, without contradiction, since her understanding of the identity "women of color" reconceptualizes the notion of "identity" itself. Unlike postmodernist feminists who understand the concept of identity as inherently and perniciously foundational, Moraga understands identities as relational and grounded in the historically produced social categories that constitute social locations.

Ironically, Moraga and other women of color are often called on in postmodernist feminist accounts of identity to delegitimize any theoretical project that attends to the linkages between identity (with its experiential and epistemic components) and social location (the particular nexus of gender, race, class, and sexuality in which a given individual exists in the world). Such projects are derided by postmodernist feminists as theoretically mistaken and dangerously "exclusionary" — particularly in relation to women of color themselves.[2]

Accordingly, I devote the first section of this chapter to an examination of the theoretical misappropriation of women of color — specifically the Chicana activist and theorist Cherríe Moraga — by the influential postmodernist theorists Judith Butler and Donna Haraway. I criticize these two theorists not only because they appropriate Moraga's words without attending to her theoretical insights, but also, and more important, because they employ her work at key moments in their arguments to legitimate their respective theoretical projects. In the second section, I articulate a postpositivist realist account of Chicana identity that goes beyond essentialism by theorizing the connections among social location, experience, cultural identity, and knowledge. By demonstrating the epis-

2. In their introduction to *Feminists Theorize the Political*, Scott and Butler ask the following questions: "What are the points of convergence between a) poststructuralist criticisms of identity and b) recent theory by women of color that critically exposes the unified or coherent subject as a prerogative of white theory?"; "To what extent do the terms used to defend the universal subject encode fears about those cultural minorities excluded in and by the construction of that subject; to what extent is the outcry against the 'postmodern' a defense of culturally privileged epistemic positions that leave unexamined the excluded domains of homosexuality, race, and class?"; "What is the significance of the poststructuralist critique of binary logic for the theorization of the subaltern?"; and "How do universal theories of 'patriarchy' or phallogocentrism need to be rethought in order to avoid the consequences of a white-feminist epistemological/cultural imperialism?" My point is that such questions enact an un-self-critical enlistment of the "woman of color," the "subaltern," and the "cultural minority" to serve as legitimators of the project entailed in "postmodern" or poststructuralist criticisms of identity.

temic component of cultural identity, I underscore the possibility that some identities can be more politically progressive than others *not* because they are "transgressive" or "indeterminate" but because they provide us with a critical perspective from which we can disclose the complicated workings of ideology and oppression.

When I speak of postpositivist realism in this book, I am referring to an epistemological position and political vision being articulated by a growing number of scholars in the United States and abroad who are developing an alternative to the reductionism and inadequacy of essentialist and postmodernist approaches to identity. Broadly speaking, to be a "realist" in a given domain is to believe in a "reality" that is, at least in part, causally independent of humans' mental constructions of it. Thus, while humans' (better or worse) understandings of their world may provide their only access to "reality," their conceptual or linguistic constructions of the world do not constitute the totality of what can be considered "real." Clearly then, when realists say that something is "real," they do not mean that it is *not* socially constructed; rather, their point is that it is not *only* socially constructed. Moreover, while realists will readily acknowledge that ideologies have constitutive effects on the social world such that "the world" is what it is at least partially because of the way humans interact with and understand it, they will insist that reality is not exhausted by how any given individual or group perceives it ideologically. This is so for two reasons: first, because there are processes of the natural world which operate independently of the human mind, and which both *shape* and *place a limit on* humans' ability to "construct" or "produce" the world. Second, because the sheer variety of conflicting ideologies extant in a global society such as ours precludes any one ideology from "producing" the entirety of the social world.

Underlying the postpositivist realist epistemology is a conception of objectivity which avoids the aporias of essentialist and (ironically) postmodernist epistemologies by opposing error not to certainty but rather to objectivity as a theory-dependent, socially realizable goal. Because realists view experience (and the knowledge humans glean from that experience) as mediated from the start, they are able to avoid the sharp opposition which structures much of postmodern thought: that experience must either be self-evidently meaningful, or else it will be epistemically unreliable. By seeing experience as theory mediated, realists understand that it can be a source of real knowledge as well as of social mystification; by seeing experience as causally related to the (social and natural) world, realists provide a way to evaluate the reliability of the

knowledge humans have gained from their experiences. The realist proposal is that the truth of different theories about the world can be evaluated comparatively by seeing how accurately they refer to real features of
the world. Under this view, because of the presence of ideological distortion, "objective knowledge is the product not of disinterested theoretical
inquiry so much as of particular kinds of social practice"; it is thus context sensitive and empirically based, while being valid across social and
cultural contexts (S. P. Mohanty, *Literary Theory* 213).[3]

In the last section of the chapter, I provide my own realist reading of
Moraga and show — by resituating her work within the cultural and historical conditions from which it emerged — that Moraga's elaboration of
a "theory in the flesh" gestures toward a realist theory of identity. A realist reading of Moraga's work presents a strong case for how and why the
theoretical insights of women of color are necessary for understanding
fundamental aspects of U.S. society.

POSTMODERNIST CYBORGS
AND THE DENIAL OF SOCIAL LOCATION

In "A Manifesto for Cyborgs," Donna Haraway figures Chicanas as
exemplary cyborgs and, as such, prototypical postmodern subjects. She
identifies two paradigmatic "groups of texts" that she sees as constructing cyborg identities: "women of color and monstrous selves in feminist
science fiction" (216). Although Haraway usually employs the generic
term *women of color,* she accords Chicanas a privileged position within
her framework. According to Haraway, the primary characteristic of the
cyborg is that of a creature who transcends, confuses, or destroys boundaries. Chicanas, as the products of the intermixing of Spaniards, Indians,
and Africans, cannot claim racial or cultural purity. Their neither/nor
racial status, their unclear genealogical relationship to the history of
oppression (as descendants of both colonizer and colonized), and their
ambiguous national identity (as neither Mexican nor fully "American")
give Chicanas their signifying power within the terms of the cyborgian
myth. To demonstrate that Haraway does, in fact, figure Chicanas as

3. For a fuller discussion of what I mean by a postpositivist objectivity see the introduction to this volume. See also S. P. Mohanty, *Literary Theory,* esp. 184–93. For more on
the postpositivist realist theory of identity, see Hames-García, "Dr. Gonzo's Carnival";
Mohanty, *Literary Theory,* esp. chap. 7; Moya and Hames-García, esp. the introduction.
Other important essays written from a postpositivist realist theoretical perspective include
Babbitt, "Identity"; Barad; Roman.

exemplary cyborgs, I have juxtaposed below a few passages from Haraway's text that describe characteristics first of cyborgs (I) and then of Chicanas/women of color (II). Notice how Haraway's figuration of Chicanas, instead of liberating them from a historically determined discursive position, ironically traps them — as well as their living counterparts in the real world — within a specific *signifying* function.

I. Cyborg writing must not be about the Fall, the imagination of a once-upon-a-time wholeness before language, before writing, before Man. (217)

II. Malinche was the mother here, not Eve before eating the forbidden fruit. Writing affirms Sister Outsider, not the Woman-before-the-Fall-into-Writing needed by the phallogocentric Family of Man. (218)

I. A cyborg body is not innocent; it was not born in a garden; it does not seek unitary identity and so generates antagonistic dualisms without end (or until the world ends); it takes irony for granted . . . (222)

II. Cherríe Moraga in *Loving in the War Years* explores the themes of identity when one never possessed the original language, never told the original story, never resided in the harmony of legitimate heterosexuality in the garden of culture, and so cannot base identity on a myth or a fall from innocence and right to natural names, mother's or father's. (217)

I. Writing is preeminently the technology of cyborgs, etched surfaces of the late twentieth century. Cyborg politics is the struggle for language and the struggle against perfect communication, against the one code that translates all meaning perfectly, the central dogma of phallogocentrism. (218)

II. Figuratively and literally, language politics pervade the struggles of women of color, and stories about language have a special power in the rich contemporary writing by U.S. women of color. . . . Moraga's writing, her superb literacy, is presented in her poetry as the same kind of violation as Malinche's mastery of the conqueror's language — a violation, an illegitimate production, that allows survival. (217–18)

Haraway claims that "women of color" can be understood as a "cyborg identity, a potent subjectivity synthesized from fusions of outsider identities" (217). She bases her claim, in part, on her appropriation and misreading of the Mexicano/Chicano myth of Malinche — a misreading that allows her to celebrate the symbolic birth of a new "bastard" race and the death of the founding myth of original wholeness.

For example, retellings of the story of the indigenous woman Malinche, mother of the mestizo "bastard" race of the new world, master of languages, and mistress of Cortés, carry special meaning for Chicana constructions of identity. . . . Sister Outsider hints at the possibility of world survival not because of her innocence, but because of her ability to live on the boundaries, to write without the founding myth of original wholeness, . . . Malinche was mother here, not Eve before eating the forbidden fruit. Writing affirms Sister Outsider, not the Woman-before-the-Fall-into-Writing needed by the phallogocentric Family of Man. (217–18)[4]

La Malinche, also referred to as Doña Marina or Malintzín Tenepal, was the Indian woman who served as translator for Hernán Cortés during the decisive period of the fall of the Aztec empire. According to the memoirs of Bernal Díaz del Castillo, who participated in and chronicled the conquest of the Aztec empire, Malintzín was born the daughter of *caciques* (Aztec nobility) (85). After the death of her father, and while she was still a young girl, her mother and stepfather sold her into captivity, ostensibly to leave the succession to the position of *cacique* free for her younger half brother. According to Díaz, she was sold to Indians from Xicalango who then gave or sold her to the Indians of Tabasco (85).

After the battle of Cintla, which took place shortly after Cortés landed at Cozumel, Malintzín was given to Cortés by the Tabascan Indians along with nineteen other women as a part of the spoils of war. From the Tabascans she learned to speak Chontal Maya, and it was her bilingualism that made her invaluable to Cortés. Cortés was able to speak Spanish to the Spaniard Aguilar (who had spent several years as a slave to the Mayan Indians), who then spoke Chontal Maya to Doña Marina, who translated into Nahuatl for Moctezuma and his numerous vassals (Diaz 86–87). It was in this manner that Cortés effected the communication that was so critical to his conquest of Mexico.

Today, La Malinche lives on as a symbol of enormous cultural significance for Mexicanas and Chicanas. As the mother of Cortés's son, she is figured as the symbolic mother of *mestizaje,* the mixing of Spanish and Indian blood. As the "dark" mother, the "fucked one," the "betrayer of her race," she is the figure against which women of Mexican descent have had to define themselves.[5] As the whore of the virgin/whore dichotomy in a culture that reveres La Virgen, she has been despised and reviled.

4. The name "Sister Outsider" derives from Lorde's book of the same name. Haraway's easy substitution of the name "Sister Outsider" for that of "Malinche," and her conflation of Chicana with Malinche with Sister Outsider signals her inattention to the differences (temporal, historical, and material) that exist between the three distinct constructions of identity.

5. See Paz, "Sons of La Malinche." In the process of describing her in his essay, Paz has served to confirm Malinche's position as the "Mexican Eve."

From the 1970s on, Mexicana and Chicana feminists have addressed the myth of Malinche, and several have attempted to recuperate and revalue her as a figure of empowering or empowered womanhood.[6] Such recuperations are generally problematic, inasmuch as attempts to absolve or empower the historical figure can result in reductive interpretations of what is a very complex situation. Cherríe Moraga's treatment of Malinche is neither naive nor reductive; she confronts the myth and examines its implications for the sexual and social situation of Chicanas today. In her essay "A Long Line of Vendidas," she looks carefully at "this myth of the inherent unreliability of women, our natural propensity for treachery, which has been carved into the very bone of Mexican/ Chicano collective psychology" (*Loving* 101), and addresses the continuing painful effects of the Malinche myth.

> The potential accusation of "traitor" or "vendida" is what hangs above the heads and beats in the hearts of most Chicanas seeking to develop our own autonomous sense of ourselves, particularly through sex and sexuality. Even if a Chicana knew no Mexican history, the concept of betraying one's race through sex and sexual politics is as common as corn. As cultural myths reflect the economics, mores, and social structures of a society, every Chicana suffers from their effects. (*Loving* 103)

Haraway's reading of the Malinche myth erases the complexity of the situation. She concludes her discussion of Malinche by claiming that "stripped of identity, the bastard race teaches about the power of the margins and the importance of a mother like Malinche. Women of color have transformed her from the evil mother of masculinist fear into the originally literate mother who teaches survival" (218–19). With this statement, Haraway conceals the painful legacy of the Malinche myth and overinvests the figure of Malinche with a questionable agency. Moreover, Haraway uncritically affirms a positionality (the margins) and a mode of existence (survival) that actual Chicanas have found to be rather less (instead of more) affirming. I do not mean to suggest that marginality and survival are not important and valuable. Certainly survival is valuable wherever the alternative is extinction. And, as I will argue, the experience and the theorizing of marginalized or oppressed people is important for arriving at a more objective understanding of the world. But I would suggest that neither marginality nor survival is a suf-

---

6. Alarcón, in "Traddutora, traditora" and "Chicana's Feminist Literature," provides a useful analysis of some of these attempts, as does Moraga in "A Long Line of Vendidas," in *Loving.* See also Candelaria; del Castillo; Gonzales; Phillips.

ficient goal for a feminist project and that no theoretical account of feminist identity can be based exclusively on such goals.

Haraway's conflation of cyborgs with women of color raises serious theoretical and political issues, because she conceives the social identities of women of color in overly idealized terms. As previously noted, Haraway's conception of a cyborg is that of a creature who transcends or destroys boundaries. It is "the illegitimate offspring of militarism and patriarchal capitalism," "a kind of disassembled and reassembled, postmodern collective and personal self," a being "committed to partiality, irony, intimacy and perversity," who is "not afraid of permanently partial identities and contradictory standpoints" and who is "related [to other cyborgs] not by blood but by *choice*" (193, 205, 192, 196, emphasis added). The porosity and polysemy of the category "cyborg," in effect, leaves no criteria to determine who might *not* be a cyborg. Furthermore, since Haraway sees a lack of any essential criterion for determining who is a woman of color, anyone can be a woman of color. Thus all cyborgs can be women of color and all women of color can be cyborgs. By sheer force of will (by "choice" as Haraway puts it) and by committing oneself (or refusing to commit oneself) to "permanently partial identities and contradictory standpoints," *anyone* can be either one or the other — or neither.[7]

The key theoretical problem here is Haraway's understanding of identity as a willful construction, as independent of the limiting effects of social location. Because she lacks an analysis of how the social categories that make up our social locations are causally relevant for the experiences we have, as well as of how those experiences inform our cultural identities, Haraway cannot conceive of a way to ground identities without essentializing them. Although she correctly ascertains that people are not *uniformly* determined by any *one* social category, she wrongly concludes that social categories (such as gender or race) can be irrelevant to the identities we choose. Haraway's refusal to grant women of color

---

7. Alcoff has suggested to me that Haraway might not intend to imply that "all cyborgs can be women of color" — that she means only that "women of color" is one particular *kind* of cyborg identity. If so, we are left with "women of color cyborgs" and "white women cyborgs" (and perhaps other *kinds* of male cyborgs, as well). In that case, of what use is the figure of the cyborg? Unless the figure of the cyborg can effectively dismantle "difference" (and the effect "difference" has on our experiences of the world), it is at best innocuous and at worst quite dangerous. We must acknowledge that a cyborg identity has the potential to become simply another veil to hide behind in order not to have to examine the differences that both constitute and challenge our self-conceptions.

grounded identities has the effect of rendering *all* claims to a woman of color identity equally valid. This theoretical stance allows Haraway to make the political move of assuming the position of the authoritative speaking subject with respect to women of color.

> From the perspective of cyborgs, freed of the need to ground politics in "our" privileged position of the oppression that incorporates all other dominations, the innocence of the merely violated, the ground of those closer to nature, we can see powerful possibilities. . . . With no available original dream of a common language or original symbiosis promising protection from hostile "masculine" separation, but written into the play of a text that has no finally privileged reading or salvation history, to recognize "oneself" as fully implicated in the world, frees us of the need to root politics in identification, vanguard parties, purity, and mothering. Stripped of identity, the bastard race teaches about the power of the margins and the importance of a mother like Malinche. Women of color have transformed her from the evil mother of masculinist fear into the originally literate mother who teaches survival. (219)

By freeing herself of the obligation to ground identity in social location, Haraway is able to arrogate the meaning of the term *woman of color.* With this misappropriation, Haraway authorizes herself to speak for actual women of color, to dismiss our own interpretations of our experiences of oppression, our "need to root politics in identification," and even our identities. Furthermore, she employs several rhetorical strategies designed to undermine "identity" as a concept and "identity politics" as a practice. First, she (incorrectly) implies that players of identity politics necessarily claim the "privileged position of the oppression that incorporates all other dominations"; she then impoverishes the discussion by linking identity politics to naive forms of essentialism that base themselves in "vanguard parties, purity, and mothering." The fact that most women of color (including Moraga) continue to organize and theorize on the basis of their identities as women of color — and that their identities *as* women of color are intimately tied to the social categories (race, gender, etc.) that make up their individual social locations — completely drops from sight in Haraway's representation of their work. It is worth noting that even within the terms of Haraway's cyborgian myth, the "bastard race" is not "stripped of identity" inasmuch as "bastard race" is itself a term of identification.

Although far more cursory, Judith Butler's treatment of Moraga's writings is also a highly questionable attempt to enlist women of color for a postmodernist agenda. In her early and highly influential book

Gender Trouble, Butler extracts one sentence from Moraga, buries it in a footnote, and then misreads it in order to justify her own inability in that text to account for the complex interrelations that structure various forms of human identity (see 153 n. 24). She reads Moraga's statement that "the danger lies in ranking the oppressions" to mean that we have no way of adjudicating among different kinds of oppressions — that any attempt to relate causally or hierarchize the varieties of oppressions people suffer constitutes an imperializing, colonizing, or totalizing gesture that renders the effort invalid. This misreading of Moraga follows on the heels of Butler's dismissal of Luce Irigaray's notion of phallogocentrism (as globalizing and exclusionary) and clears the way for her to do away with the category of "women" altogether. Thus, although Butler at first appears to have understood the critiques of women (primarily of color) who have been historically precluded from occupying the position of the "subject" of feminism, it becomes clear that their voices have been merely instrumental to her. She writes,

> The opening discussion in this chapter argues that this globalizing gesture [to find universally shared structures of oppression along an axis of sexual difference] has spawned a number of criticisms from women who claim that the category of "women" is normative and exclusionary and is invoked with the unmarked dimensions of class and racial privilege intact. In other words, the insistence upon the coherence and unity of the category of women has effectively refused the multiplicity of cultural, social and political intersections in which the concrete array of "women" are constructed. (14)

Butler's response to this critique is not to rethink her understanding of the category "women" but rather to radically undermine it as a valid political or analytical category. Underlying her logic are the assumptions that because the varieties of oppressions cannot be "summarily" ranked, they cannot be ranked at all; because epistemological projects have been totalizing and imperializing, they are always and necessarily so; and unless a given category (such as "women") is transhistorical, transcultural, stable, and uncontestable, it is not a valid analytical and political category.[8]

8. In her more recent work, Butler has shifted her position slightly on the question of identity. Whereas in *Gender Trouble* she argued for a subversion of identity, in *The Psychic Life of Power,* she figures identities as unavoidable, if pernicious, facts of social existence. Although I would find it interesting to detail the points of convergence and divergence between Butler's reformulated thesis on identity and the realist theory of identity, I will not take the space to do it here. In this chapter, I focus on *Gender Trouble* because it is Butler's argument in this book that continues to influence current debates about identity.

It should be emphasized that the passage in Moraga that Butler cites provides no actual support for Butler's argument. To read Moraga the way Butler reads her is to ignore the italicized statement that immediately follows the caution against ranking oppressions, namely, *"The danger lies in failing to acknowledge the specificity of the oppression,"* as well as to ignore the statement that immediately follows that one, "The danger lies in attempting to deal with oppression purely from a theoretical base" *(Bridge* 52). When Moraga talks about ranking the oppressions in the context from which this sentence is extracted, she is referring to the necessity of theorizing the connections between (and not simply ranking) the different kinds of oppressions people suffer.[9] More specifically, she is referring to the situation in which militant women of color with feminist convictions often find themselves. Militant men of color claim their first loyalty on the basis of race and disparage their involvement with feminism, which is, the men insist, a "white women" thing. Meanwhile, their white feminist sisters claim their first loyalty on the basis of gender, urging women of color to see the way in which they are being exploited by their own fathers, husbands, and brothers.[10] When Moraga writes that the "danger lies in ranking the oppressions," she is warning against the reductive theoretical tendency (whether it be Marxist, feminist, or cultural nationalist) to posit one kind of oppression as primary for all time and in all places. She is not advocating an admission of defeat in the project of trying to figure out how the varieties of oppressions suffered by the woman of color intersect with, or are determined by, each other.

Common to both Haraway's and Butler's accounts of identity is the assumption of a postmodern "subject" of feminism whose identity is unstable, shifting, and contradictory: "she" can claim no grounded tie to any aspect of "her" identit(ies) because "her" anti-imperialist, shifting, and contradictory politics have no epistemic basis in *experience.* Ironi-

9. See "A Long Line of Vendidas," in which Moraga talks about the necessity of theorizing the "simultaneity of oppression," by which she means taking "race, ethnicity and class into account in determining where women are at sexually," and in which she clearly acknowledges that some people "suffer more" than others (*Loving* 128).

10. For a more developed explanation of this phenomenon, see the section "Who Are My People" in Anzaldúa's essay "La Prieta." Anzaldúa writes of those who insist on viewing the different parts of her in isolation: "They would chop me up into little fragments and tag each piece with a label." She then goes on to affirm her oneness, "Only your labels split me" (*Bridge* 205). Rather than giving way to fragmentation, she insists upon holding it all together: "The mixture of bloods and affinities, rather than confusing or unbalancing me, has forced me to achieve a kind of equilibrium. . . . I walk the tightrope with ease and grace. I span abysses . . . I walk the rope — an acrobat in equipoise, expert at the Balancing Act" (209).

cally, although both Haraway and Butler lay claim to an anti-imperialist project, their strategies of resistance to oppression lack efficacy in a material world. Their attempts to disrupt gender categories (Butler) or to conjure away identity politics (Haraway) make it difficult to figure out who is "us" and who is "them," who is the "oppressed" and who is the "oppressor," who shares our interests and whose interests are opposed to ours.[11] Distinctions dissolve as all beings (human, plant, animal, and machine) are granted citizenship in the radically fragmented, unstable society of the postmodern world. "Difference" is magically subverted, and we find out that we really are all the same after all!

The key theoretical issue turns on Haraway's and Butler's disavowals of the link between identity (with its experiential and epistemic components) and social location (the particular nexus of gender, race, class, and sexuality in which a given individual exists in the world). Haraway and Butler err in the assumption that because there is no *one-to-one* correspondence between social location and identity or knowledge, there is simply *no* connection between social location and identity or knowledge. I agree that in theory boundaries are infinitely permeable and power may be amorphous. The difficulty is that people do not live in an entirely abstract or discursive realm. They live as biologically and temporally limited, as well as socially situated, human beings. Furthermore, although the "postmodern" moment does represent a time of rapid social, political, economic, and discursive shifts, it does not represent a radical break with systems, structures, and meanings of the past. Power is not amorphous since oppression is systematic and structural. A politics of discourse that does not provide for some sort of bodily or concrete action outside the realm of the academic text will forever be inadequate to change the difficult "reality" of our lives. Only by acknowledging the specificity and "simultaneity of oppression," and the fact that some people are more oppressed than others, can we begin to understand the systems and structures that perpetuate oppression and thereby place ourselves in a position to contest and change them (Moraga, *Loving* 128).[12]

---

11. As long as our world is hierarchically organized along relations of domination, categories such as "us" and "them," or "oppressed" and "oppressor" will retain their explanatory function. This is not because any one group belongs, in an essential way, to a particular category, but rather because the terms describe positions within prevailing social and economic relations.

12. For a compatible critique of how Butler and Haraway use women of color to justify their postmodernist theoretical projects, see Homans.

Until we do so, Cherríe Moraga, together with other women of color, will find herself leaving from Guatemala only to arrive at Guatepeor.[13] She will find herself caught in the dilemma of being reduced to her Chicana lesbian body or having to deny her social location (for which her body is a compelling metaphor) as the principal place from which she derives her insights. Moraga's dilemma appears as a contradiction to the theorist who recognizes a choice only between essentialist and postmodernist accounts of identity and knowledge. On the one hand, Moraga is articulating a "theory in the flesh," derived from "the physical realities of [women of color's] lives — [their] skin color, the land or concrete [they] grew up on, [their] sexual longings" *(Bridge* 23); on the other hand, she reminds us that "sex and race do not define a person's politics" *(Last Generation* 149). How can a theory be derived from the "physical realities of [women of color's] lives" if "sex and race do not define a person's politics"? When we examine this paradox from a realist perspective, the contradiction is dissolved. Theory, knowledge, and understanding can be linked to "our skin color, the land or concrete we grew up on, our sexual longings" without being uniformly determined by them. Rather, those "physical realities of our lives" will profoundly *inform* the contours and the context of both our theories and our knowledge.[14] The effects that the "physical realities of our lives" have on us, then, are what need to be addressed — not dismissed or dispersed — by theorists of social identity.

TOWARD A REALIST THEORY OF CHICANA IDENTITY

In this section I draw on Satya Mohanty's important book, *Literary Theory and the Claims of History,* to articulate a postpositivist realist

13. The Spanish-language proverb "Salir de Guatemala para entrar en Guatepeor" plays with the word fragment "*mala*" in "Guatemala" to suggest the dilemma of a person caught between a bad (*mala*) and a worse (*peor*) situation. The proverb roughly approximates the English-language proverb "To go from the frying pan into the fire."

14. At the risk of stating what should be obvious, this is as true for the white heterosexual politically conservative antifeminist as it is for the radical feminist lesbian of color. And yet, it is primarily women who address gender issues, and primarily people of color who address racial issues (both inside the academy and out). The unspoken assumption is that only women have gender and only people of color are racialized beings. This assumption reflects itself in the work of many male academics who only talk about gender when they are referring to women, and in the work of many white academics who only talk about race when they are referring to people of color. A manifestation of this phenomenon can be found in Butler's book *Bodies That Matter,* where she only theorizes race in the two chapters in which she discusses artistic productions by or about people of color.

account of Chicana identity that theorizes the linkages among social location, experience, epistemic privilege, and cultural identity. I must emphasize that this project is not an attempt to rehabilitate an essentialist view of identity. The critiques of essentialism are numerous; the aporias of an essentialist notion of identity have been well documented.[15] The mistake lies in assuming that our options for theorizing identities are inscribed within the postmodernism/essentialism binary — that we are either completely fixed and unitary or completely unstable and fragmented selves. The advantage of a realist theory of identity is that it allows for an acknowledgment of how the social categories of race, class, gender, and sexuality function in individual lives without *reducing* individuals to those social determinants.

I begin by clarifying my claims and defining some terms. *Epistemic privilege,* as I use it in this book, refers to a special advantage with respect to possessing or acquiring knowledge about how fundamental aspects of our society (such as race, class, gender, and sexuality) operate to sustain matrices of power. Although I will claim that oppressed groups may have epistemic privilege, I am not implying that social locations have epistemic or political meanings in a self-evident way. The simple fact of having been born a person of color in the United States or of having suffered the effects of heterosexism or of economic deprivation does not, in and of itself, give someone a better understanding or knowledge of the structure of our society. The key to claiming epistemic privilege for people who have been oppressed in a particular way stems from an acknowledgment that they have experiences — experiences that people who are not oppressed in the same way usually lack — that *can* provide them with information we all need to understand how hierarchies of race, class, gender, and sexuality operate to uphold existing regimes of power in our society. Thus what is being claimed is not any a priori link between social location or identity and knowledge, but a link that is historically variable and mediated through the interpretation of experience.

Experience here refers to the fact of personally observing, encountering, or undergoing a particular event or situation. By this definition, experience is admittedly subjective. Experiences are not wholly external events; they do not just happen. Experiences happen to us, and it is our theoretically mediated interpretation of an event that makes it an "experience." The meanings we give our experiences are inescapably condi-

---

15. For one poststructuralist critique of essentialism that does not quite escape the postmodernist tendency I am critiquing, see Fuss.

tioned by the ideologies and "theories" through which we view the world. But the crucial claim in my argument is not that experience is theoretically mediated, but rather that experience *in its mediated form* contains an epistemic component through which we can gain access to knowledge of the world. It is this contention, that it is "precisely in this *mediated* way that [personal experience] yields knowledge," that signals a theoretical departure from the opposed camps of essentialism and postmodernism (Mohanty, *Literary Theory* 205–6).

The first claim of a postpositivist realist theory of identity is that the different social categories (such as gender, race, class, and sexuality) that together constitute an individual's social location are causally related to the experiences she will have. Thus a person who is racially coded as "white" in our society will usually face situations and have experiences that are significantly different from those of a person who is racially coded as "black."[16] Similarly, a person who is racially coded as "black" and who has ample financial resources at her disposal will usually face situations and have experiences that are significantly different from those of a person who is racially coded as "black" and lacks those resources. The examples can proliferate and become increasingly complex, but the basic point is this: the experiences a person is likely to have will be largely determined by her social location in a given society. In order to appreciate the structural causality of the experiences of any given individual, we must take into account the mutual interaction of *all* the relevant social categories that constitute her social location and situate them within the particular social, cultural, and historical matrix in which she exists.

The second basic claim of a postpositivist realist theory of identity is that an individual's experiences will influence, but not entirely determine, the formation of her cultural identity. Thus, while I am suggesting that members of a group may have similar experiences as a result of their (voluntary or involuntary) membership in that group, I am not suggesting that they all come to the same conclusions about those experiences.[17] Because the theories through which humans interpret their experiences vary from

16. This can happen even if both individuals in the example are born into an African American community and consider themselves "black." It should be clear that I am not talking about race as a biological category. I am talking about people who, for one reason for another, appear to others as "white" or "black." As I will demonstrate in my discussion of Moraga's work, this is an important distinction for theorizing the link between experience and cultural identity for people with real, but not visible, biological or cultural connections to minority communities.

17. It is not even necessary that they recognize themselves as members of that group. For example, a dark-skinned migrant from Puerto Rico who refuses identification with

individual to individual, from time to time, and from situation to situation, it follows that different people's interpretations of the same kind of
event will differ. For example, one woman may interpret her jealous husband's monitoring of her interaction with other men as a sign that "he
really loves her," while another may interpret it in terms of the social relations of gender domination, in which a man may be socialized to see himself as both responsible for and in control of his wife's behavior. The kinds
of identities these women construct for themselves will both condition and
be conditioned by the kinds of interpretations they give to the experiences
they have. The first woman may see herself as a treasured wife, while the
second may see herself as the victim in a hierarchically organized society in
which, by virtue of her gender, she exists in a subordinate position.

The third claim of a postpositivist realist theory of identity is that
there is an epistemic component to identity that allows for the possibility
of error and of accuracy in interpreting the things that happen to us. It is
a feature of theoretically mediated experience that one person's understanding of the same situation may undergo revision over the course of
time, thus rendering her subsequent interpretations of that situation
more or less accurate. I have as an example my own experience of the
fact that the other women in my freshman dorm at Yale treated me differently than they treated each other. My initial interpretation of the situation led me to conclude that they just did not like me — the individual,
the particular package of hopes, dreams, habits, and mannerisms that I
was. Never having had much trouble making friends, I found this experience both troubling and humbling. As a "Spanish" girl from New
Mexico, I did not consider race or racism as social realities relevant to
me. I might have wondered (but I did not) why I ended up spending my
first semester at Yale with the other brown-skinned, Spanish-surnamed
woman in my residential college. It was only after I moved to Texas,
where prejudice against Mexicans is much more overt, that I realized that
regardless of how I saw myself, other people saw me as "Mexican." Reflecting back, I came to understand that while I had not seen the other
women in my dorm as being particularly different from me, the reverse
was not the case. Simultaneous with that understanding came the suspicion that my claim to a Spanish identity might be both factually and ide-

African Americans may nevertheless suffer racist experiences arising from the history of
black/white race relations within the United States due to mainland U.S. citizens' inability
to distinguish between the two distinct cultural groups.

ologically suspect. A little digging proved my suspicion correct.[18] In Texas, then, I became belatedly and unceremoniously Mexican American. All this to illustrate the point that identities both condition and are conditioned by the kinds of interpretations people give to the experiences they have. As Mohanty says, "identities are ways of making sense of our experiences." They are "theoretical constructions that enable us to read the world in specific ways" (*Literary Theory* 216).

The fourth claim of a postpositivist realist theory of identity is that some identities, because they can more adequately account for the social categories constituting an individual's social location, have greater epistemic value than some others that the same individual might claim. If, as in the case of my Spanish identity, I am forced to ignore certain salient aspects of my social location in order to maintain my self-conception, we can fairly conclude that my identity is epistemically distorted. While my Spanish identity may have a measure of epistemic validity (mine is a Spanish surname; I undoubtedly have some "Spanish blood"), we can consider it less valid than an alternative identity that takes into consideration the ignored social aspects (my "Indian blood"; my Mexican cultural heritage) together with all the other social categories that are causally relevant for the experiences I might have. Identities have more or less epistemic validity to the extent that they "refer" outward to the world, that they accurately describe and explain the complex interactions between the multiple determinants of an individual's social location.[19] According to the realist theory of identity, identities are not self-evident, unchanging, and uncontestable, nor are they absolutely fragmented, contradictory, and unstable. Rather, identities are subject to multiple determinations and to a continual process of verification that takes place over the course of an individual's life through her interaction with the society she lives in. It is in this process of verification that identities can be (and often are) contested and that they can (and often do) change.

I want to consider now the possibility that my identity as a "Chicana" can grant me a knowledge about the world that is "truer" and more "objective" than an alternative identity I might claim as a "Mexican

18. For an explanation of the historical origins of the myth that Spanish-surnamed residents of New Mexico are direct descendants of Spanish *conquistadores,* see Acuña, esp. 55–60; J. R. Chávez, esp. 85–106; González, esp. 78–83.

19. Identities can be evaluated, according to Mohanty, "using the same complex epistemic criteria we use to evaluate 'theories.' " He explains, "Since different experiences and identities refer to different aspects of one world, one complex causal structure that we call 'social reality,' the realist theory of identity implies that we can evaluate them comparatively by considering how adequately they explain this structure" (*Literary Theory* 230–31).

American," a "Hispanic," or an "American" (who happens to be of Mexican descent). When I refer to a Mexican American, I am referring to a person of Mexican heritage born and/or raised in the United States whose nationality is U.S. American. The term for me is descriptive, rather than political. The term *Hispanic* is generally used to refer to a person of Spanish, Mexican, Puerto Rican, Dominican, Cuban, Chilean, Peruvian, and so on, heritage who may or may not have a Spanish surname, who may or may not speak Spanish, who can be of any racial extraction, and who resides in the United States. As it is currently deployed, the term is so general as to be virtually useless as a descriptive or analytical tool. Moreover, the term has been shunned by progressive intellectuals for its overt privileging of the "Spanish" part of what for many of the people it claims to describe is a racially and culturally mixed heritage.[20] A Chicana, according to the usage of women who identify that way, is a politically aware woman of Mexican heritage who is at least partially descended from the indigenous people of Mesoamerica and who was born and/or raised in the United States. What distinguishes a Chicana from a Mexican American, a Hispanic, or an American of Mexican descent is not her ancestry or her cultural upbringing. Rather it is her political awareness; her recognition of her disadvantaged position in a hierarchically organized society arranged according to categories of class, race, gender, and sexuality; and her propensity to engage in political struggle aimed at subverting and changing those structures.[21]

20. For excellent discussions about the difficulties involved in homogenizing "Hispanics," as well as choosing a label by which to identify them, see Oboler, esp. chaps. 2, 4; Gracia, esp. chap. 1. For an argument in favor of the term *Hispanic,* see Gracia, esp. chap. 3. In that chapter, Gracia provides a fairly compelling historical argument in favor of a "Hispanic" identity. He asserts that the ethnic group with which we identify should be comprised of "the inhabitants of the countries of the Iberian peninsula after 1492 and what were to become the colonies of those countries after the encounter between Iberia and America took place, and by the descendants of these people who live in other countries (e.g. the United States) but preserve some link to those people" (48). I maintain, in contrast, that such an ethnic grouping is generally too large and heterogeneous to be analytically or politically useful for either the cultural critic or the activist. The category of "Hispanic" may indeed be useful for Gracia's purpose, which is to identify the group of people from whom "Hispanic philosophy" has emerged. But people's lived identities do not necessarily correspond to philosophical categories or intellectual traditions. Much more salient for a person's identity is her historical sense (which is generally more localized than Gracia would allow), her experience of being racialized and gendered within the society she grew up in, her cultural practices involving music and food, her socioeconomic status, and the values she holds. For a more sustained critique of Gracia's argument, see Moya, "Why I Am Not Hispanic."

21. Historically, the term *Chicano* was a pejorative name applied to lower class Mexican Americans. Like the term *black,* it was consciously appropriated and revalued by

The fifth claim of a postpositivist realist theory of identity is that our ability to understand fundamental aspects of our world will depend on our ability to acknowledge and understand the social, political, economic, and epistemic consequences of our own social location. If we can agree that our *one* social world is, as Mohanty asserts, "constitutively defined by relations of domination" (*Literary Theory* 232), then we can begin to see how my cultural identity as a Chicana, which takes into account an acknowledgment and understanding of those relations, may be more epistemically valid than an alternative identity I might claim as a Mexican American, a Hispanic, or an American. While a description of myself as a Mexican American is not technically incorrect, it implies a structural equivalence with other ethnic Americans (Italian Americans, German Americans, African Americans, etc.) that erases the differential social, political, and economic relations that obtain for different groups. This erasure is even more marked in the cultural identity of the Hispanic or American (of Mexican descent), whose self-conception often depends on the idea that she is a member of one more assimilable ethnic group in what is simply a nation of immigrants.[22] Factors of race, gender, and class get obscured in these identities, while a normative heterosexuality is simply presumed. We find that, to maintain her identity, the Hispanic or American (of Mexican descent) may have to repress or misinterpret her own or others' experiences of oppression. Moreover, she will most likely view her material situation (her "success" or "failure") as entirely a result of her individual merit and dismiss structural relations of domination as irrelevant to her personal situation. Thus my claim that social locations have epistemic consequences is not the same as claiming that a particular kind of knowledge inheres in a particular social location. An individual's understanding of herself and the world will be mediated, more or less accurately, through her cultural identity.

The sixth and final claim of a postpositivist realist theory of identity is

---

(primarily) students during the 1960s. According to the *Plan de Santa Barbara* (see note 24) the term specifically implies a politics of resistance to Anglo-American domination.

22. An example of the assimilationist "Hispanic" is Linda Chávez. In her book, *Out of the Barrio,* Chávez suggests that Hispanics, like "previous" white ethnic groups, are rapidly assimilating into the mainstream of U.S. culture and society (2). Not only does she play fast and loose with sociological and historical evidence, but her thesis cannot account for the social category of race. She does not mention race as being causally relevant for the experiences of Hispanics, and she repeatedly refers to "non-Hispanic whites," a grammatical formulation which assumes that all Hispanics are white. She accounts for Puerto Ricans and Dominicans by considering them as "dysfunctional" "exceptions" to the white-Hispanic rule (139–59).

that oppositional struggle is fundamental to our ability to understand the world more accurately. Mohanty, drawing on the work of Sandra Harding and Richard Boyd, explains this Marxian idea in this way:

> In the case of social phenomena like sexism and racism, whose distorted representation benefits the powerful and the established groups and institutions, an attempt at an objective explanation is necessarily continuous with oppositional political struggles. Objective knowledge of such social phenomena is in fact often dependent on the theoretical knowledge that activism creates. For without these alternative constructions and accounts our capacity to interpret and understand the dominant ideologies and institutions is limited to those created or sanctioned by these very ideologies and institutions. (*Literary Theory* 213)

The "alternative constructions and accounts" generated through oppositional struggle provide new ways of looking at our world that always complicate and often challenge dominant conceptions of what is "right," "true," and "beautiful." They call to account the distorted representations of peoples, ideas, and practices whose subjugation is fundamental to the colonial, neocolonial, imperialist, or capitalist project. Furthermore, because the well-being (and sometimes even survival) of the groups or individuals who engage in oppositional struggle depends on their ability to refute or dismantle dominant ideologies and institutions, their vision is usually more critical, their efforts more diligent, and their arguments more comprehensive than those of individuals or groups whose well-being is predicated on the maintenance of the status quo. Oppressed groups and individuals have a stake in knowing "what it would take to change [our world, and in] . . . identifying the central relations of power and privilege that sustain it and make the world what it is" (Mohanty, *Literary Theory* 214). This is why "granting the possibility of epistemic privilege to the oppressed might be more than a sentimental gesture; in many cases in fact it is the only way to push us toward greater social objectivity" (232–33). Thus a realist theory of identity demands oppositional struggle as a necessary (although not sufficient) step toward the achievement of an epistemically privileged position.

A realist theory of identity, in contrast to a postmodernist one, thus insists that we acknowledge and interrogate the consequences — social, political, economic, and *epistemic* — of social location. To do this, we must first acknowledge the reality of those social categories (race, class, gender, and sexuality) that together make up an individual's social location. We do not need to see these categories as uncontestable or absolutely fixed to acknowledge their ontological status. We *do*, however, need to recognize that they have real material effects and that their effects are systematic rather than accidental. A realist theory of identity understands that while identities are not fixed, neither are they random. There is a non-arbitrary limit to the range of identities we can plausibly "construct" or "choose" for any individual in a given society.

"THEORY IN THE FLESH": CHERRÍE MORAGA'S REALIST FEMINISM

Yvonne Yarbro-Bejarano, in her essay "Gloria Anzaldúa's *Borderlands/La frontera*," captures the exasperation and frustration of many Chicana/o academics who have been witness to the way Anzaldúa's work has been used and abused in the service of a postmodern celebration-cum-deconstruction of "difference." Yarbro-Bejarano's concern is that post-modernists have appropriated Anzaldúa's powerful image of the "border" and her theory of "mestiza consciousness" without attending to the social, cultural, and historical conditions that produced her thought. Yarbro-Bejarano critiques "the isolation of this text from its conceptual community and the pitfalls in universalizing the theory of *mestiza* or border consciousness, which the text painstakingly grounds in specific historical and cultural experiences" (7). Taking Yarbro-Bejarano's cue, my goal is twofold: to resituate Moraga's work within the conceptual community from which it emerges by regrounding it in her specific historical and cultural experiences; and to demonstrate that Moraga's theoretical framework is consistent with a realist theory of identity.

Partly as an outgrowth of ongoing struggles (from 1845) of resistance to American domination, and partly in conjunction with civil rights and other left liberation movements taking place during the 1960s, the Chicano movement, as a distinct historical and political phenomenon, was born. Some of the most visible manifestations of the Chicano movement were the New Mexico-based La Alianza Federal de Mercedes, led by Reies López Tijerina; the California-based United Farm Workers' (UFW) movement, headed by César Chávez and Dolores Huerta; the university-based Chicano Student Youth Movement; the Colorado-based Crusade for Justice, led by Rodolfo "Corky" Gonzáles; and, later, the La Raza Unida party, headed in Colorado by Gonzáles and in South Texas by José Ángel Gutiérrez.[23]

23. For histories of the Chicano movement, see Acuña; García, "Development of Chicana Feminist Discourse"; Gutiérrez; López; Muñoz; Ruíz.

Within a larger framework of resistance to Anglo-American hegemony, the groups that formed the Chicano movement employed distinct
strategies and worked toward different goals. La Alianza and the UFW
were primarily class- or labor-based movements working toward the economic improvement of the communities they represented. La Raza Unida
emphasized electoral politics and working within existing democratic
structures and institutions. The Chicano Student Youth Movement
focused on Chicanos' lack of access to education and the problems associated with racial and cultural discrimination. Participants in the youth
movement worked to establish Chicano studies programs within existing
institutions of higher education and to increase cultural consciousness
and pride.[24]

The Chicano movement in general and the Chicano Student Youth
Movement in particular fostered the development of a cultural nationalist discourse that emphasized the importance of the family in the project
of cultural survival. The sociologist Alma García explains, "Historically,
as well as during the 1960s and 1970s, the Chicano family represented a
source of cultural and political resistance to the various types of discrimination experienced in American society. At the cultural level, the
Chicano movement emphasized the need to safeguard the value of family
loyalty. At the political level, the Chicano movement used the family as a
strategic organizational tool for protest activities" ("Development of
Chicana Feminist Discourse" 219). The Chicano nationalist emphasis on
the importance of family loyalty assigned Chicanas a subordinate and
circumscribed role within the movement. They were often relegated to
traditional female roles and denied decision-making power. Moreover,
although Chicanas were active at every stage and at every level of the
Chicano movement, their participation was rarely acknowledged or
recorded.

The cultural nationalist emphasis on cultural survival in an Anglo-
dominated society further instituted strict controls on the sexual autonomy of Chicanas. Chicanas who dated or married white men were often
criticized as *vendidas* and *malinchistas* responsible for perpetuating the
legacy of rape handed down to the Chicano community from the conquest of Mexico. This same standard did not apply to males, whose relations with white women were often seen as rectifying an unjust legacy of

24. The *Plan de Santa Barbara*, written in the spring of 1969 at a California statewide
conference in Santa Barbara, launched MEChA (Movimiento Estudiantil Chicano de
Aztlán) and is probably the definitive position paper of the Chicano Student Youth
Movement. It appears as an appendix in Muñoz, 191–202.

emasculation at the hands of the white man. Chicana lesbians were viewed as the greatest threat to the cultural integrity of the Chicano community. By engaging in sexual practices that render the male irrelevant, and by refusing to inhabit the culturally mandated subject position of the good wife and mother, Chicana lesbians create the possibility for a resistant Chicana subjectivity that exists outside the boundaries of culturally inscribed notions of Chicana womanhood.[25]

Chicano cultural nationalism found its most eloquent expression within the Chicano Student Youth Movement, and it is from within that segment of the movement that what is frequently recognized as Chicana feminism emerged.[26] The Chicana feminist response to the kind of treatment they received from their Chicano brothers was to point out the contradictions inherent in maintaining one form of oppression in the service of abolishing another. Those who were explicit about their feminist convictions found themselves charged with "selling out" to white women's liberation. They were urged by their compañeros to drop their "divisive ideology" and to attend to the "primary" oppression facing all Chicanos — that is, racism. Chicanos often viewed an analysis of sexism within the Chicano movement or community as a threat not only to the movement, but to the culture itself.

Some Chicana feminists, disillusioned with Chicano cultural nationalism, began to work within white women's liberation movements in the 1970s. Long-term coalitions never developed, largely because most white women could not or would not recognize the class and race biases inherent in the structures of their own organizations. Furthermore, white feminists often replicated, in another realm, the same kind of privileging of one kind of oppression over another that had frustrated Chicanas in relation to movement Chicanos. Insisting on the primacy of gender oppression, most white feminist organizations disregarded or diminished the class- and race-based oppression suffered by most Chicanas. This resulted, in the 1980s, in Chicana feminists, together with feminists of

25. For more information on how both heterosexual and lesbian Chicanas fared within the Chicano movement, see García, *Chicana Feminist Thought,* esp. the introduction; García, "Development of Chicana Feminist Discourse"; Gutiérrez; López; Moraga, *Loving,* esp. 105–11; Saldívar-Hull, esp. 29–34; Trujillo.

26. This is not to say that Chicanas outside the university were not asserting themselves and coming to consciousness about their disadvantaged positions — just that the most consistently documented and published expressions of Chicana feminism have emerged from within the academy. For documentation of this claim, see García, "Development of Chicana Feminist Discourse"; Gutiérrez; López; Pesquera and Segura.

other nonwhite racial groups, turning to their own experience as a ground for theorizing their multiple forms of oppression.

Moraga presents an interesting case because she did not participate in the Chicano movement but has been at the forefront of the Chicana feminist response to both Chicano cultural nationalism and Anglo-American feminism.[27] Her position in the forefront can be explained both by the strength of her writings and by the fact that she was initially published and distributed through white feminist presses. Moraga is an important figure for Chicana feminists in the academy today because she is one of two Chicanas (the other being Gloria Anzaldúa) whose work is more than occasionally taken up outside the field of Chicana/o studies. As such, she is one of the few Chicanas called on to "represent" Chicanas in women's studies and feminist theory courses throughout the United States. How she is read, then, is crucial for how we understand the position of Chicanas in U.S. society.

Moraga's third world feminist political project takes as its starting point the transformation of the experience of women of color. This transformation can be accomplished, Moraga argues, only when women of color understand how their experiences are shaped by the relations of domination within which they live. Thus, while Moraga does not take the acquisition of knowledge as her goal, she sees the acquisition of knowledge — about women of color and their place in the world — as fundamental to her theoretical project. To that end, Moraga does not advocate turning away from, but toward, the bodies of women of color to develop what she calls a "theory in the flesh."[28]

Moraga's theoretical project, which is consonant with her interest in

27. Moraga explains, "During the late 60s and early 70s, I was not an active part of la causa. I never managed to get myself to walk in the marches in East Los Angeles (I merely watched from the sidelines); I never went to one meeting of MECHA on campus. No soy tonta. I would have been murdered in El Movimiento — light-skinned, unable to speak Spanish well enough to hang; miserably attracted to women and fighting it; and constantly questioning all authority, including men's. I felt I did not belong there. Maybe I had really come to believe that 'Chicanos' were 'different,' not 'like us,' as my mother would say. But I fully knew that there was a part of me that was a part of that movement, but it seemed that part would have to go unexpressed until the time I could be a Chicano and the woman I had to be, too" (Loving 113).

28. That I regard Cherríe Moraga as a "theorist" may surprise some academics who associate that honorific with a long list of publications from well-established university presses. Saldívar-Hull has argued, however, that "because [Chicana feminists'] work has been ignored by the men and women in charge of cultural modes of production, we must be innovative in our search. Hegemony has so constructed the ideas of method and theory that often we cannot recognize anything that is different from what the dominant discourse constructs. As a consequence, we have to look in nontraditional places for our theories: in the

building a movement of/for radical women of color, involves a heartfelt examination and analysis of the sources of her oppression and her pain. Haraway is correct when she says that Moraga never claims the "innocence of the merely violated." What Moraga *does* claim is a knowledge that derives from an interpretation of that violation. In a 1986 interview with Norma Alarcón, Moraga described the contours of her theoretical framework.

> I began to see that, in fact, *[Loving in the War Years]* is very much a love story about my family because they made me the lover I am. And also the belief in political change is similar because it can't be theoretical. It's got to be from your heart. They all seem related to me, and I feel that what happened since *Bridge* came out is that I got closer to my own dilemma and struggle — being both Chicana and lesbian. I really feel that all along that's been the heart of the book. I could see that this book was about trying to make some sense of what is supposed to be a contradiction, but you know it ain't cause it lives in your body. ("Interview" 129)

Condensed in this short passage are five concepts central to Moraga's theoretical approach: (1) the family as the primary instrument of socialization ("my family . . . made me the lover I am"); (2) the need for theory to be grounded in emotional investment ("political change . . . can't be theoretical. It's got to be from your heart"); (3) the link between social location and experience (Moraga represents being Chicana and lesbian in her society as a "dilemma"); (4) the body as a source of knowledge ("you know it ain't cause it lives in your body"); and (5) the centrality of struggle to the formation of her political consciousness. Both in this interview and throughout her writings, Moraga makes clear that it was through her struggles — to deny her *chicanidad* and then to reclaim it; to repress her lesbianism and then to express it; to escape sexism and heterosexism within a Chicano/a cultural context and then to combat racism and classism within an Anglo-American feminist movement — that she comes to understand the necessity for a nonessentialist feminist theory that can explain the political and theoretical salience of social location.

According to Moraga, a "theory in the flesh means one where the physical realities of our lives — our skin color, the land or concrete we

---

prefaces to anthologies, in the interstices of autobiographies, in our cultural artifacts (the cuentos), and, if we are fortunate enough to have access to a good library, in the essays published in marginalized journals not widely distributed by the dominant institutions" (46). Moraga's preface to *Bridge* as well as other of her essays that I discuss are precisely such sites of Chicana theory.

grew up on, our sexual longings — all fuse to create a politic born out of necessity" (*Bridge* 23). It attempts to describe "the ways in which Third World women derive a feminist political theory specifically from [their] racial/cultural background and experience" (*Bridge* xxiv). Implicit in these formulations are the realist insights that the different social categories of a woman's existence are relevant for the experiences she will have and that those experiences will inform her understanding of the world and the development of her politics. Moraga's contribution to the practice she names has been to recognize it and describe it as *theoretically mediated*. Unlike some other feminists of color whose writings seem to imply a self-evident relationship among social location, knowledge, and identity, Moraga explicitly posits that relationship as theoretically mediated through the interpretation of experience in the ways I have outlined.

As we have seen, Moraga's refusal to assume a self-evident or one-to-one correspondence between social location and knowledge opens her work to co-optation by postmodernist feminist critiques of identity. But what postmodernist interpretations of Moraga's writings fail to take into account is her emphasis on bodies and her insistence on the necessity of theorizing from the "flesh and blood experiences of the woman of color" (*Bridge* 23). In her own articulation of a theory in the flesh, Moraga emphasizes the materiality of the body by conceptualizing "flesh" as the site on or within which the woman of color experiences the painful material effects of living in her particular social location (*Bridge* xviii). Her focus on women of color's vulnerability to pain starkly emphasizes the way they experience themselves as embodied beings. Over the course of their lives, women of color face situations and have experiences that arise as a result of how other people misrecognize them. Others routinely react to women of color with preconceived ideas about the meanings their bodies convey. These misrecognitions can be amusing; often they are painful. Moreover, the way others misrecognize women of color can affect the kind of jobs they will "qualify" for, or where they might be able to live. The material effects these misrecognitions have are why postmodernist theories of identity that do not account for the causal connection between social location and experience have no real liberatory potential for women of color or other multiply oppressed individuals.

Moraga's personal example illustrates that a woman of color's response to her socially disadvantaged position is not uniform and can change over time. Moraga's initial prereflective and visceral response to being Chicana and lesbian was to deny her *chicanidad* and repress her lesbianism. This response represented an attempt on Moraga's part to claim access to the privilege that whiteness and heterosexuality are accorded in U.S. society. In her essay "La Güera," Moraga talks about how the fact of her white skin facilitated her early denial of her Mexican cultural heritage: "I was educated, and wore it with a keen sense of pride and satisfaction, my head propped up with the knowledge, from my mother, that my life would be easier than hers. I was educated; but more than this, I was 'la güera': fair-skinned. Born with the features of my Chicana mother, but the skin of my Anglo father, I had it made" (*Bridge* 28).[29]

As a young girl, Moraga shared her mother's concern that she be in a position to transcend the barriers faced by individuals in U.S. society who are situated as "poor, uneducated, and Chicana." The best way she and her mother could see for Moraga to accomplish this goal was for her to leave behind her Mexican cultural heritage — the presumed "cause" of her poverty and powerlessness. Their unstated goal was for Moraga to become "anglocized," a condition that, they assumed, would give her access to power and privilege. In the conceptual universe within which they were working, Moraga's white skin, her Anglo surname, and her education would be her tickets to the promised land.

Moraga's "anglocization" was at first encouraged by her growing awareness of her lesbian sexuality. The product of a strict Mexican and Catholic upbringing, Moraga concluded at the age of twelve that her strong emotional attachments to women, which she had started to identify as sexual, must be "impure" and "sinful" (*Loving* 119). Her response to this conclusion was to beat a terrified retreat into the region of religion, thus abandoning the body that was beginning to betray her biological femaleness. In the article she wrote with Amber Hollibaugh, "What We're Rollin Around in Bed With," Moraga reveals her alarm at the changes her body went through during puberty: "I didn't really think of myself as female, or male. I thought of myself as this hybrid or something. I just kinda thought of myself as this free agent until I got tits. Then I thought, '*oh, oh, some problem has occurred here . . .*'" (60). Moraga's growing awareness of her own biological femaleness, and the inability to act that she associated with that femaleness, caused her to feel "crucially and critically alone and powerless" (*Loving* 120). This aware-

29. The fact of Moraga's "whiteness" is central to an accurate mapping of her social location and crucial to an understanding of the formation of her cultural identity. The fact that her "whiteness" has been systematically overlooked by postmodernist readings of Moraga's work is symptomatic of the failure of postmodernist theories of identity to take account of the complex interactions among the multiple determinants of human identity.

ness, combined with the realization that her sexual feelings for women were inappropriate according to the standards of the society in which she lived, prompted Moraga to disavow her racialized and sexualized body. She writes that "in order to not embody the *chingada*, nor the femalized, and therefore perverse, version of the *chingón*, I became pure spirit — bodiless" (*Loving* 120).[30]

For years Moraga lived in a state of what she describes as "an absent inarticulate terror" (*Loving* 121). Her feelings for women, which she had tried so hard to suppress, did not fully reawaken until she became sexually active with men. Even then, Moraga could not face her lesbianism. She explains, "The sheer prospect of being a lesbian was too great to bear, fully believing that giving into such desires would find me shot-up with bullets or drugs in a gutter somewhere" (*Loving* 122). She began to be revisited by "feelings of outsiderhood"; she saw herself as "half-animal/half-human, hairy-rumped and cloven-hoofed, como el diablo" (*Loving* 124). It took a series of breakdowns before Moraga could begin the process of learning to live with her sexual desire for women. In that process, she became further alienated from her Chicana/o community. Because Moraga experienced her sexuality as contrary to the social mores of a Chicana/o community, it was that particular community she needed to leave in order to, in the words of Anzaldúa, "come out as the person [she] really was" (*Loving* 116). Moraga explains, "I became anglocized because I thought it was the only option available to me toward gaining autonomy as a person without being sexually stigmatized ... I instinctively made choices which I thought would allow me greater freedom of movement in the future" (*Loving* 99).

Given the urgency of her need to come to terms with her sexual identity, Moraga became, as if by default, "white." As the light-skinned daughter of a dark-skinned Mexican-origin woman, Moraga had a choice, of sorts, as to which "race" she would identify with. According to the logic of what the anthropologist Marvin Harris calls hypo-descent, Moraga is Mexican, and therefore nonwhite (56). The empirical fact that there is no "Mexican" race, that "Mexican" denotes a nationality and not a race, and that some Mexicans are phenotypically "white" seems to have little bearing on the ethnic/racial classification of Mexican-origin people in the United States. Practically speaking, the "racial" clas-

30. The Spanish verb *chingar* is stronger than the English verb "to fuck." A highly gendered word, it carries within it connotations of the English verb "to rape." Thus, *chingón* refers to the (active) male rapist/fucker and *chingada* refers to the (passive) female who is raped/fucked.

sification into which any given individual is placed in the United States today is predicated much more on how they look, speak, act, walk, think, and identify, than on the word or words on their birth certificates. Thus, Moraga can be seen as "white" by those who do not know her well and as a "woman of color" by those who do.

Moraga's identification as "white" was at least partially motivated by two underlying assumptions at work in the conceptual universe from which she emerged. The first assumption is that homosexuality belongs, in an essential way, to white people. Moraga explains that homosexuality is seen by many Chicana/os as "*his* [the white man's] disease with which he sinisterly infects Third World people, men and women alike" (*Loving* 114). The second assumption, which follows from the first, is that a woman cannot be a Chicana and a lesbian at the same time. These two assumptions, combined with the fact that Moraga was still clinging to the privilege (here figured as "freedom of movement") that the color of her skin might afford her, precluded any understanding of what it meant for her to be a *Chicana* lesbian. As long as Moraga avoided examining how the various social categories that constituted her social location intersected with, and were determined by, each other, she could conceive of her sexuality in isolation from her race. Moraga had not yet acknowledged how her Chicano "family . . . made [her] the lover [she is]" (*Loving* 129).

Moraga's eventual coming to terms with her Chicana identity was facilitated by her experience of marginalization within the women's movement.[31] However "white" she might have felt in relation to a Chicano community, she felt a sense of cultural dislocation when other women of color were not present in the feminist organizations in which she was active. However accepting of lesbianism the feminist movement tried to be, it did not deal adequately with the ways in which race and class have shaped women's sexuality.[32] Moraga realized that a feminist movement with an exclusive focus on gender oppression could not provide the home she was looking for (*Loving* 125).

In 1981, partly as a result of the alienation each had suffered within

31. Although I use the term *women's movement* in the singular, I am aware that the various feminisms are diverse and multidimensional. If I am vague, it is because Moraga does not specify which feminist group(s) she involved herself with. Throughout most of her writings, Moraga equates the "women's movement" or "feminism" with an unspecified and predominantly middle-class white women's movement. She does, at one point, specifically critique "Radical Feminism" (*Loving* 125–30).

32. See Hollibaugh and Moraga. In this conversation, Moraga and Hollibaugh address the failure of feminist theory and rhetoric to deal adequately with women's lived experiences

the women's movement, Moraga and Anzaldúa published *This Bridge Called My Back*. Although the collection was originally conceived as an anthology to be written *by* women of color and addressed *to* white women for the purpose of exposing the race and class biases inherent in many feminist organizations and theories, it evolved into "a positive affirmation of the commitment of women of color to [their] *own* feminism" (xxiii). The project was transformative, especially for the women involved in its conception and execution. For Moraga, at least, an examination of the racism, classism, and heterosexism she saw in the society around her entailed an examination of the racism, classism, and homophobia she had internalized from that society. Following Audre Lorde's suggestion that "each one of us . . . reach down into that deep place of knowledge inside herself and touch that terror and loathing of difference that lives there," Moraga turned her attention to the sources of her own oppression and pain (*Bridge* xvi). It was this self-reflexive examination that allowed Moraga finally to make the connections between the sexual and the racial aspects of her cultural identity. By examining her own experience with oppression, Moraga was able to come to an empathetic understanding of the (different yet similar) experience of oppression suffered by her mother (*Bridge* 28–30). Moraga's understanding and empathy thus worked to free her from the internalized racism and classism that had kept her from claiming a Chicana identity.

Moraga's example illustrates the possibility of coming to understand someone else's experience of oppression through empathetic identification — what Moraga, following Emma Goldman, calls "entering into the lives of others" (*Bridge* 27). Her example also illustrates the point that however dependent empathetic identification is on personal experience, the simple fact of experiencing oppression is not sufficient for understanding someone else's oppressive situation. Moraga's initial (and largely unexamined) reaction to her own experiences of oppression at first prevented her from empathizing with her mother's plight. It was not until she *reinterpreted* her experiences according to a different and more

---

of sexuality. They accuse the feminist movement of desexualizing women's sexuality by confusing sexuality with sexual oppression. They suggest that the refusal to acknowledge butch/femme roles in lesbian relationships, and the failure to understand how those sexual identities influence and condition sexual behavior, have led to (1) a delegitimization of sexual desire and (2) bad theory. They contend that a woman's sexual identity, which is necessarily influenced by her race and class background, can tell us something fundamental about the way she constitutes herself/is constituted as a woman.

accurate theoretical framework that she was able to empathize with and understand her mother's position. In other words, "experience is epistemically indispensable but never epistemically sufficient" for arriving at a more objective understanding of a situation (Alcoff, "Elimination of Experience" 6). How objectively it is understood will depend on the adequacy of the "theory" that explains the intersecting social, economic, and political relations that constitute the subject and object of knowledge. This suggests that in order to evaluate how accurately we understand a particular event or happening, we must first examine our interpretation of that event. Rather than argue, as postmodernist feminists do, that the theoretically mediated nature of experience renders it epistemically unreliable, we should address ourselves to the adequacy of the theoretical mediations that inform the different interpretations we give to our knowledge-generating experiences.

When, in her writings, Moraga talks about the need for people to "deal with the primary source of [their] own oppression . . . [and] to emotionally come to terms with what it feels like to be a victim," she is not advocating the kind of narcissistic navel-gazing that equates victimhood with innocence (*Bridge* 30). As Haraway rightly suggests, Moraga does not claim the "privileged position of the oppression that incorporates all other dominations," or the self-righteous "innocence of the merely violated." Central to Moraga's understanding of oppression is that it is a physical, material, psychological, and/or rhetorical manifestation of the intersecting relations of domination that constitute our shared world. To the extent that individuals are differentially situated within those relations, they may be simultaneously constituted as both oppressor *and* oppressed. So, an upper-class white woman can be oppressed by patriarchy at the same time that she oppresses others (such as poor *men* of color) through the privilege afforded to her by her race and class. Moraga would further argue that relinquishing the notion that there is a "privileged position of the oppression that incorporates all other dominations" does not free us of the need to relate causally the intersecting relations of domination that condition our experiences of oppression. And since the exercise of oppression is systematic and relations of domination are structural, Moraga understands that an examination of oppression is simultaneously an examination of fundamental aspects of a world that is hierarchically organized according to categories of class, race, gender, and sexuality. Thus, Moraga's call for women of color to examine their own lives is ultimately a call for women of color to under-

stand the oppressive systems and structures within which they live as part
of their larger project to "change the world" (*Bridge,* Foreword). [33]

Moraga is aware that what she is asking for will not be easy. She
understands why we are often afraid to examine how *we* are implicated
in relations of domination: "*the sources of oppression form not only our
radicalism, but also our pain.* Therefore, they are often the places we feel
we must protect unexamined at all costs" (*Loving* 134). To do the kind
of self-reflexive examination Moraga calls for can mean having to admit
"how deeply 'the man's' words have been ingrained in us" (*Bridge* 32).
The project of examining our own location within the relations of domination becomes even riskier when we realize that doing so might mean
giving up "whatever privileges we have managed to squeeze out of this
society by virtue of our gender, race, class or sexuality" (*Bridge* 30). We
are afraid to admit that we have benefited from the oppression of others.
"[We fear] the immobilization threatened by [our] own incipient guilt."
We fear we might have to "change [our lives] once [we] have seen [our-
selves] in the bodies of the people [we have] called different. [We fear] the
hatred, anger, and vengeance of those [we have] hurt" (*Loving* 56–57).

Moraga's self-interrogation involved acknowledging how she has been
guilty of working her own privilege, "ignorantly, at the expense of others" (*Bridge* 34). Moraga *now,* unlike many other white-skinned "Hispanics," has come to understand — through making connections between
her experience as a woman in a male world and a lesbian in a heterosexual world — how what functions as the privilege of looking "white" in
U.S. society has significantly shaped her experience of the world. The consequences, for Moraga, have been both positive and negative. On the one
hand, she credits her light skin and Anglo surname with pushing her into
the college prep "A" group in high school and with making her and her
siblings "*the* success stories of the family," and, on the other, she has had
to "push up against a wall of resistance from [her] own people" in her
attempts to claim a Chicana/o identity (*Loving* 96–97; *Bridge* 33–34).

What should be clear from my analysis of Moraga's work is that her
"theory in the flesh" is derived from, although not uniformly determined
by, "the physical realities" of her life, her "social location." I have shown
that the social categories that make up her particular social location are

33. The centrality of experiences of subordination to Chicana feminist theorizing is elegantly illustrated by Saldívar-Hull, especially in her autobiographical first chapter.
Although Saldívar-Hull is careful to avoid a positivist conception of experience, she nevertheless maintains, "As Chicanas, however, our specific experiences as working-class-origin,
ethnic women under the law of the fathers undergird our theories" (12).

causally relevant for the experiences she has had, and demonstrated that Moraga's cultural identity both conditions and is conditioned by her interpretations of those experiences. I have also shown how and why Moraga's interpretations of her experiences have changed over time. Moraga's understanding of the world — her knowledge — has been mediated through her cultural identity, which is indissolubly linked, through her experiences, to the various social categories of her particular material existence.

A realist theory of identity thus provides women of color with a nonessentialist way to ground their identities. It gives us a way of knowing and acting from within our own social location or "flesh." Like Moraga, we will no longer have to aspire to a bodiless, genderless, raceless, and sexless existence (an existence that has traditionally been conceptualized in terms of the unmarked but nevertheless privileged heterosexual white male) to claim justifiable knowledge of the world around us. A realist theory of identity gives women of color a way to substantiate that we *do* possess knowledge — knowledge important not only for ourselves but also for all who wish to more accurately understand the world — and that we possess it partly as a result of the fact that we *are* women of color.

CHAPTER 2

Chicana Feminism and Postmodernist Theory

For over a decade, a growing number of feminists have challenged the view that postmodernism is the most productive theoretical framework for feminist discourse. Barbara Christian, in her 1987 essay "The Race for Theory," and bell hooks, in her 1991 essay "Essentialism and Experience," were among the first to express reservations about the usefulness of a poststructuralist-influenced literary theory for their own critical projects.[1] Other feminists followed close behind: as early as 1992, Linda Singer sounded cautionary warnings about the "regulative effect" that postmodernism seemed to be having on feminist theorizing, and in 1994, Maria Lugones made a point of dissociating her theoretical account of multiplicity from postmodernist theorizing of the same. Both Judith Roof ("Lesbians and Lyotard") and Linda Martín Alcoff ("Politics") urged feminists to recognize the epistemological denial apparent in postmodernist projects that rely on unacknowledged legitimating metanarratives to establish the "truth value" of no truth. More recently, Jacqui Alexander and Chandra Talpade Mohanty suggested that "postmodernist theory . . . has generated a series of epistemological confusions regarding the interconnections between location, identity, and the construction of knowledge" (xvii). Even Linda Nicholson, undeniably one of

---

1. See also Rosaura Sánchez, "Postmodernism and Chicano Literature," which, while not focusing on Chicana feminism, succinctly evaluates the implications of postmodernist theory for liberatory political practices.

postmodernism's staunchest defenders and the editor of the collection *Feminism/Postmodernism*, found it necessary in the introduction to her co-edited 1995 anthology *Social Postmodernism* to acknowledge (in the hopes of remedying) some of postmodernism's political and theoretical limitations (8–9).

There have been, of course, a number of different reactions to the predicaments of postmodernism that these critics have identified — including the various reactions of the many theorists who never accepted its epistemological premises in the first place. But even among those feminists who have engaged seriously with postmodernist theory and who remain wary of positivist or idealist conceptions of objectivity and knowledge, a call for a new kind of theoretical "pragmatism" that attempts to avoid the normative deficits of postmodernist theory has emerged. For instance, Nancy Fraser calls for the development of an "eclectic, neopragmatist feminist theory" that permits both dereifying and normative critique even as it avoids metaphysical entanglements (167–68). Similarly, Rita Felski suggests that feminist theorists need to de-ontologize difference by "offering a redescription of the status of equality and difference that is framed in pragmatic rather than meta-physical terms" (2). Even Judith Butler — whose work in *Gender Trouble* and *Feminists Theorize the Political* can be held accountable for autho-rizing the wholesale dismissal by a generation of young feminist scholars of any feminist project that betrays a concern for "truth," "identity," "experience," or "knowledge" — has recently acknowledged that "in order to set political goals, it is necessary to assert normative judge-ments" (Butler, "For a Careful Reading" 141). Of course, like Fraser and Felski, Butler is careful not to "ground" her normative judgments in metaphysical commitments, preferring to base her politics of subversive citation and redeployment instead on a contingent " 'foundation' that moves, and which changes in the course of that movement" (141).

One of the questions I pose in this chapter is whether a purely "prag-matist" feminist theory is sufficient for a liberatory feminism. By a prag-matist feminist theory, I mean one that refuses to make any objective metaphysical claims — even limited ones — about the nature of either the world or of human beings and that, consequently, must justify its nor-mative claims in purely conventional or strategic terms.[2] By way of an

---

2. Pragmatism as a solution to postmodernist predicaments, despite the impression cre-ated by these essays, is not new. To the extent that these feminists continue to eschew even limited metaphysical claims, they will reproduce the pragmatist impulses that have long

answer, I suggest that, insofar as it tacitly presupposes the same positivist conception of objectivity and knowledge that serves as a straw person for postmodernist theory, the kind of pragmatist feminist theory that these critics propose is inadequate for theorizing and authorizing effective progressive political strategies. As part of an ongoing effort to reconceptualize (within postpositivist realist terms) concepts such as identity, experience, knowledge, and truth, I argue for the necessity of revisiting the problem of justification. I assert that progressive feminist theorists need to acknowledge that some of our ethical and political goals might indeed be based on reliable, objective knowledge of ourselves and our world. Rather than refusing to ground our politics, then, we need to ask what grounds might, in fact, be worth defending.

These are the larger theoretical concerns and questions that have informed my thinking as I have explored the influence of postmodernism on Chicana feminist theory. In my quest to find the best available language for theorizing feminist — and particularly, Chicana feminist — subjectivity and identity, I have examined two influential Chicana theorists whose work has been significantly shaped by, and has contributed to the shaping of, the "postmodern turn": Norma Alarcón and Chela Sandoval. Consistent with the way I have used the term throughout this book, I will define postmodernism as a theoretical position that incorporates such diverse elements as the decentering of the subject, the jettisoning of "grand theories," a turn toward local and even nonrational knowledges, a textualizing of the social, a valorization of flux and mobility, and a substitution of a politics of difference for a politics of liberation.[3] I have found that these two Chicana theorists demonstrate an ambivalent relationship to postmodernist theory even as they accept many of its presuppositions and claims.[4] They appreciate its dismantling

been a part of postmodernist theory. Sánchez noted in 1987 that "what seems to be gaining ground among some postmodernists who reject the old forms of legitimizing reason is a new pragmatism that defends a consensus-view of truth, one determined by the dominant bourgeois discourses, one that ensures the maintenance of the status quo" ("Postmodernism and Chicano Literature" 4–5). She concludes that the discourses generated by the postmodernist crisis in epistemology and ideology "are not contestatory at the economic or political level" (5).

3. For a fuller definition of what I mean by the term *postmodernism*, see note 9 in the introduction to this book.

4. This ambivalence toward postmodernism is one that they themselves acknowledge; this fact might prompt some critics to deny that their theories should be considered postmodernist. Part of what I will show in this chapter, however, is that their key theoretical assumptions are in fact recognizably postmodernist. As a consequence, Alarcón's attempts

of the transcendental subject of reason, for instance, while remaining committed to an account of subjectivity that allows some form of identity-based (i.e., "Chicana" or "woman of color") agency. Over the course of this chapter, I show that their attempts to theorize the experience and agency of Chicanas and other women of color are not supported by the postmodernist presuppositions they employ. I expect that my position will generate some resistance among those scholars (Chicana or not) who are already committed to postmodernism, especially to poststructuralist-influenced theories of subject formation. But I argue that the alternative theoretical framework I describe in chapter one — postpositivist realist — would better serve these two thinkers' attempts to analyze and theorize the situation of Chicanas. My purpose in foregrounding this alternative theoretical framework is to contribute in a substantive way to ongoing theoretical discussions among feminists regarding the status of "truth," knowledge, and experience, as well as the political and epistemic salience of the concept of identity.

I draw on the postpositivist realist theory of identity in order to suggest alternatives to the recognizably postmodernist positions that Alarcón and Sandoval take. For example, in response to Alarcón's postmodernist view that Chicanas are at their most radical when they symbolize a principle of abstract oppositionality, I show how two of the Chicana feminists that she uses to illustrate her contention in fact attempt to work through the conflicts they experience in order to imagine a concrete social alternative. They thus justify their efforts to create a qualitatively new and better social order with reference to a normative conception of the human good. Similarly, in response to Sandoval's postmodernist assertion that all truth claims are complicit with oppressive authoritarianism, I suggest that when truth claims are understood in a realist way as fallible and subject to verification and revision, they can contribute dialectically to the development of reliable knowledge about the world. By rethinking, from an alternative theoretical perspective, notions of agency and truth, I hope to reinvigorate discussions among Chicana and other feminists about the relationship between theory and practice, between intellectual inquiry and our ongoing attempts to transform ourselves and our world.

I begin the chapter with a necessarily brief overview of the historical context from which Chicana feminism emerged. By situating historically

---

to avoid a "clearcut postmodern agenda" are largely unsuccessful, while Sandoval's strongest insights are undermined by her postmodernist presuppositions.

the kinds of questions being asked and problems being addressed within Chicana feminist theory, I hope to show that just as Chicanas' political activism and struggles are often based on a certain theoretical knowledge, that knowledge is frequently produced in their experiences of political struggle. So, although the works I focus on in this chapter can be seen as formal expressions of Chicana feminist theory, they are not the only, or necessarily the most important, places where the theoretical insights arrived at by Chicanas and other women of color originate or are formulated and expressed. In refusing to draw a firm distinction between Chicana feminism and Chicana feminist theory, I am following Satya Mohanty, Sandra Harding, and Richard Boyd in making the more general Marxian theoretical point that knowledge is produced not in isolation from the world but through engagement with it.[5] My second purpose in invoking the context from which Chicana feminism emerged is to acknowledge the degree to which my thinking has been significantly shaped by my Chicana foremothers. I have inherited certain kinds of intellectual questions and issues that would not have been available to me without the important work of some of the same activist/theorists with whose theoretical approaches I now take issue.

In the second section of the chapter I begin my theoretical argument with a discussion of Alarcón's theory of multiple subjectivities and her attempts to remain on the margins — what she calls the "interstices" — between incompatible theoretical frameworks. I then turn, in the third section, to Sandoval's oft-cited essay "U.S. Third World Feminism: The Theory and Method of Oppositional Consciousness in the Postmodern World" to show both that Sandoval's postmodernist presuppositions partially undermine her project of theorizing the experiences of women of color and also that her most cogent insights are compatible with a postpositivist realist theory of identity. In the last section, I return to the question of whether a purely "pragmatist" feminist theory is sufficient for a liberatory feminist politics. I look to the writings of Chicana authors Cherríe Moraga and Gloria Anzaldúa for a more appropriate theoretical trajectory for the cultural critic concerned with representing the cultural productions and experiences of women of color. In that section, I examine Chicana identity from within a postpositivist realist theoretical framework, positing Chicana identity not as a principle of abstract oppositionality but as a historically and materially grounded

5. See R. N. Boyd, "How to Be a Moral Realist," esp. 203–6; Harding, *Whose Science? Whose Knowledge?* esp. 123–27; S. P. Mohanty, *Literary Theory,* esp. 212–15.

perspective from which feminists can work to disclose the complicated workings of oppression and resistance.

THE EMERGENCE OF CHICANA FEMINISM

Chicana feminism, as a distinct social movement, emerged primarily in response to the sexism Chicanas experienced within the Chicano civil rights movement.[6] Together with their fathers, husbands, and brothers, Chicana civil rights workers of the 1960s and 1970s were engaged in a struggle against the various forms of oppression and discrimination that their Chicana/o communities have historically experienced. Like their Mexicana and Chicana foremothers, Chicanas active in *el movimiento* did not distinguish their empowerment as women from the empowerment of their families and communities. In their activism and their writings they advocated for welfare rights, government-funded (but community-controlled) child care, nondiscriminatory health care, expanded legal rights, and control over their own reproductive capacities. They struggled for better working conditions and attacked racial and sexual stereotypes, frequently articulating the connections between the discrimination they faced as women, as workers, and as members of a racial minority group.[7] Nevertheless, as noted in chapter one, Chicanas in the Chicano movement were disturbed when the rights for which they were fighting continued to be unfairly distributed along gender lines within their own communities. Accordingly, throughout the 1970s, Chicanas became increasingly vocal about their dissatisfaction at being expected to defer to and serve their Chicano brothers while being expected to perform a disproportionate share of the work required for successful political organizing.[8]

Despite their commitment to *la causa,* it became increasingly apparent to Chicana feminists that their interest in achieving gender equality within the Chicano community stood in direct opposition to a discourse of nationalism that emphasized the value of family loyalty in the project

6. I use the term *Chicana* in this book to refer to a woman of Mexican ancestry who was born and/or raised in the United States and who possesses a radical political consciousness.

7. For an excellent account of the continuity between Mexican American women's activism and feminism within Mexican American communities, see Ruíz, *From Out of the Shadows,* esp. chaps. 4–6. See also Cotera.

8. For more on the development of Chicana feminist thought, see Córdova, "Roots and Resistance"; García, *Chicana Feminist Thought,* esp. the introduction; García, "Development of Chicana Feminist Discourse."

of cultural survival. In response to what they perceived as cultural genocide, Chicano cultural nationalists had self-consciously taken up a series of Mexican cultural icons in order to project an alternative, and more affirming, Mexicano/Chicano cultural reality. Among these were three female icons — La Virgen de Guadalupe, La Malinche, and La Llorona — which, taken together, shaped the boundaries of traditional Chicana womanhood.[9] Partly because of the imagined links, symbolically conveyed by these three icons, between female sexual abnegation and cultural fidelity on the one hand, and female sexual desire and cultural betrayal on the other, attacks by Chicano nationalists on Chicanas who refused to toe the party line were often couched in terms of sexuality. Chicanas who were explicit about their feminist convictions or who dated or married white men were, as noted in chapter one, criticized as *vendidas* and *malinchistas*. These invocations of La Malinche, the mistress of and translator for the Spanish conquistador Hernán Cortés, were designed to hold "unfaithful" Chicanas responsible for perpetuating the legacy of rape handed down from the conquest of Mexico. This same standard often did not apply to the men, whose relations with white women were seen as rectifying an unjust legacy of emasculation at the hands of white men. The double standard, of course, did not escape the attention of Chicana feminists, who were quick to point out its hypocrisy.[10] As the designated reproducers of culture, Chicanas in the movement were under greater pressure to conform to more traditional

9. For an extended discussion of the symbolic meaning of La Malinche for Chicanas, see chapter one. La Virgen de Guadalupe is Mexico's indigenous version of the Virgin Mary. She is believed to have appeared in what is now Mexico City to the Indian Juan Diego in 1531. As the paradigmatic spirit of female sexual and personal abnegation, *la virgen* is the revered mother and patron saint of Mexico. La Llorona is a legendary figure who symbolizes unnatural motherhood and (always) inappropriate female sexual desire. Although there are many different versions of the Llorona legend, the basic plot is this: La Llorona is a mother who drowned her children either to take revenge on her unfaithful husband or to be free to pursue her own adulterous affair. For her crime, she is condemned to wander forever in the streams and riverbeds of northern Mexico and the southwestern United States calling to and crying for her children. The legend of La Llorona is still told to children throughout that region to scare them into avoiding potentially dangerous situations with water and to encourage them to come into the house before it gets dark. For a fascinating analysis of the legend of La Llorona, together with deft readings of how the writers Sandra Cisneros and Helena María Viramontes have reworked the legend in their fiction, see Saldívar-Hull, esp. 117–23 and 156–59.

10. For three wonderful poems written by Chicanas active in the Chicano movement that successfully convey the hypocrisy to which I allude, see Cervantes, "You Cramp My Style, Baby"; Lucero-Trujillo, "Machismo Is Part of Our Culture"; Zamora, "Notes from a Chicana 'Coed.'"

models of conduct than were men. Thus, Chicana feminists were trying to break out of traditional roles as biological and cultural reproducers at the exact moment that Chicano nationalists were attempting to reinscribe them into those roles. Although a few either were pushed out of Chicano organizations or left to form their own autonomous groups, most Chicana activists continued to struggle within Chicano movement organizations as long as those organizations remained viable. As a result, the earliest expressions of what would come to constitute the origins of Chicana feminism were couched as intramural criticism designed to strengthen *el movimiento*. Chicana critiques of "macho" attitudes were presented as contributions to an ideological self-critique, and Chicana struggles against gender oppression were undertaken in the service of destroying "a serious obstacle to women anxious to play a role in the struggle for Chicano liberation" (Vidal 23).[11]

Although most Chicanas placed their primary energies in the service of the Chicano movement, some began in the late 1970s to work within white women's liberation movements. But because many white feminist organizations retained a primary focus on gender, the analyses they provided, and the political projects they undertook, proved inadequate for Chicanas who were simultaneously struggling against race- and class-based forms of oppression. Consequently, in the 1980s, Chicana feminists, together with feminists of other nonwhite racial groups who had had similar experiences within their own ethnic nationalist movements and the white women's movement, turned to their own experience as a ground for theorizing their multiple forms of oppression. In the process, a new political identity — women of color — emerged. Chicanas joined African American, Asian American, Latina, and other "third world" feminists in a variety of efforts to challenge both the racism of Anglo American feminism and the sexism of ethnic nationalist movements. Some of the most significant writings of the women of color movement include the groundbreaking anthology edited by Cherríe Moraga and Gloria Anzaldúa *This Bridge Called My Back: Writings by Radical Women of Color,* the follow-up anthology edited by Gloria Anzaldúa *Making Face, Making Soul/Haciendo Caras: Creative and Critical Perspectives by Women of Color,* and the more scholarly anthology *Third World Women and the Politics of Feminism,* edited by Chandra

11. For more information about Chicanas in the Chicano movement, see Córdova; Cotera; García, *Chicana Feminist Thought;* García, "Development of Chicana Feminist Discourse"; Gutiérrez; López; Moraga, *Loving,* esp. 105–11; Ruíz; Trujillo, "Chicana Lesbians."

Talpade Mohanty, Ann Russo, and Lourdes Torres. The important development of a women of color identity and politics, which was seen as supplementing but not replacing a Chicana identity and politics, allowed Chicana feminists to engage in coalitional politics even as they retained at the center of their politics an analysis of the interrelationship of race, class, gender, and sexuality in explaining the particular conditions of their lives in the United States.[12]

NORMA ALARCÓN'S POSTMODERNIST FEMINISM

Like other theorists who adopted the political identity "woman of color" in the 1980s and early 1990s, Chicana critic Norma Alarcón is justifiably wary of invoking any idealized feminist subject, such as the autonomous, self-determining, self-defining and, "unified subject organized oppositionally to men from the perspective of gender differences" ("Theoretical Subject(s)" 28). She argues that this autonomous and unified "subject of consciousness" comes into being through a logic of either identification (with other women) or counteridentification (in opposition to men), a binary model that is inadequate because it fails to account for the "complex and multiple ways in which the subject and object of possible experience are constituted" ("Theoretical Subject(s)" 34). That is, a binary model that figures subject formation solely in terms of identification and/or counteridentification cannot account for the fact that in "cultures in which asymmetric race and class relations are a central organizing principle of society, one may also 'become a woman' in opposition to other women" ("Theoretical Subject(s)" 33). Because Alarcón associates this kind of binary and oppositional thinking with gender standpoint epistemology (most notably the work of Sandra Harding), she turns to postmodernist feminism's explicit deconstruction of binary oppositions and rejection of a feminine "essence" in the belief that it is better suited to theorizing the experiences of nonwhite women.[13]

12. For accounts of how women of color or third world feminism emerged from Chicanas' and other nonwhite women's frustration with some white feminist organizations, see Córdova, esp. 186; García, "Development of Chicana Feminist Discourse," esp. 538–41; Sandoval, "Feminism and Racism."

13. In this chapter, I focus on Alarcón's more recent theoretical work, published since 1990, because my focus here is how postmodernism has influenced her theorizing about Chicana subjectivity. While Alarcón's political concerns have remained more or less the same, her theoretical framework has evolved as she has been influenced by the postmodern turn. See note 15 below for a brief discussion of how Alarcón's conception of the self has evolved.

Consistent with a postmodernist theoretical orientation, Alarcón's most recent work conceptualizes the "self" as being "produced" through discourse. In "Chicana Feminism: In the Tracks of 'the' Native Woman," Alarcón describes Chicanas and other women of color as "bombarded and subjected to multiple crosscultural and contradictory ideologies" that form a "maze of discourses through which the 'I' as a racial and gendered self is hard put to emerge and runs the risk of being thought of as 'irrational' or 'deluded' in their attempt to articulate their oppression and exploitation" (253). She asserts that "women of color are *always already* positioned crossculturally and within contradictory discourses" (254, emphasis added) and that they are instantiations of the "so-called postmodern decentered subject" (252). Her key theoretical assumptions are that (1) subjects are produced entirely through discourse and (2) the different discourses which produce women of color are fundamentally contradictory.

Why does Alarcón represent Chicanas as decentered postmodern subjects produced by contradictory discourses? Although she never fully explains her premises, we can reconstruct her line of thinking. For Alarcón, Chicanas are produced as individuals by the forces of capitalism even as they are produced as members of a community — as "Mothers" — by "Chicano nationalist 'communal modes of power' " ("Chicana Feminism" 253–54). In other words, each discourse (capitalist and Chicano nationalist) implicitly produces an idealized subject. Chicano nationalism's ideal subject is a dark-skinned working-class male of Mexican origin living in the United States who is fiercely proud of his indigenous roots, who is antagonistic to capitalism, and whose success cannot be conceptualized apart from the well-being of the Chicano community. The ideal subject of capitalism, however, is an autonomous individual bearer of rights who has no communal ties apart from those formed through economic exchange and who achieves success through his individual effort. For Alarcón, the contradiction arises when different discourses produce or construct Chicanas in different and irreconcilable ways. Thus, from Alarcón's perspective, Chicanas are produced by Chicano nationalist discourse as racially marked, undifferentiated (and male-identified) "members of a community," and by capitalist discourse as individuals who sell their labor in exchange for wages. When we factor in other discourses that Chicanas are likely to be "subjected to" — such as a discourse of Anglo-American liberal feminism that would produce Chicanas as female-gendered (and implicitly white) individual subjects of consciousness — we can better understand why Alarcón conceives of Chicana subjectivity as "multiple" and "contradictory." Her key point is that the different discourses that produce Chicana subjectivity intersect in ways that preclude Chicanas from being produced as unified or coherent subjects.

Alarcón's claim that Chicanas are "always already" produced in fundamentally contradictory ways gives rise to two problems. First, she undercuts the possibility of normative critique by making the postmodernist move of treating conflict as irresolvable and aporetic. For instance, she claims that "the figure and referent of Chicanas today is positioned as conflictively as Lyotard's *'differend.'* " She explains, "Lyotard defines a *differend* as a 'case of conflict between (at least) two parties, that cannot be equitably resolved for lack of a rule of judgment applicable to both arguments. One side's legitimacy does not imply the other's lack of legitimacy' " ("Chicana Feminism" 253). When Alarcón regards the two discourses that constitute Chicanas as the arguments of two parties in conflict and claims that "one side's legitimacy does not imply the other's lack of legitimacy," she skates on the edge of relativism by disqualifying any possible means of adjudicating the claims of the disputants. She thus threatens to undermine the grounds for a normative Chicana feminist criticism by opening the possibility that there will be no adequate means for deciding between, for example, feminist and sexist discourses.[14]

Second, Alarcón mischaracterizes conflicts between discourses as fundamental social contradictions. By figuring the (at least two) different discourses through which Chicanas are constituted as always contradictory, Alarcón takes discursive inconsistencies as structural contradictions and thus moves too quickly to a high level of abstraction. It is evident that no one discourse can describe Chicanas in their entirety and that the different discourses that — together — describe them do so in overlapping and obviously inconsistent ways. Nevertheless, the discourses that

14. At times, however, Alarcón recognizes the poverty of Lyotard's concept for helping Chicanas figure out how to act in the service of their own empowerment. When she admits that Lyotard's concept "cannot inform the actual Chicana *differend* engaged in a living struggle as to how she can seize her 'I' or even her feminist 'We' to change her circumstances," Alarcón implicitly acknowledges what other critics (even those sympathetic to Lyotard's philosophical project) usually concede: that once one has decided in advance that all hierarchies (and hence all judgments about what is "good" or "better," "bad" or "worse") are epistemically unjustifiable, it is impossible to say what one "should" or "should not" do and, consequently, extremely difficult to project any course of political action ("Chicana Feminism" 253). For a cogent discussion of the debilitating effects of Lyotardian postmodernism on feminist theory and the need for a normative feminist criticism, see Alcoff, "Politics of Postmodern Feminism"; Benhabib, esp. 213–25.

Alarcón figures as constitutive of Chicana subjectivity are not actually contradictory in a systematic or structural way. There is no reason to suppose, for instance, that a Chicana cannot be both a member of the Chicano community and a feminist. It is true that she may occasionally experience conflicts that arise from differing conceptions about how she should conduct herself in relation to some aspects of her life. A heterosexual Chicana with feminist convictions, for example, may have to defend her resolution not to take her husband's name in a familial context and justify her decision not to take a better-paying job in a community away from her extended family in a feminist one, but she is a Chicana feminist in both contexts. But by assuming that conflicting discourses are inherently contradictory, Alarcón idealizes each discourse in a manner that implicitly suggests that each is internally consistent and coherent (that is, that it does not have internal contradictions that could undermine it in relation to the other) and that each is stable, fixed, and incapable of change as it comes into contact with other discourses. However, the last thirty years have seen such a transformation of both Chicano nationalist and Anglo-American feminist discourses — largely as a result of each having been subjected to critiques originating from other discourses — that it is quite natural today to speak of a Chicana feminism that incorporates key precepts from each. Alarcón reifies as the unchanging condition of possibility for Chicana subjectivity the conflicts engendered by discourses that describe Chicanas in incomplete and inconsistent ways. She effectively replaces an essentialism of the subject with an essentialism of discourse.

Alarcón's understanding of the "contradictory" nature of Chicana subjectivity has some paradoxical implications for the possibility of claiming an identity. Because she identifies no existing discourse through which Chicanas or other women of color can be produced as coherent subjects, Alarcón figures women of color as "subjects-in-process" who "must take up diverse subject positions which cannot be unified without double binds and contradictions" ("Conjugating Subjects" 136). Alarcón's woman of color can have multiple subjectivities (in that she is produced as a "subject" by multiple discourses), but she cannot have an identity because "to grasp or reclaim an identity in this culture means always already to have become a subject of consciousness" ("Theoretical Subject[s]" 37). The "woman of color" within Alarcón's theoretical framework is incapable of becoming a unitary "subject of consciousness" because the multiple and "contradictory" discourses that produce her construct her as necessarily fragmented. And, according to Alarcón, the woman of color cannot hope to grasp an identity by *innocently* synthesizing her multiple subjectivities into a coherent whole because "the theory of the subject of consciousness as a unitary and synthesizing agent of knowledge is always already a posture of domination" ("Theoretical Subject(s)" 37). Alarcón thus represents Chicanas and other women of color as "postmodern decentered subject(s)" who "must move towards provisional solidarities especially through social movements" in their efforts to forge group solidarities that can help them overcome the oppressions they face ("Chicana Feminism" 252).

If we take seriously Alarcón's pronouncement that "to be oppressed means to be disenabled not only from grasping an 'identity,' but also from reclaiming it" (Theoretical Subject(s)" 37), and if we bear in mind that (in Alarcón's line of argumentation) the discourses that produce Chicanas reduce them to exploited laborers and unrecognized nurturers, then we understand that a "Chicana" cannot claim an identity unless she ceases to be oppressed and becomes the oppressor. In that case, however, she will no longer be a Chicana. The logic of this conclusion follows from Alarcón's postmodernist refusal to recognize the existence of subjects apart from the discourses through which they are produced. Insofar as there is no "self" that exists prior to subjection to discourse, any given self exists *as itself* only as long as it retains its position in the discourses through which it is produced. Thus, within Alarcón's theoretical framework, the signifier *Chicana* refers not to a biologically female person of Mexican American parentage who self-identifies as such but rather to a disembodied and fragmented consciousness that exists always within a position of subordination. Consequently, there is no room in Alarcón's postmodernist theoretical framework for movement by, or transformation of, the "Chicana self."[15]

---

15. Presumably, the only option for the Chicana who wishes to avoid fragmentation and subordination would be for her to transform the "sociosymbolic contract" so that she exists solely within a single discourse that truly names, marks, recognizes, and describes her in her entirety. The problem is that Alarcón's poststructuralist-influenced framework provides no practical guidance as to how she could go about doing that. I am using the term *sociosymbolic contract* here in the sense that Alarcón uses it in one of her early essays to describe the way young Chicanas are socialized into an Anglo-dominated patriarchal society. In that essay, "Making 'Familia' from Scratch," Alarcón draws on Julia Kristeva's notion of the "symbolic contract" and Pierre Miranda's notion of "semantic charters" to describe the way a woman's place/meaning is overdetermined by the role (or place) she occupies under patriarchal law. Alarcón extends these notions to explain how a Chicana's socialization as a wife/mother within her specific cultural context can lead to the fragmenting of her self: "To the extent that the role she is socialized into works its psychological (or physical) violence on her, or to the extent *her own sense of self* does not correspond

Alarcón's approach leaves untheorized the causal connections between the social categories of race, class, gender, and sexuality on the one hand and subjectivity on the other. The "subject" in Alarcón's framework becomes a free-floating site of consciousness with an unspecified relationship to those social categories.[16] It is significant that Alarcón never directly addresses the problem of accounting for how and why certain people, and not others, are positioned to be "subjected" to particular discourses in the first place. Because her account of subjectivity refuses to acknowledge the existence of subjects apart from the discourses through which they are produced, it cannot explain why specific "sites of consciousness" are subjected to specific discourses. Her framework thus produces some false distinctions between different kinds of people while erasing some other very salient ones.[17] For instance, by suggesting that women of color are "sites of consciousness" who are produced as "subjects-in-process" by multiple contradictory discourses, Alarcón implies that there are other (presumably non–women of color) "sites of consciousness" who are produced by internally coherent discourses that constitute them as fully realized, coherent, and stable "subjects." Contra Alarcón, I will suggest that all people are "subjects-in-process" and that, *to the extent* that they are constituted by discourses, they are all multiple and (to some degree) incoherent.

---

to her socially prescribed role, she will experience a splitting of the self" (150, emphasis added). Alarcón suggests that in order to be a speaking subject, the Chicana "has to position herself at the margins of the 'symbolic contract' and refuse to accept definitions of 'woman' and 'man' in order to transform the contract" (157). It should be noted that whereas in this essay there appears a presocial entity (i.e., the young girl) with a more or less autonomous "sense of self" who becomes socialized into a particular cultural context, in Alarcón's later, more poststructuralist-influenced work, this presocial entity disappears in favor of disembodied sites of consciousness wholly produced by contradictory discourses.

16. Alarcón writes, "Consciousness as a site of multiple voicings is the theoretical subject, par excellence, of *Bridge*. These voicings (or thematic threads) are not viewed as necessarily originating with the subject, but as discourses that traverse consciousness and which the subject must struggle with constantly" ("Theoretical Subject(s)" 38). The vagueness of Alarcón's formulation leaves unclear the nature of the relationship between particular "thematic threads" (e.g., the concerns expressed in *Bridge*) and particular subjects (e.g., women of color).

17. When I say that some distinctions are more salient than others, I do not mean that they are "essentially" salient or that they have the same salience at all times and in all places. Thus, when I argue for the salience of race in U.S. society, I mean to indicate something important and knowable about contemporary U.S. society rather than something essential about race. Similarly, there is no necessary reason gender should be salient in precisely the way it is in our society. My point, however, is that as long as it is, we need to have a way to talk about the difference it makes.

Moreover, Alarcón never addresses the question of whether the differential production of "subjects-in-process" vis-à-vis "subjects" is systematic or arbitrary. This points to the crucial failure in Alarcón's theory of subjectivity. Because her theory limits itself to the discursive realm, it cannot ask what relation, if any, exists between the differential production of subjects and certain variable biological attributes such as skin color and genitalia. She thus provides no way to understand the difference that social categories of race, gender, sexuality, and class make to the realm of human experience and the production of human subjectivity. Unless we can acknowledge that embodied human beings have at least some preexisting properties that are interpreted, but not "produced," by the discursive contexts in which they live, it would seem to be purely arbitrary that, for example, I, as a native-born New Mexican, have been "produced" as a Chicana, rather than as, say, a Native or Anglo-American man. In the process of figuring the "subject-in-process" as "consciousness as a site of multiple voicings," Alarcón does not get rid of the problem of identity; she merely suppresses it ("Theoretical Subject(s)" 38).

The failure to address the problem of identity — the problem of accounting for how and why certain people are "subjected" to certain discourses — is a characteristic weakness of postmodernist feminist theories of subjectivity, and Alarcón is not the only theorist to sidestep this issue. Judith Butler's concern, in *Gender Trouble,* with establishing the disjunctures between anatomical sex, gender performance, and gender identity, for instance, leads her to bypass the possibility of theorizing the complex process of identity formation. Instead, she merely asserts the "contingency" of these three "dimensions of significant corporeality," without ever clarifying what they are contingent upon or how they are related to one another (137). Postmodernist theories of subjectivity, like the one Butler articulates in *Gender Trouble,* cannot explain the persistent correlation between certain kinds of bodies and certain kinds of identities. While we can readily concede that one is not born a woman, we might still want to ask why a significant majority of people with anatomically female bodies nonetheless become women; while we can similarly concede that race is not biologically determined, we might still want to ask why a dark-skinned person is more likely than a light-skinned one to identify as African American. These are the kinds of questions that postmodernist approaches such as Butler's do not allow. Rather than addressing the influences the social categories of race and gender have on the processes of identity formation, Butler moves to disavow the ontological status — or reality — of those categories.

If Alarcón's weaknesses in addressing the problem of identity are more obvious than Butler's, it is only because Alarcón explicitly retains some categories of identity, while Butler attempts to promote a feminism that cannot claim to represent "women" at all. Thus, despite Alarcón's repeated call for critics to take into consideration gender, race, and class when theorizing Chicana and woman of color subjectivity, her postmodernist reliance on the productivity and materiality of discourse — to the exclusion of a consideration of the productivity and materiality of what is extra- or pre-discursive — prevents her from providing an account of the causal (indeed causally hierarchical) relationships of biologically and temporally variant bodies, human-made structures of social inequality, and the differential production of different kinds of subjects.

Why, given her postmodernist predilections, does Alarcón remain committed to identity-based agency? Why, in light of her reluctance to allow anyone to claim an identity, does she continue to refer to "Chicanas" and "women of color" in her theoretical work? I suggest that the answers to these questions lie in Alarcón's political commitments: she needs the sign "Chicana," for example, to signify a woman who, because of the objective social location she occupies, has been racialized, gendered, and classed in a particular way. It is clear that Alarcón knows whom she is referring to when she talks about Chicanas, even if her theory cannot explain how or why they become differentiated from non-Chicanas. My point here is that Alarcón employs an unacknowledged raced-and-gendered, embodied Chicana referent for her disembodied "subject-in-process."[18] She needs the sign *Chicana* to signify the particular kind of embodied consciousness that her "subject-in-process" cannot adequately refer to. If Alarcón were unconcerned with the project of empowering women of color, she could do as some other postmodernist feminists have, and shun the concept of identity altogether. But Alarcón is a Chicana feminist who has worked actively in a number of different venues to promote the well-being of Chicanas and other women of color. Her commitment to a feminism that seeks to

18. Alarcón's postmodernist refusal to acknowledge that referent, however, leads her, in "Conjugating Subjects," to a somewhat awkward formulation. In the following passage, Chicanas appear, after the fact, linked to the ungrounded and discursively produced "subject-in-process" through mere textual juxtaposition: "The critical desire to undercut subject determination through structures and discourses in my view, presupposes a subject-in-process who construct [sic] *provisional* identities . . . which subsume a network of signifying practices and structural experiences imbricated in historical *and* imaginary shifting national borders of Mexico and the United States for Chicanas" (136). Note the awkward appending of the words "for Chicanas" to this otherwise quite abstract sentence.

empower women of color is demonstrated by her work as publisher and editor of Third Women Press, a small press that publishes creative and scholarly works by women of color; by her participation in identity-based organizations such as Mujeres Activas en Letras y Cambio Social (MALCS) and the National Association for Chicana and Chicano Studies (NACCS); by her mentorship of feminist Chicana and other women of color scholars throughout the United States; and by the recurring thematic concerns of her scholarship. Accordingly, Alarcón finds herself caught between the postmodernist imperative to jettison categories of identity altogether and the pragmatic need to retain them in order to specify precisely on whose behalf it is that she is working.

I must emphasize that Alarcón's refusal to acknowledge her embodied Chicana referent is not unique to her. Rather, such a refusal is a characteristic feature of postmodernist feminist critiques of subjectivity and identity. As I demonstrated in chapter one, Donna Haraway and Judith Butler both cite or "refer" to women of color in order to justify their critiques of referential theories of identity. The "woman of color" is thus introduced into their arguments as an object or trope — an unacknowledged embodied referent that works to constitute through its exclusion the identity of the disembodied subject. Significantly, I am not the only critic to have noted this. In her essay, "'Women of Color' Writers and Feminist Theory," Margaret Homans argues that Butler, Haraway, and Diana Fuss use Chicanas and black women to "do the work of embodiment or identification [so that women of color end up acting as] an alibi for poststructuralist disembodiment or the deconstructing of identity." Homans points out that

> the status of a figure of embodiment in an argument against embodied identity must finally be that of excluded other: even though these figures are enlisted in the cause of poststructuralism, they must finally be left out of it. They define it by their difference from it. The woman of color as deployed by Haraway et al is still a figure, a figure for something — a bounded identity — serving a larger cause. (87)

And Biddy Martin, whose "Sexualities without Genders and Other Queer Utopias" is more sympathetic to Butler's overall project, nevertheless notes that

> lesbian and gay work fails at times to realize its potential for reconceptualizing the complexities of identity and social relations, at moments when . . . it at least implicitly conceives gender in negative terms, in terms of fixity, miring, or subjection to the indicatively female body, with the consequence that escape

from gender, usually in the form of disembodiment and always in the form of gender crossings, becomes the goal and the putative achievement. (105)

When antifoundationalist theorists sunder gender from sexuality in order to associate sexuality positively with transgression, cross-gender identification, and performativity, Martin argues, they implicitly figure gender negatively in terms of a passive and overdetermined femininity. In these texts, "gender . . . often appears along with race as an identification that defies ambiguous performances" (109–110). She concludes: "Conceptually, then, as well as politically, something called femininity [and especially racialized femininity] becomes the tacit ground in relation to which other positions become figural and mobile" (119).

Homans and Martin demonstrate that when Butler, Haraway, and Fuss depend on the embodied woman of color to function as the tacit ground for the disembodiment and mobility of the (implicitly white) feminist subject, they do so by excluding her, as a figure of fixity, from full and equal participation in their imagined communities of privileged feminist subjects. As such, Butler, Haraway, and Fuss do not always escape the exclusionary tendencies they so often denounce in other theoretical approaches. Moreover, as with Alarcón, their postmodernist feminist theoretical frameworks predispose them to disavow the relations of identification that undergird their critiques and guide their politics. Accordingly, their "subversions" of identity do not actually dispense with the problem of identity; like Alarcón, they simply defer the issue by refusing to theorize adequately the complex process of identity formation.

The slippage between Alarcón's unacknowledged and embodied referent and her disembodied and discursively produced "subject-in-process" is further demonstrated by her treatment of "racialized women theorists" vis-à-vis her "subjects-in-process." Over the course of the essay "Conjugating Subjects," she conflates the theoretical practice of "racialized women theorists" with the political practice of "subjects-in-process." According to Alarcón, theorizing by "racialized women theorists" represents a "process of 'determinate negation' a naysaying of the variety of the 'not yet,' that's not it." She writes,

By working through the "identity-in-difference" paradox, many racialized women theorists have implicitly worked in the interstice/interface of (existentialist) "identity politics" and "postmodernism" without a clearcut postmodern agenda. Neither Audre Lorde's nor Chela Sandoval's notion of difference/differential consciously subsumes a Derridean theorization —

though resonance cannot be denied and must be explored — so much as represent a process of "determinate negation" a naysaying of the "not yet," that's not it. (127)

Similarly, the political agency exercised by "subjects-in-process" is deconstructive and derives primarily from their ability to disrupt identity narratives by exhibiting themselves as examples of constitutive contradiction:

> A bi- or multi-ethnicized, raced, and gendered subject-in-process may be called upon to take up diverse subject positions which cannot be unified without double binds and contradictions. . . . The paradoxes and contradictions between subject positions move the subject to recognize, reorganize, reconstruct, and exploit difference through political resistance and cultural productions in order to reflect the subject-in-process. ("Conjugating Subjects" 136)

Here, Alarcón suggests that the most salient political agency of subjects-in-process derives from their invariable status as paradigmatic manifestations of contradiction and difference. She further suggests that the subject-in-process (read "racialized woman theorist") might be capable of affirmative agency — presumably through the process of determinate negation — through the reorganization and reconstruction of that which her difference deconstructs.[19] This suggestion, however, is finally undermined by Alarcón's reluctance, further on, to allow either the theorist or the subject-in-process to create a "theory" that will allow her to transcend or transform the "irreducible difference" that Alarcón sees as women of color's constitutive condition. Alarcón writes, "The very contingent currents through which the geopolitical subject-in-process is dislocated and forced into (im)migration will retain an irreducible difference that refuses to neatly correspond to the subject's account of herself and the theory we produce to account for her appearance" (137). It is worth noting that Alarcón grants agency not to subjects-in-process but to the "very contingent currents" that force them into "(im)migration" and disrupt the identity narratives through which they come into being. Thus, Alarcón's subjects-in-process possess agency, but it is an agency that derives from and is limited by the contradictory discourses through which they are produced. What we are left with, then, is a situation in

19. The Hegelian concept of determinate negation can be distinguished from total or radical skepticism in that it implies particular or specific negation. Since determinate negation is a specific negation, such that it exists in dialectical interdependence to affirmation, it has the potential to guide our understanding in a specific direction. What Alarcón's use of the concept of determinate negation finally refuses is the movement toward transcendence.

which Alarcón's "racialized women theorists" and her "subjects-in-process" possess a political agency that is severely restricted and inevitably reactive: they can transgress every boundary, call into question every category, and work in the "interstice/interface of (existentialist) 'identity politics' and 'postmodernism' " (127). However, Alarcón's framework does not allow either "racialized women theorists" or "subjects-in-process" to claim even a minimally coherent identity, to stake a preemptive political position, or to act affirmatively to work through the conflicts they experience. Moreover, theory has become a substitute for politics. Implied by Alarcón's framework is the idea that Chicanas and other women of color, as the paradigmatic manifestations of contradiction and difference, are at their most radical when they symbolize a principle of abstract oppositionality. What she leaves out is a way for Chicanas and other women of color living in the world to indicate (and begin to rectify) the systematic and causal links between socially produced categories of identity and the unequal distribution of power, goods, and resources.

From a realist perspective, I will suggest that while Chicana and other women of color feminists acknowledge the conflicts they experience, they attempt to work through them to create a qualitatively new and better social order. Furthermore, they do so in ways that require them to stake out political positions — positions that are generally justified with reference to a normative conception of the human good. In addition to engaging in direct political action as members and leaders of labor unions, community organizers, journalists, editors, educators, and so on, Chicana feminist activists and theorists are actively engaged in what, following Paul Gilroy, I call a politics of transfiguration — a transformative exercise by which historically oppressed people are engaged in imagining "the emergence of qualitatively new desires, social relations, and modes of association" both among themselves and between themselves and their oppressors (*Black Atlantic* 37). Cherríe Moraga, for example, engages in a politics of transfiguration in her essay "Queer Aztlán," in which she imagines a "Chicano homeland that could embrace *all* its people, including its jotería" (*Last Generation* 147). For Moraga, Queer Aztlán is not a territorial region but an imagined homeland where Chicanos and Chicanas of all colors, classes, and sexualities work together in the service of decolonization. Moraga does not reject Chicano nationalism per se, but wants to "expand it to meet a broader and wiser revolution," one capable of embracing a "full range of racial diversities, human sexualities, and expressions of gender" (150, 164). Implicit in

Moraga's conception of Queer Aztlán is a non-relativist realist claim that it is wrong to discriminate unfairly against people on the basis of race, gender, and sexuality. The "wiser" revolution that she imagines is not a "strategic" or "pragmatic" approach but is based on her own deeply felt conviction as to what is needed to make the world not merely different but better. Anzaldúa does something similar in her essay "La conciencia de la mestiza," in which she imagines the development of a new Chicana consciousness that turns the "ambivalence" engendered by living within contradictory frameworks into "something else" (*Borderlands* 79). Anzaldúa acknowledges, and figures brilliantly, the *choque,* or cultural collision, caused when two incompatible frames of reference come together, but she ultimately refuses to remain caught in a place of negativity and contradiction. She figures mestiza consciousness as a place where the self attempts to work out a synthesis between opposing frameworks, one in which the result is "greater than the sum of its severed parts" (79–80). Significantly, Anzaldúa's conception of mestiza consciousness provides her with a more accurate perspective on the world than she previously had, enabling her to see the "Chicana anew in light of her history" and to see through "the fictions of white supremacy" (87). Moreover, Anzaldúa explains that she is motivated by a quest for objective knowledge about herself and her place in the world: "I seek our woman's face, our true features, the positive and the negative seen clearly, free of the tainted biases of male dominance. I seek new images of identity, new beliefs about ourselves, our humanity and worth no longer in question" (87). While I do not claim that such imaginative exercises are, in themselves, sufficient to "change the world," I do argue that such affirmative imaginings are a necessary complement to engaging in direct political action designed to do just that. At a very basic level, efforts to imagine a better world help us to chart the paths down which we, as Chicana feminists, are going: they help us to decide what actions we should take, how we should prioritize our efforts, and whether and when we should consider changing directions.

CHELA SANDOVAL'S THEORY OF DIFFERENTIAL CONSCIOUSNESS

In "U.S. Third World Feminism: The Theory and Method of Oppositional Consciousness in the Postmodern World," Chela Sandoval draws on the work of writers such as Moraga, María Lugones, Audre Lorde, Bernice Johnson Reagon, and Anzaldúa to describe what she sees as a previously unrecognized kind of postmodern consciousness and political practice employed by U.S. third world feminists.[20] To lay the groundwork for her argument Sandoval proposes a topography of "oppositional consciousness" onto which all forms of oppositional consciousness and activity can be mapped. She identifies five general oppositional sites, each of which presupposes its own political program: "equal rights," "revolutionary," "supremacist," "separatist," and "differential." Sandoval is careful to note that these sites of resistance are not temporally situated, and she suggests that each position is potentially as effective as any other. However, she privileges differential consciousness over the others because she locates it on another register altogether. Whereas equal rights, revolutionary, supremacist, and separatist modes of consciousness and resistance imply coherent ideologies with fixed political programs, differential consciousness involves switching among the other four sites as the conditions of oppression or the shape of power changes. Its value, according to Sandoval, lies in its practitioners' unique ability to respond to the rapidly changing conditions of the postmodern world.

Differential consciousness, she argues, implies a new kind of subjectivity developed under conditions of multiple oppression. This new subjectivity, kinetic and self-consciously mobile, manifests itself in the political practices of U.S. third world feminists. Because nonwhite women have long been multiply oppressed, as part of their political coming-to-consciousness they have had to learn to highlight (or obscure) different aspects of themselves to be able to work effectively within political organizations. For example, if a U.S. third world feminist wants to work effectively or feel comfortable in a group organized on the basis of race, she will have to highlight the racialized aspects of her personal identity and de-emphasize the gendered ones. Conversely, if she wants to work effectively or feel included in white feminist organizations, she will have to de-emphasize or ignore the interests generated from the racialized aspect of her identity. As a result of having to continually privilege or de-emphasize different aspects of themselves in different situations, Sandoval says, U.S. third world feminists have become practiced at shift-

20. Sandoval uses the term *U.S. third world feminists* to refer to those nonwhite feminists living and working in the United States who came together in the late 1970s and early 1980s in an effort to complicate the gender- and race-based foci of white feminist and ethnic nationalist social movements. It is a term that is roughly synonymous and is often used interchangeably with *women of color*. In an effort to be faithful to Sandoval's text, I use her term when I paraphrase her argument and *women of color* in my own argument to refer to the same group of people.

ing their ideologies and identities in response to different configurations
of power.

> Differential consciousness requires grace, flexibility, and strength: enough
> strength to confidently commit to a well-defined structure of identity for one
> hour, day, week, month, year; enough flexibility to self-consciously trans-
> form that identity according to the requisites of another oppositional ideo-
> logical tactic if readings of power's formation require it; enough grace to rec-
> ognize alliance with others committed to egalitarian social relations and
> race, gender, and class justice, when their readings of power call for alter-
> native oppositional stands. . . . As the clutch of a car provides the driver the
> ability to shift gears, differential consciousness permits the practitioner to
> choose tactical positions, that is, to self-consciously break and reform ties to
> ideology, activities which are imperative for the psychological and political
> practices that permit the achievement of coalition across differences. (15)

Sandoval's schema is notable for the measure of self-consciousness it
attributes to political agents. She proposes that U.S. third world feminists
who participated in exclusively gender-based organizations during the
heyday of the women's movement never did so naively or because they
were caught within the all-encompassing web of ideology. Rather, they
were conscious of the temporary and strategic need to privilege one
aspect of themselves over others in the service of political or social
change. Their behavior was self-conscious, a strategic tactic they used to
mobilize more effectively against the particular oppressive power with
which they were struggling at the moment.[21] As a result of their differential consciousness, according to Sandoval, U.S. third world feminists
were unlikely to adopt "the kind of fervid belief systems and identity politics" typically demanded by hegemonic feminist organizations operating
under one of the other four modes of oppositional consciousness (13).
Contrary to many white women's assumptions, then, the tenuousness of
the relation between U.S. third world feminists and any particular type of
women's group was due not to disloyalty or betrayal but rather to their
self-conscious activity of weaving "between and among" various kinds
of oppositional ideologies and political strategies (13–14).

The significance for others (non–U.S. third world feminists) of
Sandoval's argument derives from her claim that while nonwhite women
have long lived within the conditions that enable and necessitate differ-

21. Sandoval writes, "The differential mode of consciousness depends upon the ability
to read the current situation of power and of self-consciously choosing and adopting the
ideological form best suited to push against its configurations, a survival skill well known
to oppressed peoples" ("U.S. Third World Feminism" 15).

ential consciousness, most Americans now exist within these same fragmenting and disabling cultural conditions. Sandoval suggests that, as a
result of a shift in the cultural logic of contemporary capitalism, differential consciousness — which hitherto was enacted almost exclusively by
U.S. third world feminists — is now available to "all first world citizens"
(22 n. 50). She explains, "The praxis of U.S. third world feminism represented by the differential form of oppositional consciousness is threaded
throughout the experience of social marginality. As such, it is also being
woven into the fabric of experiences belonging to more and more citizens
who are caught in the crisis of late capitalist conditions and expressed in
the cultural angst most often referred to as the postmodern dilemma"
(17). Sandoval thus sees U.S. third world feminists as having generated a
"common speech, a theoretical structure" that "provides access to a different way of conceptualizing not only U.S. feminist consciousness but
oppositional activity in general" (1). Her theory demands a "new subjectivity, a political revision that denies any one ideology as the final
answer, while instead positing a *tactical subjectivity* with the capacity to
recenter depending upon the kinds of oppression to be confronted" (14).
The U.S. third world feminist — the paradigmatic possessor of this tactical subjectivity — thus prefigures what Sandoval posits as the "new subject of history":

> Differential consciousness under postmodern conditions is not possible
> without the creation of another ethics, a new morality, which will bring
> about a new subject of history. Movement into this realm is heralded by the
> claims of U.S. third world feminists, . . . But to think of the activities of U.S.
> third world feminism thus is only a metaphorical avenue which allows one
> conceptual access to the threshold of this other realm, a realm accessible to
> all people. (23 n. 58)

The beautiful audacity of Sandoval's project is precisely this: the
heretofore lowly and despised U.S. third world feminist is at the political
and theoretical forefront of present-day progressive politics.[22] All oppositional others must now follow the U.S. third world feminist into the
realm of differential consciousness, for its enactment is "*imperative* for
the psychological and political practices that permit the achievement of
coalition across difference" (15, emphasis added). Those who do not —
those who remain stubbornly committed to equal rights, revolutionary,

---

22. In fact, I do not disagree with Sandoval's claim that women of color are at the forefront of progressive politics. However, I do disagree with aspects of her explanation of how
and why they are at the forefront, as will become clearer in the course of this chapter.

supremacist, or separatist modes of oppositional ideology — will in-evitably reproduce the oppressive ideologies and practices that they oppose. Any of these liberation ideologies, Sandoval claims, is "destined to repeat the oppressive authoritarianism from which it is attempting to free itself and become trapped inside a drive for truth which can only end in producing its own brand of dominations" (14).

At this point, I want to step back from Sandoval's argument in order to highlight the elements of it that derive specifically from a postmod-ernist theoretical framework. Her work, I maintain, is a blend of realist insights and postmodernist assumptions. Her most cogent insights are compatible with the kind of realist framework I propose, while her post-modernist presuppositions unnecessarily limit her project of apprehend-ing and representing the experiences of women of color.

Sandoval's first postmodernist assumption, that identities are radi-cally unstable, predisposes her to see shifts in behavior, or changes in emphasis, as shifts in identity. A working-class mother of Mexican her-itage who invests her sexual and erotic energy primarily in other women may present herself as a "Chicana" in one context, a "woman of color" in another, a "mother" in a third, a "lesbian" in a fourth, and a "worker" in a fifth. In each context, she highlights different aspects of her social identity, and, as a result, names herself differently. According to Sandoval's theory of differential consciousness, she undergoes several successive shifts in identity. A realist theory of identity, by contrast, would acknowledge that different aspects of the woman's social identity become more and less visible in different situations, but would see that identity as remaining more or less constant over the course of her move-ments.[23] Throughout Sandoval's argument, in fact, U.S. third world fem-inists remain U.S. third world feminists. In the course of enacting differential consciousness, they do not become white men, or white women, or children, or nonfeminists. They may privilege one or more aspects of their identity (gender, sexuality, race, class) over others at var-ious times and in various situations, but they do not actually "shift" their relatively stable social identities.[24] Thus, the claim that practitioners

23. For an illuminating account of the way different aspects of the self become visible in different situations, see Hames-García, " 'Who are our own people?' "

24. Of course, I do not mean to suggest that women of color never change the way they identify themselves. My point is that the self-designations they discard and take up tend to remain within a range of identities defensible within a realist framework. For the most part, they acknowledge the salience of gender and race as determining factors of social identity

of differential consciousness continually shift identities is not supported within the terms of Sandoval's own argument.

Furthermore, I disagree with Sandoval's contention that practitioners of differential consciousness shift ideologies. The measure of self-consciousness that Sandoval attributes to U.S. third world feminist political agents precludes that possibility. If, as she intimates, U.S. third world feminists are perfectly self-conscious about what they are doing — if they know that their alliance with any one group is strategic and temporary — then they are working from within an ideology of flux and cannot be said to be shifting ideologies. As Sandoval herself describes it, differential consciousness implies its own overriding ideology. Its practitioner participates in the activities implied by the other four oppositional sites, but she remains aloof to their ideologies, refusing to adopt their "fervid belief systems" because the overriding differential ideology denies any other ideology "as the final answer" (13, 14). Thus, she remains committed to an ideology of flux and, by refusing "any one ideology as the final answer," paradoxically participates in a denial of her own particular conception of truth.

Sandoval's own epistemological denial shows up in her statement that any "drive for truth . . . can only end in producing its own brand of dominations" (14).[25] With this statement, Sandoval exhibits a readiness — characteristic of postmodernist theoretical projects — to attribute oppressive motivations or effects to any project associated with a quest for truth or the acquisition of knowledge. Postmodernist theorists typically deride epistemological projects by suggesting that anyone who wishes to avoid acting in an oppressive way will suspend judgment and refuse to decide between competing narratives about the world. Their logic pro-

---

and remain cognizant of the referential and dialectical nature of social identity. For a realist account of how and why two women of color changed the way they identified themselves in response to their changed understanding of their world, see chapter one. Moreover, although Sandoval may mean something different by the term *identity* than I do, I will defend my criticism by suggesting that Sandoval's use of the term to designate the different aspects of an individual whose self-conception remains relatively stable over time is misleading and has the effect of obscuring the unequal salience of different aspects of identity.

25. I borrow the phrase from Alcoff, who identifies postmodernism's "epistemological denial" as its "unwillingness (with few exceptions) to acknowledge, take responsibility for, or indeed, to interrogate its own concern with truth, or more importantly, its own implicit invocation of some specific concept of truth by which it critiques more naive, more realist, philosophical accounts" ("Politics of Postmodern Feminism" 12). Alcoff's response to postmodernism's epistemological denial, with which I concur, is that any "project of interrogation is always situated, and implies some orientation" (24).

ceeds something like this: everything we know about the world — including what can be considered true, beautiful, good, and right — comes to us through the distorting lens of ideology conditioned by the particular cultural and/or linguistic universe within which we exist. Because we have no unmediated access to the world, we will always be uncertain about whether or not our conception of truth, beauty, good, and right is true for everyone — particularly those cultural "others" who do not share our linguistic universe — and not just for us. Because we cannot know for sure that we are right, and because the difference between "us" and "them" appears to be "incommensurable," we must refuse to impose "our" beliefs on "them" so as to avoid participating in colonizing, globalizing, and totalizing projects. The relativist stance I have just described appears to be an ethical one, but as many critics have pointed out, the logic on which it is based is fundamentally flawed. Judith Roof, for instance, notes that an analysis predicated on the "loss of metanarrative relies upon an unrecognized legitimating metanarrative that establishes the 'truth value' of no truth" (59).[26] One metanarrative is thus replaced by another; one conception of truth is dismissed in favor of one that cannot be acknowledged.[27]

Sandoval, like every other theorist who makes an argument (postmodernist or not), draws on a specific conception of truth in order to criticize other accounts. Her critique of hegemonic feminist accounts of the stages of feminism includes the following truth claims: (1) certain identifiable groups of people have engaged in the wrongful oppression and exploitation of other groups of people in systematic ways over long periods of time; (2) white (hegemonic) feminists have illegitimately appropriated the work of (oppressed) U.S. third world feminists in such a way as to render their theoretical insights invisible; and (3) exploited

26. Roof continues, "If we know that we cannot know, if we distrust representation and understand that the value of knowledge has become linked to its performativity, then our knowing that we cannot know becomes the point of knowing, becomes the legitimating uncertainty about knowledge that provides us with a certainty about knowledge's uncertainty. To see [Lyotard's conception of] paralogy as desirable — to see a lack of totality as a condition for potential change — is to inscribe uncertainty in the place of truth in the same liberating metanarratives about knowledge that see truth as human liberation" (59).

27. Mohanty deepens the critique by showing that the postmodernist response to the theory-mediatedness of knowledge "turns out to reveal a disguised form of foundationalism, for it remains within a specifically positivist conception of objectivity and knowledge. It assumes that the only kind of objective knowledge we can have is one that is independent of (socially produced and revisable) theoretical presuppositions, and concludes that the theory dependence of experience is evidence that it is always epistemically suspect" (*Literary Theory* 209).

and oppressed peoples (including U.S. third world feminists) have engaged in morally defensible resistant conduct and, as a consequence of their efforts to ameliorate the painful effects of their unfair and oppressive situations, have developed successful oppositional ideologies. These truth claims and value judgments are but a few of the most important in Sandoval's essay — without them, her argument would be incoherent and her essay meaningless. Thus, while I am not suggesting that Sandoval's claims and judgments are wrong and should be abandoned, I am saying that they should be acknowledged for what they are — namely, truth claims and value judgments. Sandoval presents her claims and judgments in such a way as to suggest that they have the status of truth; her argument presumes that what she is saying is so not only for her, but for everyone. If it were not, Sandoval would have no grounds for her injunction that others (non–U.S. third world feminists) *must* follow the U.S. third world feminist into the realm of differential consciousness.

Despite her commitment to postmodernism, Sandoval offers some cogent insights that help reveal the theoretical and political value of what she calls U.S. third world feminism. As Sandoval asserts, there is indeed a specific social movement — one she calls U.S. third world feminism, but that is more commonly thought of now as women of color feminism — whose characteristic feature is the capacity to form coalitions across difference. Moreover, she is perspicacious in her observation that the ability of women of color to work across difference (together with the underlying theoretical and political achievements implied by that ability) puts them at the forefront of present-day progressive politics. As the world's disparate economies become increasingly linked through the circuits of global capitalism, and as previously distant societies are brought closer together by rapidly developing technological advances in both communications and travel, the earth's citizens are more frequently confronted with their own and others' "otherness." As it becomes increasingly difficult for different kinds of people to remain separate, it becomes more and more important for everyone to learn the skills involved in acknowledging, negotiating, accommodating, celebrating, and, in some cases, transcending difference. As Sandoval demonstrates, women of color, for some time now, have been perfecting these very skills. And, as she proposes, they have generated knowledge out of the experiences they have had with forming coalitions across difference. It is this knowledge and these skills that women of color have to offer a world that is only now coming to grips with the fact that confronting difference entails changing the "self."

A REALIST READING OF *LA FACULTAD*

At this point I want to propose what I think is a more appropriate trajectory for the feminist critic concerned with theorizing the cultural productions and experiences of Chicanas and other women of color. Realists argue that a crucial task of the cultural critic is to attend to the links between social location and identity by theorizing the process of identity formation.[28] According to a realist theory of identity, identities are politically and epistemically significant because they can trace the links between individuals and groups and the central organizing principles of a society. Consequently, theorizing the process of identity formation can reveal the complicated workings of ideology and oppression. This task, however, requires a conception of identity that can account for the epistemic status — in terms of enlightenment *and* mystification — of identities. I approach this task by sketching out some basic premises of the postpositivist realist theory of identity before reexamining some of Sandoval's claims regarding the theoretical and political practices of women of color; I end by providing a postpositivist realist account of those practices.

The most basic claim of the postpositivist realist theory of identity is that identities are both *constructed* and *real*: identities are constructed because they are based on interpreted experience and on theories that explain the social and natural world, but they are also real because they refer outward to causally significant features of the world. Identities are thus context-specific ideological constructs, even though they may refer in non-arbitrary ways to verifiable aspects of the world such as skin color, physiognomy, anatomical sex, and socioeconomic status. Because identities refer — sometimes in partial and inaccurate ways — to the changing but relatively stable contexts from which they emerge, they are neither self-evident, immutable, and essential nor radically unstable or arbitrary. Rather, they are socially significant constructs that become intelligible from within specific historical and material contexts.[29]

According to the realist theory, an individual's identity, her experience, and her knowledge are inextricably connected. This conclusion is based on the premises that an individual's social location (the particular nexus

28. By *identity* I mean the non-essential and evolving product that emerges from the dialectic between how a subject of consciousness identifies herself and how she is identified by others. By *subject of consciousness* I mean she who identifies herself and/or is identified by others as a self-conscious evolving entity existing continuously across time.

29. See Mohanty, *Literary Theory*, esp. 202–34; Hau, "On Representing Others," esp. 33–46.

of race, class, gender, and sexuality in which she exists in the world) is causally relevant for the experiences she will have and that an individual's experiences will influence, although not determine, the formation of her social identity.[30] Because identities are, in part, theoretically mediated constructions that refer outward to the societies from which they emerge, they provide their bearers with particular perspectives on the world. As such, identities provide people with frameworks (the epistemic value of which varies widely) for interpreting their experiences. In other words, a person's interpretation of an event will be at least partially dependent for its meaning on her self-conception — her understanding of her particular relation to the people and happenings surrounding that event.

A key postpositivist realist insight is that the epistemic status of different identities can be evaluated by seeing how well they work as explanations or descriptions of the social and natural world from which they emerge. The epistemic value of particular identities can be revealed by seeing how well they "refer" to verifiable aspects of the world they claim to describe. To the extent that identities do not work well as explanations of the world — to the extent that they fail to "refer" adequately to the societies from which they emerge — they can help to reveal the contradictions and mystifications within which the members of those societies live.[31]

I turn back now to a consideration of Sandoval's arguments in order to show how her postmodernist presuppositions partially undermine her realist insights. If we look carefully at Sandoval's argument, it is clear that the differential consciousness she describes is thoroughly grounded in a specific type of consciousness that she understands as being common to women of color. Sandoval, quoting Moraga, asserts that women of color have learned to "measure and weigh what is to be said and when, what is to be done and how, and to whom, . . . daily deciding/risking who it is we can call an ally, call a friend (whatever that person's skin, sex, or sexuality)."[32] Sandoval is referring to the experientially acquired knowledge that manifests itself in the "survival tactic" described by

30. For six basic claims of the postpositivist realist theory of identity, see chapter one, especially the section entitled "Toward a Realist Theory of Chicana Identity."

31. For an in-depth consideration of the dialectical relation between error and objectivity, see chaps. 6 and 7 of Mohanty, *Literary Theory*, esp. 184–94, 206–16; Hau, "On Representing Others," esp. 33–56; Wilkerson, "Is There Something You Need to Tell Me?" esp. 5–22, 31–34.

32. The quote, which appears on page 15 of Sandoval's "U.S. Third World Feminism," comes from Moraga's preface to the second edition of *This Bridge Called My Back* xviii–xix.

Anzaldúa as *"la facultad,"* a skill developed by marginalized people whose well-being is often dependent on the goodwill of others (*Borderlands* 38). Anzaldúa describes it variously as a "vestige of a proximity sense," an "acute awareness mediated by the part of the psyche that does not speak," and a "shift in perception" honed by pain and developed most readily by "those who do not feel psychologically or physically safe in the world" (*Borderlands* 38–39). As a survival skill, *la facultad* allows such people to adjust quickly and gracefully to changing (and often threatening) circumstances. With origins in experiences of pain and trauma, *la facultad* involves a loss of innocence and an initiation into an awareness of discrimination, fear, depression, illness, and death.

Perhaps in an effort to avoid charges of essentialism, Sandoval abstracts the experientially acquired knowledge and consciousness of women of color in order to make it accessible to "all people" ("U.S. Third World Feminism" 23 n. 58). In order to do this, however, she must weaken the link between social location, experiences of oppression, and the development of differential consciousness.[33] In the process, Sandoval covers over the pain involved in Anzaldúa's account of the development of *la facultad* and presents an idealized portrait of the mobile subjectivity she sees as characteristic of differential consciousness.

> The consciousness which typifies la facultad is not naive to the moves of power: it is constantly surveying and negotiating its moves. Often dismissed as "intuition," this kind of "perceptiveness," "sensitivity," consciousness if you will, is not determined by race, sex, or any other genetic status, neither does its activity belong solely to the "proletariat," the "feminist," nor to the oppressed, if the oppressed is considered a unitary category, but it is a learned emotional and intellectual skill which is developed amidst hegemonic powers. . . . In order for this survival skill to provide the basis for a differential and unifying methodology, it must be remembered that la facultad is a process. Answers may be only temporarily effective, so that wedded to the process of la facultad is a flexibility that continually woos change. (22–23 n. 57)

Thus, Sandoval sees *la facultad* as the basis for the differential methodol-

---

33. Sandoval writes, "Citizenship in this political realm is comprised of strategy and risk. Within the realm of differential consciousness there are no ultimate answers, no terminal utopia (though the imagination of utopias can motivate its tactics), no predictable final outcomes. *Its practice is not biologically determined, restricted to any class or group,* nor must it become static. The fact that it is a process capable of freezing into a repressive order — or of disintegrating into relativism — should not shadow its radical activity" (23 n. 58, emphasis added).

ogy she promotes. Moreover, she views the mode of behavior that char-
acterizes *la facultad* as being consistent with that of differential consciousness: both involve a *"tactical subjectivity* with the capacity to
recenter depending upon the kinds of oppresssion to be confronted" (14).

Analyzing *la facultad* within a postpositivist realist framework rather
than a postmodernist one allows us to acknowledge its non-essential
nature and its epistemic significance without either severing the ties
between social location, experience, and identity or idealizing *la facultad's* knowledge-generating potential. The postpositivist realist readily
agrees that *la facultad* is not "determined by race, sex, or any other
genetic status" and that there are marginalized individuals (people who
by virtue of some combination of race, class, gender, or sexuality might
claim oppressed status) who do not develop *la facultad*. Similarly, she
concedes that the skill does not "belong" to the "proletariat," the "feminist," or to "the oppressed, *if the oppressed is considered a unitary category . . .*" (23, emphasis added). Furthermore, the realist agrees with
Sandoval that it would be a mistake to consider "the oppressed" as a unitary (and, by implication, "essential") category. Her reasons for reaching
this conclusion, however, are different from Sandoval's. Unlike Sandoval,
whose postmodernist presuppositions lead her to weaken the links
among identity, experience, and social location so as to avoid the infer-
ence that they have any kind of essential connection, the realist insists on
the inextricable — but complex and variable — connections between
them. The realist would point out that when we do not consider the
oppressed as a unitary category — when we take into account the multiple determinations and the theoretically mediated formation of social
identity — we can still identify non-arbitrary experiential connections
between being oppressed and developing *la facultad*. [34] Furthermore, the
realist would be wary about idealizing the knowledge-generating component of *la facultad*. Because an awareness of oppression or pain may
lead to survival tactics that do not necessarily explain the world's social,
political, and economic workings, the realist would be reluctant to use *la
facultad* as the basis for a new feminist epistemology. As I will illustrate

34. The realist claim that there is a non-arbitrary experiential connection between being
oppressed and the development of *la facultad* does not presuppose that all persons who are
oppressed in the same way develop the same political consciousness. The claim is more limited, and speaks to the necessary, but not sufficient, role of experience in the development
of *la facultad*. The failure of a multiply oppressed individual to develop *la facultad* raises
the issue of error in the interpretation of one's own experience. An in-depth consideration
of error in interpretation is beyond the scope of this chapter; I refer the reader to the works
cited in note 31 above.

in an example taken from Moraga later in this chapter, feelings of fear and alienation are not, in themselves, sufficient for an adequate understanding of one's social, political, and economic situation.

I should emphasize that, unlike the "ideal" postmodernist I am positing, Sandoval does not completely deny the connections among identity, experience, and social location. Nevertheless, she weakens them by minimizing the differences between the experiences of multiply oppressed people (such as nonwhite women) and "all first world citizens" who are caught in the crisis of late capitalism (17, 22 n. 50, 23 n. 58). Her refusal to take a firm stand regarding the role of multiple oppression in the development of *la facultad* makes her work susceptible to the kind of criticism to which I am subjecting it. My point is that just as we want to avoid making the connections too secure, so should we avoid making them too elastic. Only by conducting a careful examination of how, when, and under what conditions *la facultad* develops will we adequately understand the latent epistemic privilege of the oppressed.[35]

So, while I would agree with Sandoval that women of color both develop and display the intuitive capabilities of the kind described by Moraga and named by Anzaldúa, I disagree with Sandoval's implication that the knowledge and skills acquired by women of color can be arrived at, in any sort of willful way, by people who do not share their same social locations. Being multiply oppressed is a necessary — although not sufficient — condition for developing *la facultad*. Two realist premises are most relevant here. (1) As long as our world is hierarchically organized along enduring relations of domination, people occupying different social locations will experience the world in systematically different ways; and (2) it is a consequence of theory-mediated knowledge that not everyone who has the same kind of experience will react in the same way or come to the same conclusions about that experience. When taken

---

35. In my usage, *epistemic privilege* refers to a special advantage with respect to possessing or acquiring knowledge about how fundamental aspects of our society (such as race, class, gender, and sexuality) operate to sustain matrices of power. The key to claiming epistemic privilege for people who have been oppressed in a particular way stems from an acknowledgment that they have experiences — experiences that people who are not oppressed in that same way usually lack — that *can* provide them with information we all need to understand how hierarchies of race, class, gender, and sexuality operate to uphold existing regimes of power in our society. What is being claimed is not an a priori link between social location and knowledge but a link that is historically variable and mediated through the interpretation of experience. Under this definition, *la facultad* can be understood as a partial manifestation of the epistemic privilege that most nonwhite women are situated to possess as a result of being subject to a multitude of oppressions.

together, these two realist assumptions allow the claim that some people are better situated than others to develop *la facultad,* without falling into the essentialist trap of assuming a determinative relationship between social location and consciousness.

Sandoval does make some claims in her discussion of *la facultad* that can be read as realist. By acknowledging that those who possess *la facultad* have learned it as an "emotional and intellectual skill which is developed amidst hegemonic powers" (22 n. 57), Sandoval points to the theoretically mediated nature of experientially acquired knowledge. Moreover, her contention that *la facultad* is "a process" does not preclude the realist claim that experience has real theoretical and epistemic importance. The answers at which a woman of color arrives may be "temporarily effective" not because her answers lack some kind of truth value but because her situation changes, or her particular understanding of the world needs to be refined, revised, or fine-tuned. Within a realist conception of knowledge, error is not antithetical to, but constitutive of, postpositivist objectivity.

Within a realist framework, oppositional ideologies (and the identities they engender) are more than sites of political and theoretical resistance to be pragmatically or strategically occupied or abandoned. Rather, they are ways individuals or groups perceive, interpret, and interact with the world around them. Thus, a change in ideology or identity can represent a movement toward a better (or worse) understanding of the social world. To the extent that the ideological framework through which a person views the world adequately explains that world's social, political, and economic workings, or to the extent that the identity she claims accurately describes the complex interactions between the multiple determinants of her particular social location, that ideology or identity will be epistemically (not just "strategically") justified — it will constitute "objective" and reliable knowledge. Whether an identity has more (or less) epistemic value than a previous ideology or identity is not something that can be determined in advance — ideologies and identities must be compared with other (competing) ideologies and identities, evaluated for logical consistency, and tested empirically against the world they claim to describe. Thus, the realist claim is not that humans are always successful in their efforts to make successive approximations toward the truth — just that they *can* be.[36]

36. My claim is *not* that ideologies are mere lenses through which we view an already existing world but that some ideologies are better than others at describing the complex

Let me illustrate the realist theoretical point I am making. As fallible human beings with no immediate access to the world, women of color have been as subject to mystification and error as anyone else. Consequently, they may have participated in race-based organizations without attending to the interests of their gender — not because they were enacting differential consciousness, but because they had not yet figured out that their gender brings with it a set of interests. Angela Davis, in a keynote address given at SUNY Oneonta in April 1996, admitted that during her participation in the black power movement of the 1960s she was largely unaware of the conflicts between the interests of her gender and the masculinist rhetoric of the movement. Similarly, some women who now identify as women of color may have participated in gender-based political movements without fully understanding that such organizations systematically neglected the race and class interests central to the lives of most nonwhite women. Moraga is a case in point: she had to work through to an understanding of the interests generated by the racialized aspect of her identity. During her participation in the women's movement during the 1970s and prior to her identification as a woman of color, she was not initially conscious that she was neglecting those interests. The realization came to her gradually, and manifested itself, at first, in discomfort — in the sense that something was missing, something was wrong. In the preface to the first edition of *This Bridge Called My Back,* Moraga recounts her coming to consciousness as a woman of color:

> A few days ago, an old friend said to me how when she first met me, I seemed so white to her. I said in honesty, I used to feel more white. You know, I really did. But at the meeting last night, dealing with white women here on this trip, I have felt so very dark: dark with anger, with silence, with the feeling of being walked over.
> I wrote in my journal: "My growing consciousness as a woman of color is surely seeming to transform my experience. How could it be that the more I feel with other women of color, the more I feel myself Chicana, the more susceptible I am to racist attack!" (xv)

Here, Moraga describes a growing awareness of her difference from white women. In the process of interacting with them, Moraga learns more about herself; she reconnects with the racialized aspect of her identity that she had previously denied. Her "transformation of experience"

---

network of human interactions and natural phenomena which constitute the totality of our (constructed and discovered) reality.

is thus a consequence of her reinterpretation of the things that happen/ have happened to her in light of her new (and more accurate) perspective on the social world within which that experience has meaning. Importantly, Moraga does not merely "choose" to be a woman of color, nor does she mentally "construct" the racialized aspect of her heritage (her Mexican ancestry) on which she identifies as a woman of color. Of course—inasmuch as the identity "woman of color" is a political construct, and is only one among a range of identities defensible within a realist framework available to her—Moraga does have a choice. But her choice is not arbitrary or idealist; it is not unconnected to those social categories (race, class, gender, sexuality) that constitute her social location and influence her experience of the world. The realist argument is this: as a result of her expanded, and more accurate, understanding of the social world, Moraga's self-conception and her identity change. Moraga's newfound identity, "woman of color," is more epistemically and politically salient than her former identity—implicitly white "woman"—insofar as it more accurately refers to the complexity and multiplicity of Moraga's social location. This is not to say that there could not be another identity that might also, or more accurately, refer to the complex being she is. The realist claim I am making here is limited: not all identities a given individual can claim have equal political or epistemic salience.

Without diminishing the importance and relevance of *la facultad,* I would locate it at the level of quasi-self-consciousness, rather than the level of full self-consciousness that Sandoval implies in her theory of differential consciousness. Within the realm of *la facultad,* theoretical understanding is preceded by fear, alienation, and pain. All too often, nonwhite women know that something is wrong: we feel it in our gut, in our spine, in our neck. But it takes time, sometimes distance, and occasionally education or a consciousness-raising group for us to figure out what is wrong or missing. Having her consciousness raised is, in effect, what Moraga describes in her essay "La Güera" when she relates an incident that took place in an apple orchard in Sonoma. In an effort to help Moraga understand her "total alienation from and fear of [her] classmates," a friend said to her: "Cherríe, no wonder you felt like such a nut in school. Most of the people there were white and rich" (*Bridge* 30–31). Prior to her friend's statement, Moraga had not fully realized that white and rich was something that she was not. More precisely, she had not yet come to acknowledge the salience of race or class in U.S. society—she had not come to understand how much difference those social categories make to an individual's experience of the world.

All along I had felt the difference, but not until I had put the words "class" and "color" to the experience, did my feelings make any sense. For years, I had berated myself for not being as "free" as my classmates. I completely bought that they simply had more guts than I did — to rebel against their parents and run around the country hitch-hiking, reading books and study-ing "art." They had enough privilege to be atheists, for chrissake. . . . But I knew nothing about "privilege" then. White was right. Period. I could pass. If I got educated enough, there would never be any telling. (*Bridge* 31)

In hindsight, and from the perspective of a woman of color, Moraga embeds three realist insights regarding the theory-mediatedness of expe-rience and the epistemic status of identity into her discussion of this past event. First, she realizes that a person's social location is causally relevant to the experiences she will have. She reports that the source of her "total alienation" from her classmates was her lower socioeconomic status and her Mexican ancestry (*Bridge* 30). Second, she recognizes that a person's interpretation of her experience is influenced by her identity. She notes that as long as she identified with her "white and rich" classmates — as long as she did not acknowledge the socially significant ways her social location differed from theirs — she was unable to understand her feelings of alienation. Moraga's third realist insight follows from the second: if a person's self-conception (or identity) refers inaccurately or only partially to the social and natural world from which it emerges, her interpreta-tions of her experiences will be epistemically impoverished. She explains that "all along [she] had felt the difference" between herself and her classmates, but it was not until she reinterpreted her college experience through a different theoretical framework — one that incorporated the concepts of race and class as salient analytical categories — did her expe-rience "make any sense" (*Bridge* 31). When Moraga's identity more accurately referred to her social location, her perspective on the world became correspondingly more objective. So, while it is clear that Moraga's intuitions — her feelings of fear and alienation — were necessary to the development of her political and theoretical knowledge, it is also clear that they were not, in themselves, sufficient for an adequate under-standing of her social, political, and economic situation. I submit that this insufficiency poses a serious challenge to Sandoval's effort to develop a model of feminist consciousness based on the prototype of *la facultad*.

Viewing Moraga's coming-to-consciousness as a woman of color from a realist perspective shows that her changing political commitments are tied to her evolving conception of what her place in society *is* versus what it *should be*. At the end of "La Güera," Moraga articulates the desire to work through the fragmenting conditions she has faced in her own life. She writes, "I think: what is my responsibility to my roots — both white and brown, Spanish-speaking and English? I am a woman with a foot in both worlds; *and I refuse the split*. I feel the necessity for dialogue. Sometimes I feel it urgently" (*Bridge* 34, emphasis added). Refusing to be split by her various positions, Moraga contradicts Sandoval's postmodernist contention that women of color "shift" back and forth between competing ideologies or make an emotional commitment to the "shattering of the unitary sense of self" for the purpose of developing a mobile identity ("U.S. Third World Feminism" 23 n. 58). Moraga and the other women of color whose work I admire and teach understand that instability is not necessarily a comfortable or desirable situation in which to exist; life on the margins or in the interstices, while potentially exhilarating and creative, also can be difficult and exhausting. As a result, they struggle to find a way to bring all of the disparate aspects of their social identities together into integrated or synthesized selves.[37] Certainly, one of the major victories to date of women of color feminism is the ability some women of color now have to conceptualize themselves as nonfragmented beings constituted neither by lack nor by excess.

I contend that when these women of color change ideologies and identities, they are motivated by a genuine concern for truth and the hope of creating an objectively better world. In saying that they have a genuine concern for truth or objectivity, I am not suggesting that they are therefore naive, inflexible, or authoritarian. On the contrary, it is their *nonrelativist* commitment to truth that enables their insights and facilitates the development of their cross-cultural political achievements. Moraga, for example, concludes "La Güera" by explaining her choice to practice women of color politics in terms that are recognizably realist. On the one hand, Moraga believes that a woman of color identity provides her with a better perspective from which to "recognize" and thus fight against the oppressive effects of race and class "privilege." On the other, she hopes that by coming together with other women of color who are similarly willing to confront their own ideological mystifications, she will be able to participate in a dialogue that will enable women of color to forge a truly liberatory feminist collective. Moraga's choice to identify as a

---

37. See, e.g., Anzaldúa's description of the culmination of the Coatlicue state, that place of contradictions, where she describes everything "rushing to a center, a nucleus. . . . All the lost pieces of myself come flying . . . magnetized toward that center," and where she feels "*completa*" and "not afraid" (*Borderlands* 51).

woman of color is thus not "strategic" or "pragmatic"; it is based on her best estimation of what she must do to help create a non-oppressive world in which women of color, too, can have "joy in [their] lives" (*Bridge* 33–34). Women like Moraga, as individuals whose social location generally places them in a subordinate position within prevailing relations of domination, have a personal stake in knowing "what it would take to change [our world, and in] . . . identifying the central relations of power and privilege that sustain it and make the world what it is" (Mohanty, *Literary Theory* 214). As a result, women of color like Moraga who work for social change generally do so with a great degree of seriousness, and a steadfast commitment to discerning what is true from what is false for the purpose of perfecting their political practice.

It seems to me that the call by some critics for a "pragmatist" feminist theory is at least partially motivated by the desire to avoid the positivist versions of truth and objectivity that postmodernists have long attributed to all epistemological projects. These feminists do not want to risk the possibility of making theoretically dogmatic truth claims that might turn out to have oppressive effects. So, in an effort to avoid being "wrong," they decide to avoid any overt commitment to what might be "right." They thus retain a positivist conception of truth and objectivity in their tendency to oppose the possibility of error to absolute certainty. From a postpositivist realist perspective, however, it would be a mistake to assume that a commitment to truth invariably leads to theoretical dogmatism. In the course of making a theoretical argument, I regularly make a number of truth claims. I understand them, however, to be fallible claims; they are open to contestation and revision. What makes them specifically *truth* claims is that I understand them to be true, and I cannot abandon them until I have an experience that causes me to rethink my position, or until someone, using argumentation and presenting evidence, persuades me that I have been partially or completely in error. At that point, I will acknowledge that the truth claims I have been making need to be abandoned or revised. I will then develop a new (and hopefully more accurate) conception of truth and continue to understand my (new) truth claims as being true.

The distinction between saying that my truth claims are infallible and saying that they are fallible is important and bears elaboration. The first stance, which corresponds to a positivist epistemology, presupposes that truth exists, and that I have unmediated access to it. This stance leads to naivete, inflexibility, and domination. The second stance, which corresponds to a postpositivist epistemology, assumes that truth exists and that I can make successive approximations toward it.[38] I acknowledge that I have no immediate access to truth and that, as a result, my ideas are subject to mystification and error. As such, I am required (if I care very much about truth at all) to consider alternative conceptions of what the truth is. I further realize that considering alternative versions of the truth may make me profoundly uncomfortable. I may — more precisely, *will* — have to question the very foundation of my being: my sense of my self, my understanding of what is or is not beautiful, what is or is not good. I will have to reevaluate all that I hold dear, everything that makes life meaningful. Indeed, I will have to ask whether human life has any meaning at all. The advantage of a postpositivist realist framework is thus that it incorporates the possibility of self-critique: insofar as the realist attempts to justify her normative judgments with reference to some acknowledged metaphysical claims about the nature of the world or of human beings, she is in a better position to question and revise those claims. The postmodernist or pragmatist, by contrast, having justified her normative judgments with reference to what is strategically useful or politically expedient, is forced inevitably into a position of epistemological denial from which she is unable to question or revise her conception of truth or justice because her theoretical framework will not allow her to admit that she has one.

The radical and realist questioning of themselves and the world around them, I submit, constitutes women of color feminism's genuine contribution to the project of progressive social change.[39] The women of color whose work I admire and teach understand both the contingency and the importance of cultural values; they understand that while any one conception of truth may be culturally mediated, it cannot therefore be dismissed as a mental or discursive "construct" with no relevance to those beings located outside the culture within which it is true. As people who

38. For an account, drawn from the philosophy of science, of how objective knowledge is theory dependent and subject to continual empirical observation and verification, see R. N. Boyd, "How to Be a Moral Realist," esp. 189–92.

39. I should not have to say this, but because of the potential for being misunderstood, I will. In saying that the radical questioning of themselves and the world around them constitutes the genuine contribution of women of color feminism to the project of progressive social change I am *not* saying that this is all that women of color have to offer. Clearly, individual women of color have contributed and will continue to contribute to progressive social movements in variable and important ways. All I mean to suggest is that to the extent that we can identify a social movement that can be designated "women of color feminism," the great contribution of that social movement has been to demonstrate the viability of, and methods involved in, creating coalitions across difference.

are frequently situated on the wrong side of dichotomous constructions of truth and beauty, such women have developed a deep suspicion toward hegemonic constructions of the same. However, I have not seen that they therefore have dismissed the concepts as in themselves hegemonic. Indeed, women of color's commitment to a truth (however difficult to access) that transcends particular cultural constructions underlies their success in forming coalitions across difference. As committed as they are to the idea that they are right, women of color such as Bernice Reagon Johnson, Audre Lorde, Papusa Molina, Cherríe Moraga, Mitsuye Yamada, Chandra Talpade Mohanty, and Angela Davis have all allowed themselves, in one forum or another, to entertain the possibility that they may be (may have been) wrong — they have admitted that their own culturally constructed conceptions of truth may need to be revised, complicated, or abandoned in order to make meaningful connections with women different from themselves. This willingness to question their own conceptions of truth in the service of negotiating difference is what occasions Reagon to say, "most of the time you feel threatened to the core and if you don't, you're not really doing no coalescing" ("Coalition Politics" 356); what Lorde refers to when she says that difference must be seen as "a fund of necessary polarities between which our creativities spark like a dialectic" ("Master's Tools" 99); and what Moraga means when she says we have to look deep within ourselves and come to terms with our own suffering in order that we can challenge, and if necessary, "change ourselves, even sometimes our most cherished, block-hard convictions" (Moraga and Anzaldúa, *Bridge* preface). These and other women of color have undertaken the task of asking and seeking answers to the questions Why? When? What? Where? and How? They are, in other words, committed to a "drive for truth." I contend, moreover, that it is precisely because they are *realists,* because they take truth seriously — seriously enough to question their own truth claims — that theirs is a process incapable of "freezing into a repressive order — or of disintegrating into relativism" (Sandoval, "U.S. Third World Feminism" 23 n. 58).[40]

40. Saldívar-Hull refers to the kind of women of color feminist practice that I identify in this chapter as "feminism on the border," and calls its practitioners "fronteristas" (60). By "feminism on the border," Saldívar-Hull means a liberatory ideology and practice that takes into account race, class, gender, and sexual orientation in all their nuances and that is not bound by national or ethnic categories (34). According to Saldívar-Hull, fronteristas base their alliances on shared values rather than shared blood — they "make that final leap from filiation to affiliation, from ties to men and women of [their] own blood to political ties with peoples across national borders who enter the United States in search of political liberation" (145).

Within Chicana and Chicano studies, as in feminist and minority studies, scholars are currently facing what Linda Martín Alcoff has called an "identity crisis" ("Cultural Feminism"). How we choose to accomplish the task of theorizing the identities of minority and female subjects will have decisive implications for the future of these fields. If we choose the postmodernist approach, we run the risk, for example, of theorizing Chicana identity in terms of ambiguity and fragmentation so that the "Chicana" becomes, in effect, a figure for marginality and contradiction in the postmodern world. I would argue that the term *Chicana* should not denote a principle of abstract oppositionality. Although this kind of formulation can be politically useful, it is finally too general to have significant analytical import. If we choose the realist approach, we will work to ground the complex and variable experiences of the women who take on the identity Chicana within the concrete historical and material conditions they inhabit. Rather than a figure for contradiction or oppositionality, the "Chicana" would be a part of a believable and progressive social theory. I would like to suggest that it is only when we have a realist account of our identities, one that refers outward to the world we live in, will we be able to understand what social and political possibilities are open to us for the purpose of working to build a better society.

My postpositivist realist critique of postmodernist feminist conceptions of identity in both this chapter and chapter one illuminates something important about all identities. Identities are politically and epistemically significant because they reveal the links between individuals and groups and central organizing principles of the society. This is why theorizing the process of identity formation can provide a critical perspective from which cultural critics can disclose the complicated workings of ideology and oppression. In the next chapter, I start from this premise to show that even identities that do not work well as explanations of the social world can be epistemically valuable. Through an examination of the characteristic assumptions of four neoconservative minority writers, I show that to the extent that an identity fails to refer adequately to the central organizing principles of the society from which it emerges, it can help reveal the contradictions and mystifications within which members of that society live.

CHAPTER 3

Cultural Particularity vs. Universal Humanity

The Value of Being Asimilao

assimilated? qué assimilated,
brother, yo soy asimilao.

   Tato Laviera, "asimilao"

In the prologue to his intellectual autobiography *Hunger of Memory: The Education of Richard Rodriguez,* the author presents himself to the reader as the quintessential middle-class American man. His rags to riches scenario and his claim to have successfully assimilated into mainstream American culture (a process that, according to Rodriguez, entailed alienation from his Mexican parents and the concomitant loss of any connection to an ethnic past) are meant to indicate Rodriguez's exemplary status as a self-made American man. Over the course of the book, Rodriguez chronicles his transformation from a "socially disadvantaged" Mexican American child to an assimilated middle-class American man. He does so in a first-person "conversion" narrative that positions him squarely within a long tradition of American autobiographical narratives.[1] From within this tradition, Rodriguez affirms his American identity by emphasizing his deracinated individuality. Thus he can write, with no hint of irony, "This is my story. An American story"

1. In a piece in which he locates and defines the roots of ethnicity, Werner Sollors writes that "a latent fascination with the other in ourselves may account for the great popularity of autobiographical narratives of conversions from heretic to true believer, from criminal to social hero, or from ethnic to American. . . . It is obvious that the imagery of processive change, of a transformation from a pre-American past to an American identity . . . is patterned on the symbolism of religious conversions. There is a heathenish dimension to the past, to *any* past, in American literature, and a sacred quality to the future in America" (649).

(*Hunger* 5). And further: "I write of one life only. If my story is true, I trust it will resonate with significance for other lives" (*Hunger* 7).

Given the currency of Rodriguez's writings, Americans of all races, ethnicities, and political persuasions would do well to consider the "truth" and "significance for other lives" of Rodriguez's tale of assimilation. Although his political positions and educational prescriptives have been vehemently refuted by many other Mexican American educators, activists, and politicians, Rodriguez is frequently received by non–Mexican Americans as a native informant, and his arguments continue to influence public policy debates about politically charged minority entitlement programs such as bilingual education and affirmative action. Moreover, Rodriguez's literary success has been, by several measures, phenomenal. His controversial first book was received enthusiastically by conservative politicians and thinkers, a consequence Rodriguez successfully parlayed into a lucrative speaking and journalism career. Moreover, he has been anthologized as a representative Mexican American author in the Norton Anthology's *New Worlds of Literature: Writings from America's Many Cultures,* and his autobiography continues to be taught as a representative piece of Mexican American literature in high school and college classrooms across the country. Together with Linda Chávez, Richard Rodriguez currently occupies the position of the American mainstream media's favorite "Hispanic" representative.[2] How accurately he represents himself, then, will have continuing cultural and political consequences for Latina/os as a subordinated group.

Richard Rodriguez exemplifies the situation of the neoconservative minority intellectual in the United States. He joins Shelby Steele, Stephen Carter, Linda Chávez, and a number of other outspoken minority thinkers who have claimed for themselves the role of the new vanguard of minority public intellectuals. They see themselves as occupying a place

2. Rodriguez is frequently called upon to represent the "Hispanic" viewpoint on panels and in forums in mainstream American media that focus on cultural or racial diversity. In his role as editor of the Pacific News Service and contributing editor for *Harper's Magazine,* *U.S. News and World Report,* and the Sunday Opinion Page of the *Los Angeles Times,* and as a regular guest on the *NewsHour with Jim Lehrer,* Rodriguez regularly writes or speaks about issues concerning Latina/os and other people of color in the United States. Linda Chávez has been a weekly columnist for *USA Today* and a contributor to the *New York Times, Wall Street Journal, Washington Post, Commentary, New Republic,* and *Reader's Digest.* In March 1997, she started writing a Creators Syndicate column covering politics, education, feminism, immigration, and other topics. Her clients for that column include the *Boston Herald, Chicago Tribune, Denver Post, Detroit News, Philadelphia Inquirer,* and the *Washington Times.* She has also appeared as a guest on such programs as the *McLaughlin Group* and the *NewsHour with Jim Lehrer.*

in American society that is structurally different from the place occupied by their forebears, and they consider the political ideas and solutions they offer to be fundamentally new. Although three of the four claim to be either politically moderate or even left of center, neoconservative minorities such as Rodriguez, Steele, Carter, and Chávez take political positions that put them at odds with traditional leftist advocates of minority rights: they oppose affirmative action, decry minority set-asides, and argue in favor of cultural assimilation.[3] Their success in spreading their views can be demonstrated by their high media visibility, their access to publishing outlets, and the enthusiastic reception of their books.[4]

Left-leaning minority critics of neoconservative minority thinkers frequently attribute the success of the latter to the fact that their ideas and arguments are palatable to a white mainstream audience and useful for a U.S. media interested in maintaining the social and economic status quo. Perhaps because neoconservative minorities have been so thoroughly embraced by conservative segments of United States society, proponents of multiculturalism who are working for social change tend to reject these thinkers wholesale, without stopping to consider or analyze how or why they might have come to occupy the theoretical positions and social identities that they have. Instead, their critics accuse neoconservative minorities of "selling out" their communities of origin, of being victims of racial self-hatred, and of suffering from serious ideological delusion.[5]

3. In a 1994 interview with Postrel and Gillespie, Rodriguez states, "I think of myself as left of center." In a profile of Shelby Steele and Stanley Crouch, Gene Seymour writes that they think of themselves as "intellectual provocateurs, apple-cart shakers, professional skeptics. What they aren't, they insist, are conservatives, neo- or otherwise." For his part, Stephen Carter devotes an entire chapter, "Why 'Black Conservative' is Pejorative," to the project of explaining and justifying his political views. Carter is loath to align himself with any party or position, although he admits to sharing Steele's reluctance at being called a conservative (146). Chávez's political views are unapologetically conservative.

4. Steele's *The Content of Our Character* made the *New York Times* bestseller list and was lauded by the *Wall Street Journal* as "one of the best books on race in America to appear in the past twenty-five years." It is worth noting that although Steele's book was very favorably received by many white Americans, it was widely denounced by African American scholars and activists. For more on how Steele's ideas were received by African Americans, see Seymour.

5. Carter documents this kind of reaction to his and other black neoconservatives' views in his chapters "Silencing Dissent" and "On Contenting Oneself with Silence" (see esp. 107–11, 126). Rodriguez alludes to similar reactions in *Hunger of Memory* (see esp. 148, 161–62). Unlike Carter, who presents his opponents' views and then argues against them, Rodriguez does not give voice to the objections raised by his critics, choosing instead to label his critics "intolerant," "uncivil," and ideologically motivated. See, for instance, his characterizations of students at Cal State Northridge and UC San Diego in his 1994 interview with Postrel and Gillespie.

Consequently, their substantive claims have more frequently been celebrated or dismissed than they have been engaged.

   In this chapter, I would like to consider the possibility that in trying to
escape what they experience as the dehumanizing strictures of collective
(especially racial) identity, neoconservative minorities like Rodriguez,
Steele, Carter, and Chávez raise a valid concern about the relationship
between the culturally particular and the universally human.[6] Taking
Richard Rodriguez as exemplary, I examine the writings of neoconservative minorities in order to trace the contours of a neoconservative minority identity politics.[7] Because neoconservative minorities view collective
racial identities (that is, black or Chicana/o) as culturally particular, my
inquiry addresses directly the centerpiece of neoconservative minority
identity politics — the insistence that members of politically and culturally subordinate groups should be required to assimilate into mainstream
American society. In the process of examining the value of assimilation, I
unmask the false universality behind the ideal of assimilation defended
by neoconservative minorities and argue against the way in which they
oppose individual to collective identity. As part of my evaluative project,
I examine the central claim of Rodriguez's intellectual autobiography —
that he has been successfully assimilated. After demonstrating the role of
interpretive error in the formation of Rodriguez's neoconservative minority identity, I turn back to the postpositivist realist theory of identity I
elaborated in chapters one and two to posit one way in which progres-

   6. By considering the merits of neoconservative minority discourses, I do not intend to
overlook, downplay, or endorse the many problematic aspects of their perspectives. I do,
however, want to allow for the possibility that neoconservative minority accounts are
attractive to many white (and some nonwhite) Americans for reasons *other* than simple
racism.
   7. I define *identity politics* as a social practice in which a person or persons who identify with or are identified with a recognizable group such as "women" or "gays" make
arguments or take action with the purpose of affecting social, economic, or educational
policy relative to that group. Within this social practice, the identity of the political practitioner both motivates and is a central facet of the claim, argument, or action. Two other
terms I use throughout this and the following chapter also merit clarification. I use the term
assimilation to refer to forced, unidirectional cultural change to a white middle-class
American norm. I thus mean to distinguish the process of state-sponsored assimilation from
the uncoerced process of cross-cultural acculturation that frequently occurs when two or
more different cultural groups have sustained contact over a long period of time. Finally, by
multiculturalism I mean to refer in a general way to a late twentieth-century social movement promoting state-sanctioned support (usually in the form of public funding for multicultural education or community-based festivals) for the purpose of learning about and
encouraging the development of diverse cultures as a primary social good. For a liberal
defense of multiculturalism as a primary social good, see Kymlicka, *Liberalism,* esp. chaps.
7–9; Kymlicka, *Multicultural Citizenship,* esp. chaps. 5 and 6; Moses.

sive intellectuals might go about fostering the conditions conducive to
working toward a better society. I argue that the value of assimilation
resides in a legitimate need for productive human interaction, and suggest that all of us — members of politically and culturally subordinated
groups as well as members of politically and culturally dominant ones —
can benefit from engaging in a process of multi-directional cross-cultural
acculturation (thus becoming "asimilao"). Against neoconservative
minority claims, I show that when we pay the right kind of attention to
our own and others' particularity, we position ourselves to develop a
more productive understanding of our universal humanity.

NEOCONSERVATIVE MINORITIES AND THE
DISAVOWAL OF RACIAL IDENTITY

The value, necessity, and/or inevitability of assimilation continues to be
one of the most hotly contested political issues in the United States. This
is because social policy decisions with significant material consequences
are decided on the basis of whether policymakers believe that cultural
and racial minorities have an obligation to assimilate to mainstream
American culture. If, like Shelby Steele, an educational policymaker sup-
ports the goal of assimilation, she is unlikely to support multicultural
educational initiatives and bilingual education; if she agrees with Richard
Rodriguez that the purpose of education is to socialize children into
mainstream American society — to provide them with a set of common
cultural assumptions — she will actively oppose reform efforts to make
the curriculum representative of different cultural experiences.[8] If, like
Linda Chávez, our policymaker equates "Americans" with white middle-
class people, she will ensure that the educational system she influences
will function to deracinate minority children; only by becoming more
"American," she will insist, can minorities "move ahead" in our society.
Her decisions will have a profound effect on the lives not only of the

8. See Rodriguez, *Days of Obligation*. He writes, "The classroom will teach us a language in common. The classroom will teach us a history that implicates us with others. The
classroom will tell us that we belong to a culture" (167). Also, in his interview with Postrel
and Gillespie, Rodriguez talks about what he sees as the function of the American education system: "What the classroom should insist on is that [little Johnny] belongs to a culture, a community, a tradition, a memory, and that in fact he's related to all kinds of people
that he'll never know. That's the point of education. . . . Education is not about self-esteem.
Education is demeaning. It should be about teaching you what you don't know, what you
yet need to know, how much there is yet to do."

minorities affected by her policies, but on the lives of all Americans who fail to learn about the histories and experiences of people unlike themselves. At stake, then, is the question of the value of assimilation: what price — if any — should Americans (and especially minorities) be required to pay in order to foster a common American culture?

The obvious question to ask ourselves when considering the value of assimilation is this: Are members of minority groups who assimilate to white middle-class American culture in fact happier, healthier, and more well off than those who do not? In asking this question, we might want to consider the possibility that Richard Rodriguez has a point when he says that highly educated Chicana/os who "scorn the value and necessity of assimilation," in effect, "toy with the confusion of those Americans who cannot speak standard English as well as they can" (*Hunger* 26, 35). While Rodriguez is both unkind and inaccurate in his attribution of motives, it is apparent that those of us who "make it" do so, in part, by assimilating to dominant (that is, "white") American culture. We become skilled at negotiating the white man's way; we master his language and learn his social codes. Moreover, it is evident that the recipients of affirmative action fellowships have often been those who come from the most assimilated, least disadvantaged backgrounds. For these reasons, it could be a mistake if, in our defensiveness, we fail to acknowledge the economic and social benefits of (at least partially) sharing a "culture" with the (white) people we interact and work with. Similarly, we might want to consider the possibility that Shelby Steele is right when he suggests that in our readiness to defend cultural particularity, we overlook the importance of seeing "human universals." Steele may be communicating something of value when he suggests that a world that paid more attention to our common humanity *would* be a better world: less conflictual, more harmonious, more egalitarian, more just.

Because neoconservative minorities like Rodriguez and Steele base their conviction that minorities should be required to assimilate to a white, middle-class American norm upon their notion of what universal humanity is, it is worth looking at what neoconservatives mean when they refer to "human universals."

The neoconservative understanding of the relationship between collective (racial and, as such, particular) identity and individual (universal and, as such, raceless) identity is that the two are antithetical to each other. Specifically, they believe that racial group membership robs a person of an important aspect of her humanity — that is, her individuality. Steele, for example, sees racial identity as a "threat" to human individuality: "When [middle class blacks] first meet, we experience a trapped feeling, as if we had walked into a cage of racial expectations that would rob us of our individuality by reducing us to an exclusively racial dimension. We are a threat, at first, to one another's uniqueness" (*Content* 22–23). Like the philosopher K. Anthony Appiah, Steele understands the lives of blacks in the United States as being "too tightly scripted" (Appiah 97–99). He believes that the life scripts enabled by the identity "African American" are too negative and too culturally impoverished to allow people so identified to exercise a robust personal autonomy.

Furthermore, Steele thinks that because collective racial identities diminish a person's individuality, they can lead to a situation in which people who identify with them become less than fully human.

> In the deepest sense, the long struggle of blacks in America has always been a struggle to retrieve our full humanity. But now the reactive stance [i.e., black identity] we adopted to defend ourselves against oppression binds us to the same racial views that oppressed us in the first place. Snakelike, our defense has turned on us. I think it is now the last barrier to the kind of self-possession that will give us our full humanity, and we must overcome it ourselves. (*Content* 35)

Richard Rodriguez is similarly critical of collective racial identities and their detrimental effect on human agency. His critique, however, is curiously linked to a racialist and culturalist conception of what it is to be an "American." In a discussion of some undocumented Mexican workers he encounters one summer, Rodriguez suggests that those persons who are seen as unindividuated members of a racial collectivity are somehow deficient; insofar as they cannot advocate for themselves as individuals, they lack human agency.

> On two occasions, the contractor hired a group of Mexican aliens. . . . In all, there were six men of varying age. . . . They came and they left in a single old truck. Anonymous men. (*Hunger* 134)

> Their silence stays with me now. The wages those Mexicans received for their labor were only a measure of their disadvantaged condition. Their silence is more telling. They lack a public identity. They remain profoundly alien. Persons apart. (*Hunger* 138)

In Rodriguez's view, these "anonymous" Mexicans (albeit of varying age) cannot be differentiated from one another: they travel together and remain collectively silent. Moreover, the lump sum wages they receive measure their inability to advocate, as individuals and legitimate members of the American polity, on their own behalf. Because "those Mexicans" lack a "public identity," because they cannot speak for themselves in English and as individuals, they remain disempowered outsiders to American society.

Although Rodriguez never explicitly says what he means by "public identity," or why he considers it to be so crucial for human agency, his meditation on the importance of public individuality in "Aria" helps us to discern his intent. According to Rodriguez's account of his own process of assimilation in that chapter, it was only after he was able to "think of [himself] as an American, no longer an alien in *gringo* society, [that he could] seek the rights and opportunities for full public individuality." He needed to become indistinguishable — another one of the "members of the crowd" of white middle-class people — in order to become an agential member of the American polity (27). For Rodriguez, this entailed leaving behind the Spanish language ("the language of the alien") and denying himself the intimacy of a close cultural connection to his Mexican-origin family (34).[9] Public identity, in Rodriguez's account, thus appears indistinguishable from the identity of the white middle-class English-speaking male citizen of the American nation-state. In effect, Rodriguez collapses civic and ethnic conceptions of what it means to be a legitimate inhabitant of the United States (that is, an "American") and wrongly concludes that the Mexicans he encounters are deficient in an important element of their humanity — that is, their individuality.[10] Moreover, his choice of terminology indicates that he concurs with Steele in seeing such people as less than fully human. They are, he asserts, "profoundly alien."

The above passages demonstrate that the neoconservative minority view conveys a specific conception of what it means to be fully human. By setting collective (racial and, as such, particular) identity in opposition to individual (universal and, as such, raceless) identity, Rodriguez and Steele figure cultural, racial, or ethnic particularity as supplemental — and occasionally as inimical — to universal humanity. In the following passage, for instance, Steele portrays racial specificity as additional, not intrinsic, to the "human universals":

9. I provide a fuller reading of Rodriguez's account of his assimilation in a later section of this chapter.

10. Rodriguez is certainly not the first person to conceive of American citizenship in racialized, gendered, or class terms. For much of the history of the United States, American citizenship has been associated with propertied white males. For a cogent discussion of the history of racial, gender, and economic exclusions which have been attached to definitions of American citizenship, see Foner.

> In the writing [of *The Content of Our Character*], I have had both to re-member and forget that I am black. The forgetting was to see the human uni-versals within the memory of the racial specifics. One of the least noted facts in this era when *racial, ethnic, and gender difference* are often embraced as sacred is that being black *in no way spares one from being human. . . .* in this book I have tried to search out the human universals that explain the racial specifics. (*Content* xi, emphases added)

According to Steele's view in the above passage, that which is "human" transcends what are merely racial, ethnic, or gender trappings. In other passages, Steele takes a harsher view, portraying racial identity as harm-ful to human possibility.

> To retrieve our individuality and find opportunity, blacks today must — con-sciously or unconsciously — disregard the prevailing victim-focused black identity. Though it espouses black pride, it is actually a repressive identity that generates a victimized self-image, curbs individualism and initiative, diminishes our sense of possibility, and contributes to our demoralization and inertia. It is a skin that needs shedding. (*Content* 172)

Steele's interesting choice of metaphors ("a skin that needs shedding") in an argument that advocates the end of *black* racial identity makes explicit his underlying conception of what it means to be human. Throughout his book, Steele's ideal human appears as a deracinated (by default white), ungendered (by default male), unsexed (by default het-erosexual), postcultural (by default American) individual; he appears to be devoid of particularity and he possesses rational agency.[11] In all this, Steele's ideal human bears a telling resemblance to the European En-lightenment's all-knowing and unsituated subject of reason.

Neoconservative minorities such as Rodriguez and Steele accept the bourgeois heterosexual Euro-American male subject as the standard of universal humanity. They err, as liberal thinkers typically have, by taking one particular manifestation of humanity and positing it as universal. They do this by making the bourgeois heterosexual Euro-American male subject the norm to which all other subjects must conform, even as they

11. The anthropologist Renato Rosaldo uses the term *postcultural* to refer to dominant members of the North American middle class. His point is that people who belong to a dominant first world culture are often unable to see themselves as cultural beings. Because what they do and how they do it seem to them to be the "obvious" and "right" way to do things, and because they are unable to imagine themselves as possible objects of an anthro-pological gaze, they appear to themselves as "people without a culture." Under this view, immigrants have culture while those who have "assimilated" have moved beyond culture (209–10).

simultaneously disavow that subject's racial, gender, sexual, and cultural particularity. Rodriguez, Steele, Carter, and Chávez all understand "racial" identity as always referring to "black" or "Hispanic" (i.e., non-"white") identity. In their writings, "white" identity does not appear as a racial identity. Although they acknowledge the existence of "white" people, they do not demonstrate an awareness that persons in the United States with pale skin undergo a racialization process that produces them as "white." Similarly, "male" does not appear as a gendered identity, while heterosexuality is simply assumed.

Neoconservative minorities consistently characterize particularity as that which deviates from the middle-class heterosexual white male norm. Rodriguez, for example, derides "gay studies, women's studies, ethnic studies" as areas of inquiry that do not contribute to a fundamental understanding of who "Americans" are. According to Rodriguez, the study of gays, women, or ethnics serves merely to "flatter" the groups in question (*Days of Obligation* 169). By contrast, Rodriguez believes that the study of the European (or Euro-American) heterosexual male teaches us something fundamental about what it means to be American. Rodriguez writes, "I need to know about seventeenth-century Puritans in order to make sense of the rebellion I notice everywhere in the American city. Teach me about mad British kings so I will understand the American penchant for iconoclasm" (*Days of Obligation* 169). The difference in Rodriguez's schema between (presumably heterosexual) "mad British kings" and "gays" is, apparently, the difference between sufficiency and excess: we need to know about one; we do not need to know about the other. Thus, Rodriguez reinscribes the bourgeois heterosexual European or Euro-American male subject (here represented by seventeenth-century Puritans and mad British kings) as the unmarked standard from which gays, women, and ethnics deviate as a result of their sexual, gender, and racial particularities.

Curiously, although Rodriguez argues against gay studies, women's studies, and ethnic studies, he inadvertently suggests their value. He writes, "Did anyone attempt to protect the white middle-class student of yore from the ironies of history? Thomas Jefferson — that great democrat — was also a slave owner. Need we protect black students from complexity? Thomas Jefferson, that slave owner, was also a democrat. . . . Once you toss out Benjamin Franklin and Andrew Jackson, you toss out Navajos. You toss out immigrant women who worked the sweatshops of the Lower East Side. Once you toss out Thomas Jefferson, you toss out black history" (*Days of Obligation* 169–70). The irony behind Rodriguez's claim is that American history, as it has traditionally been taught to those "middle-class students of yore" (and to everybody else), did precisely what he suggests it did not — that is, it protected them from the ironies of history.[12]

Rodriguez and Steele further err in setting collective racial identity in opposition to individual identity. As long as the category of race remains a structuring social formation in the United States, collective racial identity will not be antithetical to individual identity; rather, they will be dependent on each other. It is as impossible to have a racial collectivity that is not made up of individuals as it is to have an individual who is not a member of some racial collective. This is because all identities, including racial ones, are inescapably relational: to know ourselves as *selves* requires us to know ourselves in relation to *others*. In the process of defining who we are, we describe ourselves as beings with certain recognizably human characteristics — characteristics shared by some and lacking in others. To the extent that we define ourselves as being like some people, and not like others, we will identify ourselves in relation to a group — even if it means defining ourselves as being outside that group.

Moreover, just as there are no individuals who are not members of some collective identity, so there are no members of any given collective identity, racial or otherwise, who are not at the same time individuals. Because every human being occupies an objective social location constituted by multiple categories of identity, every member of a collective will likely differ from every other member in one or more significant ways. This is why the social identities of individual members of a particular racial group cannot be assumed to be the same — race is but one aspect of social location. Therefore, to assume (as neoconservative minorities do) that the act of identifying as African or Mexican American deprives a person of her individuality is to fall into the essentialist (and racist) logic of assuming that race makes up the totality of her being.

---

12. For a powerful critique of the inadequacies of historical education in the United States, see Loewen. Rodriguez's discussion of education demonstrates that he misunderstands the aims and contributions of gay, women's, and ethnic studies programs. It is partly as a result of the growth of black and other ethnic studies programs that we now question the myth of the founding fathers as the great and beneficent protectors of democracy and freedom. Moreover, without the establishment of women's studies programs, it is unlikely that sufficient resources would have been dedicated to the study of, for example, immigrant women in the sweatshops of the Lower East Side, work that has furthered a more adequate understanding of the role of women's labor in the shaping of the United States economy. Contrary to what Rodriguez suggests, gay studies, women's studies, and ethnic studies programs have never been interested in "tossing out" Benjamin Franklin and

NEOCONSERVATIVE MINORITIES' IDEAL
OF ASSIMILATION

Neoconservative minorities' acceptance of the bourgeois heterosexual Euro-American male as the exemplar of universal humanity profoundly influences their conception of the best way to work toward a non-racialized society. This is because they uncritically embrace what they take to be the middle-class American cultural values synonymous with that norm. They see American society in highly idealistic terms and assume that if there are individuals who do not "fit in" to American society, those individuals, and not society, need to change. As a consequence, neoconservative minorities equate assimilation to American mainstream culture with overall societal advancement. Steele, for instance, sees assimilation as highly desirable for promoting a better world: "The work ethic, the importance of education, the value of property ownership, of respectability, of 'getting ahead,' of stable family life, of initiative, of self-reliance, et cetera — are in themselves, raceless and even assimilationist. . . . These values are almost rules for how to prosper in a democratic, free enterprise society that admires and rewards individual effort" (*Content* 95). In this passage, Steele implies that the culturally and historically situated values held by middle-class Americans represent the values all residents of this country should hold.

Rodriguez, for his part, starts out by arguing that assimilation is a necessary good and ends up by viewing it as inevitable. In *Hunger of Memory*, Rodriguez argues vigorously for the value of assimilation to a white, middle-class norm on the basis of the claim that those who are not fully assimilated are alienated from public life. In *Days of Obligation*, he suggests that assimilation is not necessary so much as it is certain: "The best metaphor of America remains the dreadful metaphor — the Melting Pot. Fall into the Melting Pot, ease into the Melting Pot, or jump into the Melting Pot — it makes no difference — you will find yourself a stranger to your parents, a stranger to your own memory of yourself" (*Days of Obligation* 161). Assimilation, Rodriguez implies, is a *natural* phenome-

---

Andrew Jackson. They have never exclusively devoted themselves to "instill[ing] in children a pride in their ancestral pasts," or producing a "pageant of exemplary slaves and black educators," even though it is well accepted in educational circles that self-esteem is an important element in successful educational efforts (*Days of Obligation* 169). Their epistemological and educational mission has always been corrective. By their very nature, they — as much or more than any other area of study — have been actively engaged in exploring the ironies of history.

non: "I don't believe in assimilation any more than I believe in the sunrise. It happens. Assimilation happens, to coin a phrase" (quoted in Pederson, "Diversity and Assimilation").

Unlike Steele and Rodriguez, Stephen Carter appears to recognize that other cultures may have other, equally valuable, ways of approaching the world. He writes,

> The ideal of merit as the route to reward should not be confused with the very different proposition that the society in which we live today is one that gives out rewards that way. Similarly, not every standard accepted in *our* society is necessary for civilization in *every* society. Even the most confirmed cultural absolutist can hardly come away from such a book as Jomo Kenyatta's *Facing Mount Kenya* without conceding that others may have customs that work for them and not for us, and that forcing them to be like us would likely destroy perfectly moral, if somewhat different, cultures. (*Reflections* 231–32)

However, having acknowledged that other — different — cultures may be "perfectly moral," Carter sets this insight aside as something that need not be considered further in his present discussion. The result is a gentle relativism by virtue of which he refuses to consider the possible relevance of other societies' cultural practices for his own life. This basically anti-intellectual move is somewhat surprising coming from someone so concerned about getting out of the preformed intellectual "box" to which his racial identity supposedly consigns him.[13] It is a move, moreover, that replicates his refusal in another section of his book to consider the "fairness" of the screening "standards" by which educational goods and economic resources get distributed. At one point he writes, "I put aside for the moment the question of the fairness of standards" (*Reflections* 51); and later he says that "most professionals of whatever color are far too busy proving themselves to spend time quibbling over the fairness of standards for medical board certification or law firm partnership" (*Reflections* 90).

Because he sets aside these important political and evaluative questions, Carter avoids the necessity of questioning his own values, and those of the dominant members of the society in which he lives. He assumes, for instance, both that "standards of excellence are a requisite

---

13. Carter's introduction opens with this concern: "To be black and an intellectual in America is to live in a box. So I live in a box, not of my own making, and on the box is a label, not of my own choosing. Most of those who have not met me, and many of those who have, see the box and read the label and imagine that they have seen me" (1). His book represents an attempt to get others to see beyond that box.

of civilization," and that "we live in a world of brilliant scientific discoveries, remarkable acts of moral and spiritual courage, profound literary achievements, and outstanding professional performances" (231). Carter's somewhat rosy view of the world (which is not false so much as only partly true) leads him to proclaim that "we live in a world that cares about excellence, needs it, and should not be afraid to judge it" (231). The problem with Carter's argument against affirmative action in a book that attempts to influence public policy with regard to hiring practices is that he never addresses the difficult issue of how exactly we should go about judging "excellence." Instead, he presumes that whatever "standards" are already in use are culturally unbiased and provide an adequate method of judging "merit" and "excellence." Rather than questioning the fairness of standards or examining the dominant values of the society he lives in, Carter suggests that we should turn our attention to cultivating what he calls "The Edge, what every professional driving toward the top of his or her chosen field wants to hold over all the others, the competition, who are grabbing for the same brass ring" (*Reflections* 90). Carter thus fails to ask himself the really challenging questions, among which might be: Is competition a good in itself? Is it productive to want to "hold" things over other persons? Is "grabbing for the same brass ring" the model of human interaction we should all be striving for? In the end, by not considering seriously the viability of alternative approaches that may foster greater solidarity and justice, Carter ends up affirming the primacy of bourgeois heterosexual Euro-American male cultural values as much as Rodriguez and Steele do.

The a priori assumption that American society is not in need of reform and that all people are equally autonomous agents acting from fully rational conscious choice leads neoconservative minorities to take reductive approaches to solving complex social problems. Because they misjudge the absolute merit of American society, they make policy recommendations that hinder, rather than facilitate, the development of productive cross-cultural interaction. The most frequent solution they proffer to problems involving racial and economic inequality is that individual members of minority groups must simply work harder. Steele insists that "individual initiative" is "the only thing that finally delivers *anyone* from poverty" (*Content* 16). Carter proposes, as an alternative (or remedy) to affirmative action, that blacks just do better. He says that "the way to turn this potential liability [the stigma of affirmative action] into a powerful asset is to make our cadre of professionals simply too good to ignore" (*Reflections* 86). Not surprisingly, the neoconservative minority perspective incorporates a "blame the victim" mentality. Chávez asserts that "only the Puerto Rican community can save itself, but the healing cannot begin until the community recognizes that many of its deadliest wounds are self-inflicted" (*Barrio* 159), while Steele piously declares that "if conditions have worsened for most of us as racism has receded, then much of the problem must be of our own making" (*Content* 15). Such sanctimoniousness on the part of neoconservative minorities ignores the role of economic forces and government policies on the lives of ordinary working people: Chávez's "analysis" of the Puerto Rican situation fails to take into account the role of the U.S. government-sponsored Operation Bootstrap in the creation of a massive Puerto Rican underclass,[14] while Steele's attempt to conjure away racism through the incantatory repetition of the phrase "as racism has receded" has had little effect on the socioeconomic situation of blacks and Latina/os living in the United States today.[15]

As a group, neoconservative minorities seriously underread the degree to which a variety of economic and social forces in our capitalist society exert control over the material conditions of the lives of ordinary people. Because they are working with an abstract individualist notion of autonomy, neoconservative minorities underestimate the constraints placed upon individual agency by unchosen aspects of any given person's social location. Consequently, they conclude incorrectly that ordinary people have the power to determine the quality of their own lives. At a minimum, neoconservative minorities assume that they can exert singular control over the formation of their identities. Rodriguez, for example, asserts that his public identity ultimately depends upon his "imagination of [himself]" (138). In the next section, I provide a close reading of Rodriguez's *Hunger of Memory* in order to expose the interpretive error that underlies his neoconservative minority identity. In the process, I add to the postpositivist realist theory of identity elaborated in chapters one and two, showing that identities based on ideological mystifications can, when examined closely, be important sources of knowledge about the world. To the extent that identities do not work well as explanations of the social world — to the extent that they refer imperfectly to salient

14. For more on how U.S. economic policy has influenced the lives and economic opportunities of Puerto Ricans, see Carr; Dietz; Sánchez Korrol.

15. See Steele's "Race-Holding" in *The Content of Our Character,* in which he repeats this phrase or a variation of it no fewer than six times. My point is that Steele relies on mere repetition to convince his reader of the truth of this claim without providing any substantive evidence for it.

aspects of the society from which they emerge — they can help reveal the fundamental contradictions and mystifications within which members of that society live.

INTERPRETATION OF MEMORY: THE ASSIMILATION OF RICHARD RODRIGUEZ

Over the course of *Hunger of Memory,* Rodriguez figures his changing relationship to the Mexican American community as a protracted and poignant drama of painful loss and consequent gain. He is careful, though, to distinguish his narrative from a call for a culturally sensitive approach to educating Mexican American children.

> My awkward childhood does not prove the necessity of bilingual education. My story discloses instead an essential myth of childhood — inevitable pain. If I rehearse here the changes in my private life after my Americanization, it is finally to emphasize the public gain. The loss implies the gain. . . . Once I learned public language [English], it would never again be easy for me to hear intimate family voices. . . . But that may only be a way of saying that the day I raised my hand in class and spoke loudly to an entire roomful of faces, my childhood started to end. (27–28)

Thus, rather than regretting the loss of the cultural connection he cherished as a child, Rodriguez figures his transition from ethnic identity to deracinated American identity in terms of a process of maturation: his "childhood started to end" when he learned to speak English. Social and political opportunity, he insists, are available only to those who, in the process of growing up, shed their ethnic identities: "Only when I was able to think of myself as an American, no longer an alien in *gringo* society, could I seek the rights and opportunities necessary for full public individuality. The social and political advantages I enjoy as a man result from the day that I came to believe that my name, indeed, is *Rich-heard Road-ree-guess*" (27). Rodriguez closes his book by refusing a "minority" identity altogether, suggesting that "minorities" are those people who are *culturally* disadvantaged. He presumes that as a highly educated person, he can no longer be considered a minority: "The reason I was no longer a minority was because I had become a student" (147). On the surface, then, *Hunger of Memory* testifies to Rodriguez's successful, if difficult, assimilation into mainstream white American society.

Despite his proclamations, Rodriguez's book testifies to the contrary. His focus on culture at the crucial moment of claiming an American identity collapses the concept of race into the concept of culture and allows him to conveniently obscure the salience of the category of race in the formation of his identity. Yet even a cursory reading of *Hunger of Memory* reveals how central his awareness of himself as a racialized being is to his sense of self. Throughout his youth, Rodriguez equates dark skin with poverty, powerlessness, and disadvantage. Hyper-aware of the color of his skin, and terrified that as a result of his complexion he will become one of *los pobres*, Rodriguez devotes a considerable amount of energy to trying to escape what he perceives to be the inexorable and unenviable fate of dark-skinned people. With the encouragement of his mother, he spends his childhood staying out of the sun to avoid making his skin darker than it already is.

In one of the most compelling passages in the book, Rodriguez employs gothic associations to convey the disgust he feels for "the dark" part of himself. He prefaces the passage by telling his reader that he felt shame and sexual inferiority because of his dark complexion, and that he thought of himself as an ugly child.

> One night when I was eleven or twelve years old, I locked myself in the bathroom and carefully regarded my reflection in the mirror over the sink. Without any pleasure I studied my skin. I turned on the faucet. (In my mind I heard the swirling voices of aunts, and even my mother's voice, whispering, whispering incessantly about lemon juice solutions and dark, *feo* children.) With a bar of soap, I fashioned a thick ball of lather. I began soaping my arms. I took my father's straight razor out of the medicine cabinet. Slowly, with steady deliberateness, I put the blade against my flesh, pressed it as close as I could without cutting, and moved it up and down across my skin to see if I could get out, somehow lessen, the dark. All I succeeded in doing, however, was in shaving my arms bare of their hair. For as I noted with disappointment, the dark would not come out. It remained. Trapped. Deep in the cells of my skin. (124–25)

Accompanied by background music (evoked through the alliteration of the letter "s" in an extended description of the "swirling voices of aunts . . . whispering, whispering incessantly"), Rodriguez's deliberately suspenseful step-by-step narration of the event positions the reader as an unwilling spectator to something possibly horrific. At this point in the book, the reader knows that Rodriguez does not like himself, knows that he has locked himself in the bathroom, and knows that he has removed his father's razor from the cabinet. Not until fully three-fourths of the way through the passage is the reader assured that Rodriguez's adolescent intent is not suicidal. The remaining fourth of the passage is devoted to Rodriguez's disappointed discovery that "the dark" is not alienable from himself. Nevertheless, Rodriguez continues to speak of it as if it were. His final statement, which is given dramatic emphasis by being split up into three separate phrases, emphasizes the distinction Rodriguez wishes to make between "the dark" and his "self." "The dark" is referred to as "it," as something separate from and alien to the "skin" that Rodriguez refers to as belonging to himself.

In the pages that follow this passage, the reader learns that when Rodriguez's attempt to "get out, somehow lessen, the dark" fails, his solution is to "[grow] divorced from [his] body" and become "insecure, overweight, listless" (124–25). As an adolescent, Rodriguez denies himself a "sensational life" explaining that "I was too ashamed of my body. I wanted to forget that I had a body because I had a brown body" (126).[16] Eventually, however, Rodriguez moves to resolve his dilemma in a manner that is less personally restrictive. Because he cannot change the color of his skin, and because denying himself "desired sensation" is not a viable long-term option for him, he decides that dark skin no longer means what he had assumed it to mean all along (131). Over time, he divests "the dark" of the negative associations he had previously attributed to it. Subsequently, he concludes, "My complexion becomes a mark of my leisure. . . . my complexion assumes its significance from the context of my life. My skin, in itself, means nothing" (137).

Although he appears to have solved his dilemma when he reinterprets the significance of his skin color, Rodriguez cannot overcome his terror of being identified with the underclass. Despite his apparent liberation from his obsession with dark skin, he still needs a way to differentiate himself from the poverty, powerlessness, and disadvantage represented by *los pobres* — those poor, pitiful laborers to whom his dark skin has linked him. Thus, he responds to this need by psychologically projecting

16. Although I do not provide a detailed analysis here, "Complexion" is as much about Rodriguez's internalized homophobia as it is about his internalized racism. His denial of his own brown body was simultaneously a denial of his socially proscribed sexual desire for the brown bodies of *los braceros*. He writes, "I'd see the Mexican gardeners. I was unwilling to admit the attraction of their lives. I tried to deny it by looking away. But what was denied become strongly desired" (*Hunger* 126). And, "It was at Stanford, one day near the end of my senior year, that a friend told me about a summer construction job he knew was available. I was quickly alert. Desire uncoiled within me. . . . I would . . . at last grasp desired sensation. No longer afraid. At last become like a *bracero*" (130–31). Significantly, Rodriguez refers to Mexican workers as *los braceros* (the laborers — literally, the ones who work with their arms) when he is describing his desire for them, and as *los pobres* (the poor, pitiful ones) when he is describing their socioeconomic status. For an excellent discussion of Richard Rodriguez's relationship to his sexuality, see Hames-García, "Mestizos in Flux."

out all the negative associations he had previously attributed to "the dark" onto what he depicts as the unindividuated and profoundly disenfranchised collective consciousness of *los pobres.*

> Their silence stays with me now. . . . They lack a public identity. They remain profoundly alien. Persons apart. People lacking a union obviously, people without grounds. . . . Their silence stays with me. I have taken these many words to describe its impact. Only: the quiet. Something uncanny about it. Its compliance. Vulnerability. Pathos. As I heard their truck rumbling away, I shuddered, my face mirrored with sweat. I had finally come face to face with *los pobres.* (*Hunger* 138–39)

Thus, when "the dark" trapped deep within the cells of Rodriguez's own skin ceases to be the frightening alien entity with the power to brand him as one of the despised, *los pobres* emerge as the "uncanny" and "profoundly alien" presence within the United States borders whose collective "silence" threatens the certainty and security of Rodriguez's "American" identity.

Besides providing an evisceratingly honest account of the phenomenon of internalized racism, Rodriguez's case presents a dramatic illustration of what can happen when a person grows up within "an impoverished 'social context of choice' " (Moses 1). According to the educational theorist Michele Moses, a good life in a just and democratic society will be characterized by a significant capacity for self-determination. By this she means that members of that society will be able to make choices about who they want to become in relation to their historical, cultural, and social contexts without being constrained by unjust societal limits. The problem with current American society, Moses suggests, is that historically entrenched structures of oppression present some people, but not others, with severely constrained social contexts of choice. Because the collective identities of African Americans and Chicana/os, for example, are more frequently denigrated than affirmed in the United States, people who are identified with these groups frequently find themselves in social contexts of choice that do not provide the kinds of personal and cultural structures that support a wide range of options for them. As long as this is the case, some African Americans and Chicana/os will feel that they must reject their home cultures and identities in order to improve their life chances. This situation can contribute to their making what Moses calls "costly" choices — that is, choices that require them to deny or distort their identities (7). Moses points out that insofar as they are unable to develop and maintain self-conceptions that incorporate significant aspects of their personal pasts, people who deny or distort their identities are often left with much-diminished capacities for self-determination. They are forced, as Rodriguez was, to reject their families and cultures of origin in a futile attempt to determine meaningfully the way their lives will go. The solution, Moses avers, will involve some state-sponsored efforts (i.e., multicultural education) to affirm a wider variety of cultures and identities as socially worthy.

Significantly, Moses and the neoconservative minorities I am critiquing here share the same long-term ideal. They are all in favor of a life characterized by a robust self-determination unconstrained by unjust societal limits — as am I. Moses differs from the neoconservative minorities, however, in her acknowledgment of the structural forces (economic, racial, and cultural) that shape people's choices. Moreover, like the postpositivist realist, she has a dialectical conception of social identity. This is in sharp contrast to Rodriguez, who tends to understand identity in purely idealist terms. If, as a boy, he imputed too much significance to the color of his skin, as a young adult, Rodriguez attributes too little. He assumes that social identity is entirely a matter of "mind"; that subjective consciousness is the most determinative feature of any person or group. He explains, "I was not one of *los pobres*. What made me different from them was an attitude of mind, my imagination of myself" (*Hunger* 138). On the basis of this same idealism, Rodriguez concludes that he is no longer a member of a "minority" group. By using the term "minority" to refer to "poorly schooled, disadvantaged Americans," and by emphasizing the advantages of his own education, Rodriguez attempts to elide the issue of race in order to escape what he perceives as the stigma of being "minority": "I was not — in a *cultural* sense — a minority, an alien from public life. (Not like *los pobres* I had encountered during my recent laboring summer.) The truth was summarized in the sense of irony I'd feel at hearing myself called a minority student: The reason I was no longer a minority was because I had become a student" (*Hunger* 147). Rodriguez's account of his identity formation thus attempts to deny the fact that, when used in a United States social context, the term "minority" generally refers to specifiable *racial* groups.[17] Instead, he attempts to

17. For an account of the historical development of the concept of race in the United States and its role in structuring the social world, see Omi and Winant. I have found their definition of race to be very helpful. They write, "race is a concept which signifies and symbolizes social conflicts and interests by referring to different types of human bodies. Although the concept of race invokes biologically based human characteristics (so-called 'phenotypes'), selection of these particular human features for purposes of racial signification is always and necessarily a social and historical process" (55).

change (and then contain) the meaning of the term by redefining it solely in terms of *culture*.

> It became easy . . . to forget that those whose lives are shaped by poverty and poor education (cultural minorities) are least able to defend themselves against social oppression. (*Hunger* 149–50)

> [Academics] should have acknowledged (the truth) that higher education is out of the reach of minorities — poorly schooled, disadvantaged Americans" (*Hunger* 153).

In effect, Rodriguez decides that by *changing his mind*, he can change his identity — and the social world to which his identity refers. He thus ignores the dialectical, referential, and *social* nature of identity, and demonstrates his unwillingness to acknowledge the political, economic, and epistemic consequences of his social location — of which race is one fundamental aspect.[18] Ironically, Rodriguez's idealist assumptions about identity echo the idealist assumptions of the postmodernist identity theorists I criticized in chapters one and two. I am thinking specifically of Donna Haraway, who suggests that people are related, "not by blood but by choice" ("Cyborgs" 196). As demonstrated in those chapters, theorists like Haraway also attempt to sever the links between identity and social categories such as race or gender.

Ultimately, and despite his best efforts, Rodriguez cannot convince the world around him that he is not a "minority." Ever since the publication of *Hunger of Memory*, it has become increasingly evident to his critics as well as to Rodriguez himself that his assimilation into white American society was not as successful as he had claimed it to be.[19] Tellingly, those intellectuals who have given Rodriguez the most sustained attention — the literary critics who have written and published papers about his work — have consistently refuted his efforts to refuse a minority identity.

18. In *Hunger of Memory*, Rodriguez claims that his upward social mobility has changed the racial meanings attached to his dark skin. He writes, "Visiting the East Coast or the gray capitals of Europe during the long months of winter, I often meet people at deluxe hotels who comment on my complexion. (In such hotels it appears nowadays a mark of leisure and wealth to have a complexion like mine.) Have I been skiing? In the Swiss Alps? Have I just returned from a Caribbean vacation? No. I say no softly but in a firm voice that intends to explain: My complexion is dark" (113). However, his subsequent book, *Days of Obligation*, testifies against the veracity of this claim insofar as it documents other Americans' continued willingness to see him as a racialized being.

19. See Alarcón, "Tropology of Hunger"; Rivera, "Richard Rodriguez' *Hunger of Memory*"; R. Saldívar, *Chicano Narrative*, esp. 145–70; J. D. Saldívar, *Border Matters*, esp. 140–51; Rosaura Sánchez, "Calculated Musings."

They note, instead, his tendency to misinterpret his own social situation. Lawrence Hogue points out that *"Hunger of Memory* shows unconsciously a Richard Rodriguez who has always been marginal to the experience of the middle class, white, American male because he is a person of color" (58). Alfredo Villanueva-Collado takes Rodriguez to task for holding the "unfounded belief that language, by itself, can achieve assimilation for individuals who are linguistically or racially different" (79). And Antonio Marquez reminds us that Rodriguez's theme is typically that of a "minority" in the United States.

> Indeed, Rodriguez's life is not unique. He is not the first to suffer the childhood trauma of inferiority. He is not the first to be torn between conflicting cultural values. He is not the first to embrace assimilation and to take the avenue of higher education toward an academic career, and consequently to be uprooted and alienated from his family and cultural roots. And he is certainly not the first to be stamped as a *vendido* for separating himself from his heritage and assuming the trappings of the Anglo bourgeoisie. . . . In brief, he has taken a common experience and given it the shape of literary art through the autobiographical form. (132)

Like so many other literary critics who treat Rodriguez's work, Marquez situates *Hunger of Memory* firmly within the tradition of Chicana/o literature — in spite of Rodriguez's protestations and claims to exceptionalism.[20] So, while Rodriguez might wish to consider himself representative of a deracinated middle-class American man — or at least *not* representative of the "typical Hispanic-American life" — his autobiographical narrative unconsciously portrays a recognizably minority experience (*Hunger* 7).

Moreover, Rodriguez's unsuccessful attempts, in *Hunger of Memory,* to escape the socially constructed meaning of his skin color testify both to his failure to understand the salience of race in American society and his unwillingness to acknowledge the consequences of his social location.[21]

---

20. When asked to teach a minority literature course at Berkeley in the early 1970s, Rodriguez declined. He explained, "I didn't think that there *was* such a thing as minority literature. Any novel or play about the lower class will necessarily be alien to the culture it portrays" (*Hunger* 161). With respect to his own autobiography, he writes, "Let the bookstore clerk puzzle over where it should be placed. (Rodriguez? Rodriguez?) Probably he will shelve it alongside specimens of that exotic new genre, 'ethnic literature.' Mistaken, the gullible reader will — in sympathy or in anger — take it that I intend to model my life as the typical Hispanic-American life. But I write of one life only. My own" (7).

21. By *social location,* I mean the particular nexus of gender, race, class, and sexuality in which an individual exists at any given time in society. For a fuller discussion of the epistemic effects of social location, see chapter one.

Unlike lighter skinned Mexican Americans who might be able to "pass" as white, Rodriguez is indelibly marked as nonwhite by his physiognomy and the color of his skin. By arguing that Rodriguez is mistaken in his refusal to acknowledge the consequences of his social location, I am not suggesting that he needs to recognize "who he really is," or that his identity was determined at birth. In fact, I am deeply sympathetic to the young Rodriguez's desire to escape a racializing gaze that sees people of color as lesser (if not less than) human beings. However, no amount of wishful thinking will effectively change either entrenched social institutions or the dialectical character of identity. Because racialized thinking is deeply interwoven into the fabric of our society, our racial designation affects our countless daily social, political, and economic interactions with others. Moreover, because identity is dialectical, our racial designation is not a purely personal affair; just because Rodriguez thinks of himself as different from *"los pobres"* does not mean that others will not assign him and them to the same racial group. To the extent that Rodriguez refuses to recognize this consequence, he is simply blinding himself to the racial dynamics that affect his psychic and material well-being without finding an effective way to insulate himself from their very real effects.

The reception of both his autobiography and his later writings testify to other Americans' continued willingness to assign racial significance to Rodriguez's physiognomy and skin color. In the final analysis, Rodriguez exists not as a deracinated individual living within the boundaries of his imagined universe (or even within the covers of his carefully wrought autobiography), but as an embodied human being whose identity has been, and continues to be, constituted in and through social interaction. Rodriguez's skillful use of literary devices to transmute the meaning of words and identities within the covers of a book proves insufficient when he loses control of the medium. At a 1995 speech he gave at a meeting of the American Society of Newspaper Editors in Dallas, Rodriguez recalled that Bill Moyers once asked him in an interview, "Do you consider yourself as Hispanic or American?" Aside from the fact that the question supposes a false dichotomy (a dichotomy Rodriguez himself reinscribes in *Hunger of Memory*), Moyers's question demonstrates that Rodriguez ultimately fails in his attempt to escape a racializing gaze. Moyers's question is intelligible only if we understand that Moyers sees Rodriguez as someone who is *not* fully "American," as someone who has *not* been successfully deracinated. Rodriguez's sarcastic response — that he is Chinese because he lives in an Asian section of San Francisco — evades the central issue (who counts as "American"?) and reveals his inability to maintain his idealist convictions about identity in the face of social interaction.

So, despite Rodriguez's assertion that he is "no longer a minority," his books are usually shelved in the Chicana/o literature section of college bookstores; in contradiction to his claim to have successfully assumed a mainstream American identity, talk show hosts and TV journalists still consider Rodriguez to be a suitable representative of Hispanics in the United States; and, in the face of his self-professed cultural alienation, Rodriguez continues to write about, speak about, and *speak for* people of Mexican origin in the United States and Mexico. For all his early attempts to disavow his connection to Mexicans and other Latina/os, Richard Rodriguez is yet considered to be a member of a racial minority group.

A close examination of Rodriguez's writings demonstrates that he has indeed undergone cultural change. He is not the same person he was as a young boy; he has become more "American." He has not, however, been successfully deracinated. Not only does Rodriguez continue to be recognized by others as a member of a racial minority group, but his writings reveal that his own thinking has been deeply shaped by the social phenomenon of race. Indeed, one of the most notable features of neoconservative minorities is how race conscious they reveal themselves to be. Thus, a critical evaluation of the underlying claims of neoconservative minority identities will reveal that race profoundly influences who they are, what they believe, and how they are regarded by others (including those who make the economic and social policy decisions that affect our daily lives). Despite the fact that race lacks a biological basis, it remains a causally significant feature of our social world.

The continuing salience of race, even to those who deny its social significance, demonstrates why a postmodernist approach — which either undermines the reality of those categories constitutive of identity (of which race is one) or undertheorizes the relationship between social location and identity — will be inadequate to our contemporary political moment. In the next section, I return to the postpositivist realist theory of identity in order to propose it as an alternative to both neoconservative and postmodernist conceptions of identity. Only with a more complex and sophisticated understanding of identity such as that provided by a postpositivist realist theory of identity can progressive social thinkers respond to the real challenges posed by the existence of cultural and other kinds of difference.

A REALIST APPROACH TO UNIVERSAL HUMANITY

My examination of the neoconservative minority approach to assimilation suggests that the problem many postmodernist critics of the Enlightenment have with the concept of the "universal" may actually be a problem with the way that concept has historically been described — specifically, with the particular *content* that has been ascribed to the universal human. If, on one hand, the universal subject is figured implicitly as the bourgeois heterosexual European male, then any feature that diverges from that norm (such as homosexuality or female gender) will be seen as culturally particular and epistemically irrelevant. But if, on the other hand, we acknowledge that the so-called universal subject that postmodernist critics have been rejecting is actually the bourgeois heterosexual European male, then we are in a better position to see him as a cultural being — an embodied being grounded in a particular time and space. A realist approach to identity recognizes the embodiedness and situatedness of all subjects, enabling us to see that cultural particularity is antithetical to universal humanity only when we have a culturally elaborated understanding of universal humanity.[22] Situating the grand "subject of reason" allows us to divest him of his universalist pretensions without doing away with the subject (and subject-based agency) altogether. The realist approach contends that cultural particularity need not be antithetical to universal humanity as long as we have a conception of universal humanity that is *not* culturally elaborated.

The suggestion proposed by Mohanty in *Literary Theory and the Claims of History* is that we should follow Kant in understanding "reason" as a practical and universal human capacity. Rather than conceptualizing reason as a fixed Enlightenment formula for achieving predetermined moral and political ends, Mohanty suggests that we see it as a universal human capacity that allows persons to continually evaluate their actions within the context of their ideas and experiences, and enables them to act purposefully in response to those ongoing evaluations (139, 199, 248). Recognizing that all humans are "rational" in this minimal way allows us to conceptualize human universality in terms of a basic capacity shared by all humans, rather than as a comprehensive

22. My point holds for any culturally elaborated understanding of universal humanity, whether that subject be the bourgeois heterosexual European male, or, let us say, a proletarian lesbian Asian female. Historically, of course, the so-called universal subject has been equated with the bourgeois heterosexual European male, which is why it is so difficult for us to see him as a particular being.

account of human nature. Under this view, one need not belong to a particular racial or cultural group in order to be considered worthy of human dignity and consideration; one need only be a part of an evolving cultural community. Moreover, this conception of universal humanity invites specification and particularization, but does not require either for support of the basic universalist claim (199–200).

This minimal notion of universal humanity suggests both the possibility and necessity of cross-cultural communication. While realists such as Mohanty acknowledge the importance — and occasional necessity — of having a common language, common values, and common priorities, they also understand that it would be a mistake to assume that they know ahead of time what that language, those values, and those priorities should be. Scholars will too often discuss the issue of diversity in either/or terms: either diversity is good, or it is not; either humans foster difference, or they attempt to eradicate it. From a realist perspective, it is a mistake to think of our options for dealing with difference in these oppositional terms. Given the fact of human diversity, we need to take the project of cross-cultural communication seriously.

Of course, any project of cross-cultural communication requires that we attend to the nature of human difference. In order to do this, we need to be able to specify what the differences are, what those differences mean to the way we choose (or are forced) to live our lives. We need a way to decide whether the differences between individuals or groups can or even *should* be resolved. We need to be able to ask what difference a given "difference" makes. It is important for us to realize that while there are some differences we can live with, there are others we cannot. For the sake of the healthy flourishing of humankind, we need to know which are which.

Consider, for example, linguistic difference. The consequences of linguistic differences range from the realm of minor annoyance to a matter of life and death. If you are in an elevator with two other people who are speaking a language you do not understand, your inability to understand them may make you feel vulnerable. You may wonder if they are talking about you (they may be) and you may be irritated. Strictly speaking, this is not a societal issue; it is your problem. You can choose whether or not to be annoyed. Not being able to understand everything everybody else says at all times is a consequence of linguistic differences that society at large can live with. There are other circumstances, however, in which it is imperative that two people share a language. It is fairly obvious, for instance, that a flight controller and the pilot of an aircraft attempting to land within that flight controller's jurisdiction must share some kind of language. Similarly, a doctor and a nurse must be able to communicate with each other in an emergency room situation. A plane crashing because the pilot cannot understand the flight controller's language or a patient dying because the doctor and nurse cannot communicate with each other are consequences of linguistic differences that society at large literally cannot "live" with. These are instances in which linguistic difference becomes a societal issue, and in which the need for a common language is quite obvious. But what is not obvious is what that common language should be. There is no reason that the speakers of one language should be forced to switch to the other — it is quite possible that the two parties could both learn a third language, or that the two languages could be combined into a pidgin or creolized language. In actuality, the issue of which language will prevail will most likely be decided by considerations of convenience or power — but it is not necessary that it be so.

Thus, the value of assimilation (insofar as it involves sharing a language, accepting received values, assuming customary habits of interaction) does not involve specifically the well-being of minorities so much as it addresses a legitimate need for productive human interaction. When minorities assimilate to white middle-class American culture, the effect is often that they learn to communicate more effectively with those who hold the keys to their economic well-being; the result is potentially rewarding for everyone involved. However, having acknowledged the value of sharing a common culture, I would nevertheless argue that it is a mistake to assume that productive human interaction is predicated on assimilation to a predetermined norm. There are two reasons for this: (1) to avoid the damage that assimilation (when conceived of as forced unidirectional cultural change) wreaks on the psyches of those individuals who are forced to abandon their own culture;[23] (2) to prevent the loss of

---

23. The philosopher Ofelia Schutte argues that when assimilation leads to an indifference toward the preservation of diversity as constituted by ethnic group membership, it violates a broader principle of social justice. Her argument in favor of group rights is derived from a "conception guided by the principles of a culturally pluralist, democratic society. Such a conception recognizes that to deprive human beings of favorable conditions by which they can be recognized for their specific linguistic and historical-cultural achievements and contributions is to inflict a degree of violence on them" (65). The philosopher and political theorist Charles Taylor makes a similar claim when he says that "nonrecognition or misrecognition can inflict harm, can be a form of oppression, imprisoning someone in a false, distorted, and reduced mode of being" (25). The idea behind such calls for recognition is that to erase (by destroying or refusing to recognize) a culture or identity is effectively to deny the full humanity of those people who have been socialized within it.

moral and epistemic possibility that follows in the wake of predetermined cultural homogeneity. From a realist perspective, people like Rodriguez, Steele, Carter, and Chávez suffer from a failure of imagination — a failure that derives at least in part from the white American ethnocentrism and racism they have internalized.[24] Consequently, they are unable to see that other cultures may have different ways of approaching problems or social arrangements that give rise to greater human flourishing. Neoconservative minorities assume ahead of time that the middle-class American values they hold are the best values of all. However, there is no reason to assume that white middle-class American values are the set of values to which all people should aspire. In fact, there is much evidence to suggest that they are not. To the extent that we are interested in working for a more socially and politically equitable world, then, our goal should be not assimilation, but rather multi-directional cross-cultural acculturation.

When neoconservative minorities point to the successes of "assimilated" minorities, they exhibit selective vision. While they see the value of cultural sharing, they fail to consider the emotional, psychological, and *epistemic* consequences of forced unidirectional cultural change. Objectively speaking, we live in a troubled society: one need only turn on the television, pick up the newspaper, or talk to one's neighbor to realize this. For this reason, if people do not fit into our society, we should consider the possibility that we need to change society instead of people. Moreover, contrary to Rodriguez's claim that assimilation is inevitable, cultural change is not always in the direction of assimilation. Cultural change always occurs, but more often in several directions.

THE VALUE OF BEING *ASIMILAO*

In his essay " 'Qué assimilated, brother, yo soy asimilao': The Structuring of Puerto Rican Identity in the U.S.," the cultural critic Juan Flores argues that Puerto Ricans living on the mainland do not assimilate as

---

24. Because he never questions the value of assimilation, Rodriguez cannot account for why so many Latina/o educators with terminal degrees in their field have what he represents as such nefarious designs on their communities of origin. Consequently, he lets slander do the work of argumentation in dismissing their substantive claims. Rodriguez calls bilingual education a "scheme" perpetrated by "middle-class ethnics" who are "filled with decadent self-pity, [and] obsessed with the burden of public life" (*Hunger* 11, 27). Rodriguez suggests that "foreign-language bilingualists" are naive and dangerous: naive because they do not "realize" that one cannot be "a public person while remaining a private person" and "dangerous" because "they romanticize public separateness and they trivialize the dilemma of the socially disadvantaged" (*Hunger* 33, 26, 34, 27).

much as they "grow together" in a strong process of cultural convergence with blacks and other migrants from the Caribbean and Latin
America (191–92). Flores notes that while outsiders often mistake this
growing together for assimilation, the process is not directed toward
incorporation into the dominant culture. What results, instead, is a pluralism that does not "involve the dissolution of national backgrounds
and cultural histories but their continued affirmation and enforcement
even as they are transformed" (192). Only from this vantage point of cultural coalescence with other non-dominant groups do Puerto Ricans
move toward interaction with Anglo-American society at large. Flores
argues that while Puerto Ricans who have undergone this cultural convergence can be readily distinguished from those who have more recently
arrived from the island, it is nevertheless "not accurate to speak of assimilation" in connection with their cultural formation. He concludes,
"Rather than being subsumed and repressed, Puerto Rican culture contributes, on its own terms and as an extension of its own traditions, to a
new amalgam of human expression. It is the existing racial, national and
class divisions in U.S. society which allow for, indeed necessitate, this
alternative course of cultural change" (192). Invoking the main theme
from nuyorican poet Tato Laviera's poem "asimilao," Flores contends
that while Puerto Ricans in North America undergo cultural change,
they do not become assimilated in the sense of becoming culturally indistinguishable from middle-class white Americans. Rather, they adapt to
their new surroundings by retaining some values and cultural practices
and by changing others—absorbing other ways of being in the world
from among the various cultural groups they come into contact with.
They become, in other words, *asimilao*.

Once we acknowledge that assimilation (when conceived of as forced,
unidirectional cultural change) is not inevitable, we are free to consider
the value of being *asimilao*. By observing actual processes of cross-
cultural interaction, we have opened the space in which to argue that
assimilation to a predetermined norm can actually impoverish society by
depriving people of the behavioral and moral insights they might gain as
a result of their respectful interaction with people from different cultural
backgrounds. To make this argument, I draw upon Mohanty's realist
idea that cultures are both repositories of and laboratories for behavioral
and moral knowledge.[25]

---

25. See S. P. Mohanty, *Literary Theory*, esp. 240–42. Kymlicka has championed a similar idea within liberal theory: "Liberals should be concerned with the fate of cultural

To understand why assimilation to a predetermined norm can be epistemically and morally detrimental, we must first remember that cultural change is not arbitrary, but is a response to changing social and economic conditions. Although such cultural change may occasionally be forced, as in the case of government-sponsored assimilation programs,[26] it can also occur as a result of (more or less) conscious choices on the part of cultural practitioners. To the extent that humans have some choice about how they will interact with their changing environment, "cultural practices — ways of living, of creating, of choosing to value one thing over another in our daily lives — are an essential form of moral inquiry" (Mohanty, *Literary Theory* 240). Cultures, Mohanty explains, "not only embody values and beliefs, they test and modify these values and beliefs in practical ways" (240). It is when we think of cultures as behavioral and moral laboratories that we can begin to understand how essential multiculturalism is to our society's ability to imagine and enact new behavioral and moral possibilities. Other people's preferred ways of living can provide us with models for other kinds of cultural practices — practices that we may not have thought of, or that we may not have had the opportunity to try — that may be more conducive to human flourishing than some of our own.[27]

Mohanty's realist conception of multiculturalism as epistemic cooperation thus provides a strong justification for the preservation of cultural diversity. It allows us to see that cultural diversity is a valuable characteristic of an ideal society — for epistemic, not merely sentimental, reasons. If we follow Mohanty in understanding cultural diversity as "the best social condition in which objective knowledge about human flour-

---

structures, not because they have some moral status of their own, but because it's only through having a rich and secure cultural structure that people can become aware, in a vivid way, of the options available to them, and intelligently examine their value" (*Liberalism* 165).

26. For information on government-sponsored efforts to "Americanize" Mexican Americans, see Deutsch; Ruíz, esp. chap. 2; G. J. Sánchez, *Becoming Mexican American,* esp. chap. 4.

27. I recognize that humans' ability to modify their cultural practices in accordance with their evolving values and beliefs will vary across time, space, and circumstance. I understand that some people, because of their objective social locations, will be less autonomous and more constrained by economic, social, or cultural constraints than some others. Furthermore, I acknowledge that what we might subjectively experience as an act of individual choice might be influenced by larger historical and economic forces. Nevertheless, I reject as unfounded the claim that any or all of us are so completely determined that some degree of voluntary and liberatory cultural change is impossible. It is in this spirit that I embrace Mohanty's conception of multiculturalism as epistemic cooperation.

ishing might be sought," then we will see that in protecting cultural diversity we are not merely avoiding a negative social consequence (inflicting violence on underrepresented groups), but promoting a positive one (nurturing the conditions that might lead to a better world) (243). Moreover, it is not necessary to argue that every multicultural situation always leads to human flourishing in order to defend the general principle that cultural diversity is conducive to humans' moral and intellectual growth. I will draw out some of the further ramifications of this realist position in a subsequent chapter on multicultural education. For now, I want to turn to the implications of my argument for the practice of identity politics.

THE EPISTEMIC SIGNIFICANCE OF IDENTITY POLITICS

Within politically progressive circles today, critics and activists alike often take for granted that identity politics as such are essentialist, theoretically retrograde, or even politically dangerous. I want to suggest that absolute dismissals of all kinds of identity politics are premature — even though such dismissals are frequently motivated by political convictions similar to those that motivate my own arguments. (To reiterate: I define identity politics as a social practice in which a person who identifies or is identified with a recognizable group such as "Chicana/os" or "lesbians" makes arguments or takes action with the purpose of affecting social, economic, or educational policy relative to that group. Within this social practice, the identity of the political practitioner both motivates and is a central facet of the claim, argument, or action.) Without defending those forms of identity politics that are predicated on the disenfranchisement of others, and with full awareness that all identities are somewhat reductive and potentially co-optable, I nevertheless contend that *some* forms of identity politics that are undertaken by members of marginalized groups in the service of creating economic, social, and political equity between different groups are epistemically and morally justifiable.[28]

---

28. I see my position as being consistent with the one taken by Schutte. She explains that the fact that "the words *woman* and *Hispanic* may be politicized or commercialized well beyond [her] taste, and even contrary to it, does not lead [her] to stop describing [herself] with these terms." What we understand is that these (and other) terms do important work for her insofar as they allow her to situate herself in relation to others. Schutte reconciles herself to the limitations of each identity category by adopting the principle of recognizing the internal heterogeneity of the groups with which she identifies. This principle allows her to identify as a member of a group without being coerced into compliance with its normative type (67). A similar logic attends Schutte's defense of retaining ethnic/cultural

Embedded in my argument is the idea that identity politics cannot be an end in themselves, but should be seen as a necessary step on the way toward creating economic, social, and political equity between different groups.[29]

My reasons for defending the practice of identity politics by members of marginalized groups are primarily epistemological. To the extent that we, as cultural critics, are interested in gaining a more accurate understanding of our social world, we must give greater weight to socially marginalized identities and non-dominant perspectives. My postpositivist realist defense of the principle of epistemic privilege draws on the idea, common to much feminist and marxist theory, that the major obstacle to the achievement of objective knowledge is blindness regarding the epistemic consequences of social location.[30] Insofar as the perspectives of people in positions of privilege and authority are refracted through distorting lenses that naturalize the existing social order, the epistemic norm of "objectivity" requires that such partial and distorted perspectives be critically examined from the standpoints of the subordinated. The idea here is not that subordinated people know better about everything, but rather that their well-being (and sometimes even survival) requires that they attend to the dynamics of the particular forces by which they are subordinated. This is in contrast to people in positions of privilege or authority, whose interest in maintaining the status quo often fosters (moral and political) blindness with regard to those institutional structures on which their privileges are based. What this means is that, to the extent that we want to have a more objective understanding of the dynamics of socially significant phenomena like racism, sexism, or heterosexism, all scholars, regardless of their own particular identities, would do well to attend to the identities and experiences of people who are located on the lower levels of a socially and economically stratified society. Unless we have access to alternative perspectives — perspectives that are formed through interpretation of personal experience — we risk being arrested in the process of our intellectual and moral growth. Since identities are indexical — since they refer outward to social structures

---

identifications. While she recognizes the potential dangers posed by group identifications, she also recognizes the value — which is supported by a broader principle of social justice — of "having a substrate of differentiating elements in cultures . . . that challenge the narrow-mindedness of patterns of behavior inherited from the past" (65).

29. For a brilliant defense of identity politics, see Alcoff, "Who's Afraid of Identity Politics?"

30. For a fuller discussion of what I mean by *epistemic privilege,* see chapter one.

and embody social relations — they are a potentially rich source of information about the world we share.

In chapter one, I argued that the recovery of the experiences of oppressed people uncovers knowledge, and ways of living, that, when shared with people who have not been oppressed or have not lived in the same way, allows oppressor and oppressed alike to have a more complex and adequate understanding of their shared world than either of them could have by themselves. I argued that as long as certain identities are devalued, those identities will be epistemically valuable and politically salient. I further demonstrated that the recovery of the experiences of oppressed peoples, and the examination of devalued identities, are necessary steps on the road toward a more objective knowledge of social relations. What I wish to add here is that the first step in the recovery of the experiences of oppressed people will involve a reexamination by oppressed peoples of their own lives. This is not standpoint epistemology in the sense of having non-oppressed people "starting from the lives" of oppressed people.[31] It is not enough to use the lives and experiences of marginalized people as the "matter" about which one theorizes. In order for a scholar to fully appreciate the epistemic significance of marginalized lives other than her own, she must pay careful attention to what the people who occupy those positions of marginalization think and feel about the meanings their lives convey. It is precisely for the failure to pay careful attention to the insights of Cherríe Moraga that I criticize Donna Haraway and Judith Butler in chapter one. Moreover, it is because I believe that identities have epistemic significance that I have tried, in this chapter, to give serious consideration to the real concerns of neoconservative minorities. Marginalized people are necessarily more aware of the processes by which their own identities become marginalized. For this reason, the project of self-examination must be carried out by oppressed peoples and then *shared* with people who have not been oppressed in the same way. Inasmuch as this examination is carried out by and from within a community of similarly oppressed people, they will necessarily practice identity-based politics.

It is my contention that neoconservative minorities — despite their unwillingness to acknowledge as much — are themselves participating in the process of self-examination entailed by identity politics. They are

31. For more information on feminist standpoint epistemology, see Calhoun, esp. chap. 6; Harding, "Rethinking Standpoint Epistemology"; Harding, *Whose Science? Whose Knowledge?*

persons identified with recognizable groups (Mexican and African American) who engage in social practices (such as writing books and granting interviews) in which they make arguments (against bilingual education or affirmative action) or take action (such as sponsoring legislation) with the purpose of affecting social, economic, or educational policy relative to their own groups. Moreover, their identities (political and racial) both motivate and are central to their claims, arguments, and actions. As such, neoconservative minorities collectively participate in the creation of a discourse and an identity identifiable as "neoconservative minority." They are not iconoclastic individualists, but rather share a tendency to take similar positions in public debates concerning multicultural education, assimilation, and racial or ethnic identity. Furthermore, although they differ in the particulars, neoconservative minorities share several basic assumptions about the egalitarian nature of United States society and the necessity for minorities to assimilate to a white middle-class American norm.

Practitioners of neoconservative minority identity politics can be identified by some of their characteristic assumptions. They have an ambivalent relationship to the minority communities with which they are identified by others. They simultaneously exploit their minority status for political and economic purposes (they allow themselves to be published and marketed as native informants) even as they attempt to disavow their "exemplary" minority status. As a general rule, neoconservative minorities overlook the structural and inegalitarian nature of society. They ignore the structural inequities that contribute to the correlation between the likelihood of incarceration and nonwhite racial status, and between poverty and female gender. Where neoconservative minorities do address such glaring social inequalities, they tend to locate the cause of such inequalities within the cultural character of the subordinated individual or group. Consistent with their focus on culture, neoconservative minorities have a liberal understanding of individual agency. Instead of seeing people as temporally and biologically limited beings with a variable measure of control over their lives, neoconservative minorities tend to see *all* people as *equally* autonomous agents acting from fully rational conscious choice. Although they invariably mention socioeconomic status as a factor influencing people's lives, they do not incorporate a class analysis into their interpretative frameworks, or deal adequately with the effect economic forces have on individual life chances. In several neoconservative minority narratives, class emerges as an issue only for the purpose of undermining the salience of race as a

determining feature of social identity. Additionally, they fail to acknowledge that in a capitalist economy, some people — no matter how hard
they work — will never attain middle- or upper-class status for the simple
reason that capitalism requires an exploitable labor force. As a result of
their tendency to overlook the structural nature of society, neoconservative minorities formulate idealist conceptions of identity. By undermining
or ignoring the political, economic, and social salience of race and gender, they focus on culture (language, habits of interaction, family structure, living arrangements) as the only determinant of social identity. They
assume that if a person changes her culture, she can change her social
identity (and, by extension, her life chances). Finally, neoconservative
minorities' focus on culture leads them to champion assimilation (forced,
unidirectional cultural change) to a white middle-class American norm.
They argue against multicultural education, affirmative action, and bilingual education in the belief that such programs hinder, rather then promote, the assimilation of minorities into American mainstream society —
a society about which they are largely uncritical.

Understanding neoconservative minorities as practitioners of identity
politics has helped me to appreciate their arguments for assimilation —
which I recognize as having been developed through self-reflection about
the meanings of their own racialized identities — as suggestions for the
best way to end or minimize race-based discrimination and inequality in
our society. I do not, for the reasons given in this chapter, agree with the
majority of their suggestions; nor do I admire most of the political and
rhetorical strategies they employ in their efforts to negotiate their own
racialized identities. I do, however, defend their practice of identity politics in the service of creating economic, social, and political equity
between different racial groups. Moreover, because I see neoconservative
minorities as fellow travelers in this worthy social, political, and epistemological project, I have been spared the necessity of either accepting or
rejecting their suggestions outright. Instead, I have been able to consider
the merits of their perspective, evaluate their arguments, and, by identifying the sources of their errors, work toward figuring out less reductive
and more effective ways of approaching the problems of race-based (and
other forms of) discrimination and inequality. The project of evaluation
and engagement with the arguments of neoconservative minorities has
led me to suggest, as an alternative to assimilation, the value of being
asimilao.

My reading of neoconservative minorities has implications for the
proper function of education in the United States. If we are concerned to

provide children and young adults with common cultural assumptions, we need to find a way to acknowledge, respect, and examine the existing cultural diversity of the United States. We have a responsibility as educators to teach students the skills they need to gather, process, and evaluate the various kinds of information with which they are presented. In the next chapter, I employ a postpositivist realist approach in my analysis of multicultural education in order to promote thinking about the best way we might do this.

CHAPTER 4

Learning How to Learn from Others

Realist Proposals for Multicultural Education

Both sides do need to be able to listen, and I contend that it is those with the most power, those in the majority, who must take the greater responsibility for initiating the process.

Lisa Delpit, "The Silenced Dialogue"

The primary and secondary public educational system in the United States is an important institution — one which, by law, most school-age children in the country pass through. Moreover, it is one of the primary vehicles through which societal values are transmitted and dispersed. It is for this reason that debates about curricular content, school funding, and the educational value of school sports and arts programs are often heated and acrimonious. Debates about schooling provide forums in which Americans can engage in debates about deeply held values: underlying the contentions behind bilingual education, prayer in schools, textbook selection, and the desirability of educating the children of illegal immigrants are differing judgments involving what kind of society we wish to live in and what sort of children we believe are worth spending our money on.

It is not surprising, then, that education has long attracted social activists and reformers of various political persuasions. In *The Irony of Early School Reform: Educational Innovation in Mid-Nineteenth Century Massachusetts*, Michael Katz argues that from its inception the public educational system in this country has been at least partially understood as a mechanism by which untutored and uncivilized children could be restrained, sorted into positions, and socialized to take up their proper positions within a hierarchically stratified society. Through an empirical study and analysis of tax books, manuscript censuses, voting records, and educational journals published in mid-century Massachusetts, Katz shows that the newly established public high schools were viewed by educational reformers and community leaders as important vehicles for managing social change. These new high schools were charged with the Herculean tasks of fostering a limited amount of social mobility (primarily for the children of the middle classes); promoting economic growth (a result of rapid industrialization); contributing to communal wealth; and inculcating habits of punctuality, industry, and moral self-restraint in the communities' emerging citizen/workers. Katz further argues that the civilizing/socializing mission was especially important with regard to common (or primary) schools.[1] He quotes a 1857–58 Boston School Committee report that captures a sentiment typical of the educators of the day. In the face of rapid social changes brought about by industrialization, urbanization, and immigration (primarily of Irish Catholics), Boston educators imagined their responsibilities to include "taking children at random from a great city, undisciplined, uninstructed, often with inveterate forwardness and obstinacy, and with the inherited stupidity of centuries of ignorant ancestors; forming them from animals into intellectual beings, and . . . from intellectual beings into spiritual beings; giving to many their first appreciation of what is wise, what is true, what is lovely and what is pure" (120). Acculturation into middle-class Protestant values was clearly an important part of the public educational system's mission.[2]

Irish Catholic children, of course, were not the only children subjected to the civilizing efforts of nineteenth-century Protestant reformers.[3] In a study that examines the late nineteenth century campaign to educate Native American children, David Wallace Adams looks at three mutually reinforcing perspectives that were essential factors in the history of Indian schooling: Protestant ideology, the civilization-savagism paradigm, and the quest for land by whites. Adams argues that reformers' efforts to educate Indian children were motivated by a belief in the necessity of fostering within them the mental and moral concept of possessive

1. See Katz, esp. pp. 33–50, 117–38.

2. For more on the role of Protestant ideology in education, see Kaestle, *Pillars of the Republic,* esp. chap. 5; Kaestle, "Ideology and American Educational History," esp. pp. 127–28.

3. As I noted in chapter three, Americans of Mexican descent were subjected to "Americanization" programs administered through the schools. For more information, see Deutsch; G. J. Sánchez, *Becoming Mexican American,* esp. chap. 4; Ruíz, esp. chap. 2.

individualism (6). By equating the capitalist values of American Prot-
estantism with "civilization," reformers were able to maintain a philan-
thropic self-conception even as they sought to "persuade the students to
accept the idea that it was inevitable and entirely justified that the
Indians lose their ancestral lands to a more progressive people" (19). The
"success" of Indian schooling could thus be measured by the degree to
which Indian students internalized the view that assimilation to Protestant values, and abandonment of their cultures of origin, was a step
toward enlightenment and salvation.

These two examples — the Irish Catholic and the Native American —
both illustrate that ideology and education have been historically insep-
arable. Socialization into a dominant ideology has always been a central
function of free public education in the United States.[4] Whether or not
participants in discussions about education have been forthcoming about
their political and social agendas, they have self-consciously sought to
promote some kinds of values and serve certain interests, while simultaneously seeking to close off the discussion of other kinds of values.

My purpose in highlighting the link between education and ideology is
not to suggest that it is always pernicious. Nor do I mean to suggest that
it is a situation we can avoid. Education cannot be purged of ideology:
schools both teach skills and transmit values. These two functions can be
analytically distinguished from each other, but they cannot be practically
separated. For example, reading is one of the skills we are supposed to
learn in the course of being educated. It is not, however, merely a skill.
How we read (declaiming to others or silently to ourselves, reading for
theme or for structure, attending to the explicit message of the text or
revealing its silences, emphasizing a text's coherence or highlighting its
semantic disjunctions) as well as *what* we read (the "great books" of the
Western tradition, ethnic literature, prayer manuals, rap music, contemporary films, or the backs of cereal boxes) inevitably involve value judgments about what reading is "for" as well as what is important or
"worth" reading. All pedagogical approaches have embedded within
them certain values which are thereby perpetuated. It is precisely for this
reason that progressive educators need to understand the ideological
underpinnings of various educational approaches. If we are to be successful in promoting a noncolonial, empowering educational system for
all our nation's children, we will need to pay careful attention to the values different educational approaches attempt to promote.

4. For a lucid discussion of the role of ideology in education, see Apple, esp. chap. 4.

In this chapter, I work forward from some of my conclusions in chapter three to extend the postpositivist realist theory of identity into the realm of multicultural education. I begin by reviewing the central debates surrounding multicultural education and by discussing the implicit claims about the nature of culture, and the value of cultural diversity, that are made by key opponents and proponents of multiculturalism. Building upon my contention that assimilation to a predetermined norm can actually impoverish society by depriving people of the behavioral and moral insights they might gain as a result of their respectful interaction with people from different cultural backgrounds, I argue that a truly multiperspectival, multicultural education is a necessary component of a just and democratic society. In response to some of the dilemmas identified by multicultural educational researchers, I propose eight postpositivist realist principles that I believe should be central to the pedagogical practice of educators and researchers who are interested in promoting a truly democratic and culturally diverse society. I conclude by showing that the realist conception of multiculturalism as cooperative cross-cultural inquiry into the nature of human welfare provides the strongest justification for multicultural education yet proposed — even as it helps us to understand why and how some initiatives that rely on a model of multiculturalism as cultural pluralism have failed.

WHY MULTICULTURAL EDUCATION?

The culture wars of the 1980s brought to the center of the American consciousness the link between politics and education. Faced with movements toward more inclusive and culturally sensitive educational curricula at the primary, secondary, and postsecondary levels — efforts brought about, in part, by the new social movements of the 1960s and early 1970s — political conservatives responded by decrying the decline of the national educational system.[5] The chief targets of their attacks were multicultural education and ethnic studies, educational reform movements aimed at remedying discrimination in education. Although such movements were originally intended to make education more accessible to racial minorities, they have expanded to address other forms of inequality as well (Sleeter and Grant, "An Analysis" 421).

Among other charges, political conservatives who oppose multicul-

---

5. See, for example, the 1983 report, *A Nation at Risk*, prepared by the National Commission on Excellence in Education.

tural education efforts accuse multiculturalists of enforcing a socially intolerant "political correctness" in the schools and on college campuses. Undergirding the debate about "political correctness" is the ahistorical and faulty assumption that multiculturally minded radicals introduced political concerns into the curriculum for the first time. Opponents of multiculturalism further argue that the resulting attentiveness to "difference" promotes balkanization, unfairly coddles minority students, discriminates against white males, and leads inevitably to a breakdown in the social order.[6] Such critics typically alternate between two approaches: either they follow the authors of the 1983 study *A Nation at Risk* and call for a back-to-basics approach to educating our nation's children, or they line up with Allan Bloom and William Bennett to advocate for a return to a study of the Western tradition for the sake of promoting common cultural assumptions and social harmony.

Both of these approaches refuse to acknowledge the inescapable link between education and ideology. Those who call for a back-to-basics approach to education assume that the teaching of skills can be isolated from the content of the curriculum. They argue that schools should not become mired in political debates, but should be concerned with providing students with the technical skills they need to succeed in an increasingly technological job market. Those who call for a return to the study of the Western tradition argue that a curriculum focusing on the "great books" transcends ideology because such works are intrinsically more valuable than the works that historically have not been taught. The "great books" have withstood the "test of time," conservative thinkers argue, because they are aesthetically superior. Teaching the "great books" is thus not a matter of advocating a particular ideology, but of acknowledging objective merit, promoting cultural advancement, and fostering social unity.[7] In the manner of the neoconservative minorities whose ideas I examined in chapter three, advocates of both these approaches attempt to deny the inextricable link between education and ideology by posing their own perspective as one that is universal and untainted by particular political concerns.

The 1990s has been largely a period of review and retrenchment for progressive educators. Political struggles over education have taken the form of efforts by conservatives to deny all but the most basic kinds of

6. See, for example, Schlesinger; Ravitch; R. Rodriguez, *Hunger;* R. Rodriguez, *Days of Obligation;* Steele.

7. See, for example, Bennett, "To Reclaim a Legacy"; Bennett, *Our Children and Our Country;* Bloom.

education to members of groups who they deem to be unworthy. At times, even that basic right has been threatened. In 1994, voters in California passed (by a margin of 59 to 41 percent) Proposition 187. That ballot measure, which was heavily funded by conservative political groups, sought to deny to the children of illegal immigrants (most of whom are assumed to be Latina/os) the right to any free public education whatsoever.[8] Affirmative action came under attack as more white Americans started to believe that minority recipients of this redress program were gaining an unfair advantage. Setbacks occurred at the postsecondary level as well. In 1992, Cheryl Hopwood, one of four white plaintiffs who sued after being denied admission to the University of Texas Law School, prevailed in her suit. Her case was subsequently upheld in 1996 by the Fifth Circuit Court of Appeals, and race-conscious affirmative action programs at Texas' public universities were declared unconstitutional.[9] Subsequently, in 1996, the passage in California of Proposition 209 decimated the state's affirmative action programs. This resulted in a precipitous drop in the number of African American, Native American, and Latina/o students who are matriculating at California's premier public institutions of higher education.[10] Similar kinds of initia-

8. The core provisions of Proposition 187 were never implemented. Temporary restraining orders were issued almost immediately in response to court challenges alleging the proposition's unconstitutionality. In November 1995, U.S. District Judge Mariana Pfaelzer ruled that the ban on elementary and high school education for illegal immigrants is unconstitutional. In March 1998, the same judge issued a final order forbidding the implementation of all core provisions of Proposition 187, including the denial of education to children of illegal immigrants. For more information see McDonnell, "California and the West"; McDonnell, "Prop. 187 Found Unconstitutional"; Lesher. At the time of this writing, efforts are under way to put a new proposition on the California state ballot that would amend the constitution to make the provisions of the act enforceable.

9. Because the Fifth Circuit Court of Appeals area includes Oklahoma, that state's institutions have been similarly affected. In 1996, the first year the Hopwood restrictions were in place, enrollment by black and Latina/o freshmen at UT's flagship campus in Austin fell 14 percent and 13 percent, respectively. Since then, the "10 percent solution" put in place by the Texas Legislature has resulted in a small reversal of some of the losses. According to the new law, graduates in the top 10 percent of any high school in the state now automatically qualify for admission to the state's public university system. At UT, minority enrollees increased to 37 percent in 1998, up from 34 percent in 1997. The effect of the Hopwood decision was more dramatic in the law and medical schools. In 1996, the UT law school saw admissions of African American students fall by 87 percent, while admissions of Latina/os fell by 46 percent. For more information see Cantor; Hoppe; Robinson.

10. For the fall of 1998, the first year race was disallowed as a factor in admissions, there was a sharp drop in the admission of African Americans and Latina/os to the three most prestigious campuses in the UC system. At Berkeley, admissions of African Americans were down 66 percent, Latina/os 53 percent, and Native Americans 39 percent. The news

tives were immediately undertaken in other states throughout the country.[11] Then, in November of 1998, the passage of Proposition 227 abolished the state's primary and secondary school bilingual education programs, mandating in their place a one-year English immersion program through which all Limited English Proficient (LEP) students are now invited to either "sink or swim."

Finally, within days of the passage of Proposition of 227, Ward Connerly, a University of California regent who was the primary force behind both the regents' 1995 decision to ban race-based admissions and the passage of Proposition 209, proposed a review of all UC ethnic

---

that Berkeley had rejected over 800 African American and Latina/o freshmen applicants who had 4.0 GPAs and SAT scores of at least 1,200 caused an outcry from minority advocates. At UCLA, there was a 43 percent decline in the number of African Americans admitted, 33 percent for Latina/os, and 43 percent for Native Americans. UC San Diego saw drops of 45 percent for African Americans, 31 percent for Latina/os, and 37 percent for Native Americans. Despite an overall increase in applications from underrepresented minorities, admissions systemwide were down 18 percent for African Americans and 7 percent for Latina/os. Following the second phase of admissions, 3,179 students who had been denied admission to the UC campus of their choice were "referred" to other UC campuses, a practice that is resulting in a redistribution of minority students to the less competitive, historically less diverse campuses of Riverside, Santa Cruz, and Irvine. However, even with the referrals, there was an overall drop of 9 percent in admissions granted to underrepresented minority students systemwide. Acceptances by underrepresented minority students who were admitted have also fallen. Systemwide, less than half of the underrepresented students who were admitted to UC have chosen to accept, resulting in a decline in acceptance for African Americans of 24 percent and for Latina/os of 6 percent. Again, the impact at the most prestigious campuses has been disproportionately severe: at Berkeley, only 98 out of the 3,660 students who planned to enroll in the fall of 1998 were African American, 264 were Latina/o, and 14 were Native American. The UC system is currently looking to Texas as a model for a possible solution to the problem of declining minority enrollments. Efforts to improve the preparation and recruitment of underrepresented minorities have resulted in some modest gains within the past two years. At Berkeley, for instance, the percentage of underrepresented minorities who were admitted increased to 13.2 percent for fall 1999 as compared to 10.5 percent in 1998. Also, at UCLA, the percentage of underrepresented minorities admitted from fall 2000 increased by 0.6 percent from 1999. The number of African Americans admitted, however, declined slightly from 3.3 percent to 3 percent. Please note: my sources for these figures are primarily newspaper stories, and, as such, are subject to the errors common to pieces produced quickly. Occasionally, my sources have contradicted each other by a few percentage points. In all cases, I have done my best to ascertain which figure is likely to be more accurate. My purpose in providing these figures is to illustrate a trend, and I make no claims for their absolute accuracy. For more information see Baye; Burdman; de Cardenas; Hayward; "New UC Berkeley Admission Figures"; Ristine, "New Data"; Ristine, "UC Figures"; Rene Sánchez, "Ban on Preferences"; and Weiss.

11. The year 1997 saw initiatives patterned after California's Proposition 209 introduced in Arizona, Colorado, Florida, Georgia, Michigan, Missouri, New Jersey, New York,

studies programs. During the press conference where he called for the review, Connerly conveyed his conviction that identity-based scholarly initiatives are politically particular and without academic significance: "Things like personal ancestry, or your heritage, to the extent that they're important, you get them at home, or you should have it in high school."[12] Connerly's comments revealed an especially strong bias against the kinds of race-based projects that he sees as contributing to the "balkanization of our society":[13] "I want to nudge the university to question why we are using race and ethnicity" as a basis for scholarship, he said, and noted that "if students who take these courses emerge more frustrated and more race-conscious than they were when they entered the university, that's a cause for concern."[14] He then called upon ethnic studies faculty members to "make the case that this is sound academic curriculum rather than the political correctness mind set," before adding, "I'm not convinced."[15]

Faced with this conservative backlash, advocates of educational initiatives that support population and curricular diversity in education have found themselves scrambling to respond adequately to the charges leveled against them. I suggest that the difficulty multiculturalists and ethnic studies scholars face is due less to the intrinsic value (or lack thereof) of these programs and more to the fact that progressive educators have not yet articulated a strong universalist defense of what appear to many Americans to be particularist (that is, segregationist) approaches to educating our nation's children. In view of widely accepted notions (rooted in philosophical liberalism) that see cultural particularity as socially divisive and epistemically suspect, a particularist or relativist defense of such programs merely weakens their already dwindling base of support among Americans who are not already inclined to accept the epistemic value of cultural diversity. This is the lesson we must take from

---

North Carolina, Oklahoma, Ohio, and South Carolina. Also in 1997, U.S. Rep. Charles Canady, R-Fla. and Sen. Mitch McConnell, R-Ky. put forth the so-called Civil Rights Act of 1997, which, had it passed, would have prohibited the use of race and gender preferences by the federal government. In the fall of 1998, Washington state voters passed I-200, a measure patterned after California's Proposition 209. Also in 1998, Rep. Frank Riggs, R-Calif., failed to amend a higher education bill that sought to end race-based affirmative action in higher education. It was the fourth such effort in six months rejected by Congress. For more information see Baye; Camia; Epstein; Sandler; "Initiative 200."

12. See Chao.
13. See Weiss, "Mixing Commencement and Culture."
14. See Lempinen.
15. See Lempinen.

the phenomenal success of the writings and initiatives of the neoconservative minorities whose assumptions I examined in chapter three.

The difficulties facing proponents of multicultural education and ethnic studies have been compounded by the fact that left-leaning cultural
critics have become increasingly wary about making substantive claims
about the political or epistemic salience of racial and gender identity. As
I have demonstrated throughout this book, the influence of postmodernist theory within literary and cultural studies has had the pernicious
effect of delegitimizing within the academy any political or knowledge
claim that is rooted in identity. In the current political climate, it is crucially important for supporters of multicultural education and ethnic
studies programs to have sound intellectual and *universalist* justifica-
tions for their programs, as well as for the salience of the identities
around which such programs are organized. In this chapter, I provide a
sketch of what such a justification might look like.

MULTICULTURALISM IN THE CLASSROOM

Before proceeding with my discussion about the implementation of various multicultural educational initiatives, I summarize below two different taxonomies of multicultural education as they have been developed
by three leading educational researchers. My purpose is to provide the
nonexpert reader with a general sense of the goals and pitfalls of such initiatives as they are understood by experts in the field of multicultural
education.

The first taxonomy I recap below was developed by Christine Sleeter
and Carl Grant after they conducted an analysis of a wide variety of U.S.
books and articles about multicultural education, grades K–12. Their
purpose in doing the analysis was to bring conceptual clarity to the field
by examining what the different scholars and advocates of multicultural
education meant by the term. They were concerned also with evaluating
the existing literature for its contributions to the theory and practice of
multicultural education. As a result of their review, Sleeter and Grant
developed a five-part taxonomy by which they categorized educational
researchers' use of the term *multicultural education*. In their discussion of
each of the five approaches, they examine how the term is understood
and note its shortcomings and oversights:

1. *Teaching the culturally different.* Authors taking this approach advocate adapting instruction to students who are linguistically or cul-

turally different for the purpose of helping them transition to mainstream language and culture. It grew out of and best describes current models of bilingual education. According to Sleeter and Grant, advocates of this approach are primarily concerned with facilitating individual achievement and social mobility. In Sleeter and Grant's view, this approach is limited because it fails to incorporate an analysis of the unequal distribution of goods and power among racial groups. Moreover, it puts the burden of eliminating racism on people of color and their teachers rather than on the population as a whole.

2. *Human relations.* This approach seeks to bring diverse groups together in order to foster understanding, respect, and more effective cross-cultural communication between them. The problem, according to Sleeter and Grant, is that the literature promoting this approach fails to address factors such as poverty, institutional discrimination, and powerlessness, and the effects these factors have on generating conflict among students. It thus lacks a solid theoretical foundation and fails in its efforts to transform society.

3. *Single group studies.* This approach focuses attention on a previously ignored racial or cultural minority group in an attempt to sensitize students to a group's victimization as well as to its accomplishments. According to Sleeter and Grant, there are two problems in the literature advocating this approach: first, authors pay little attention to what it is supposed to accomplish, perhaps because they assume that the goals are self-evident and need no elaboration; second, advocates tend to ignore multiple forms of human diversity and how are they related to each other.

4. *Multicultural education.* The primary goal of this approach is to promote equal opportunity and human diversity by analyzing the links between race, language, culture, gender, handicap, and social class as institutionalized structures of inequality. According to Sleeter and Grant, advocates of this approach are particularly good at articulating goals and recommending curricular materials, but are less successful at considering how the approach might be implemented. Sleeter and Grant also note some disagreement among advocates of this approach regarding the extent to which considerations of race and ethnicity should predominate over issues of social class, gender, and handicap in multicultural educational initiatives.

5. *Education that is multicultural and social reconstructionist.* This approach attempts to extend the multicultural education approach

described above into the realm of social action. It thus explicitly concerns itself with developing pedagogical practices that will help students to understand the causes of oppression and inequality, and to develop strategies by which they can use power for collective betterment. The advantages of this approach are that it gives more consistent attention to issues of gender and social class than other approaches. On the other hand, the literature provides few instructional models. Sleeter and Grant see this approach as the least developed of the five, and caution its advocates against expending too much energy in criticizing the shortcomings of the other approaches.

In 1989, James Banks developed a taxonomy which traces the levels of integration of ethnic content in school curricula. He understands these levels as building on one another, and as having evolved in a more or less consecutive way since the civil rights movements of the 1960s.

1. *Contributions approach.* This approach recognizes famous people, holidays, and cultural events of previously ignored racial or cultural groups by incorporating them into an already existing curriculum. An important characteristic of this approach is that the curriculum remains essentially unchanged in its structure, goals, and salient characteristics; it is thus the easiest approach for teachers to take. The downside of this approach is that it often results in the trivialization of ethnic cultures and, because it focuses on what can be perceived as strange and exotic characteristics of ethnic people, can end up reinforcing stereotypes and misconceptions.

2. *Additive approach.* This approach incorporates key concepts and themes related to recognizable minority ethnic groups into an existing curriculum; these themes are presented as being unique to the groups in question and marginal to the history of the dominant population. While this approach is better than the contributions approach in that it often entails the addition of a book, a unit, or a course to the curriculum, it shares a major disadvantage with the contributions approach in that it does not necessitate a substantial restructuring of the curriculum as a whole. This often means that the events, concepts, issues, and problems chosen for study are selected and presented using Eurocentric criteria and perspectives. As a result, the added materials are often presented without proper contextualization, and their meanings are frequently misunderstood or misrepresented.

3. *Transformation approach.* This approach is premised on the idea that our contemporary society has emerged as a result of the dynamic interaction between various cultural groups. It presents concepts and themes central to the history of the dominant group from diverse perspectives as well as introducing themes and concepts from previously marginalized groups. The key curriculum reform involves an infusion of various perspectives, frames of reference, and content material from various groups. Unlike the two previous approaches, it involves changes in the fundamental goals, structure, and perspectives of the curriculum.

4. *Decision-making and social action approach.* This approach encourages students to take what they have learned through a transformative approach to multicultural education and turn it into action designed to better their social world. Like Sleeter and Grant's multicultural/social reconstructionist approaches, this approach sees the school as an institution that should help ethnic students analyze the society they live in, teach them decision-making skills, and empower them to question, contest, and change existing ideologies, institutions, and practices within the society and the nation-state.

What becomes clear from even a cursory review of these taxonomies, and of the scholarly literature on multicultural education more generally, is that most conceptions of multicultural education focus on the benefits it has for students from marginalized groups. Even when multicultural education is understood to be appropriate for children from dominant groups (as in the case of Sleeter and Grant's human relations approach), educators as well as educational scholars generally presume that multicultural education primarily benefits *non-dominant* children, who will experience less discrimination as a result of increased cultural sensitivity. Furthermore, most multicultural initiatives focus specifically on racial and cultural difference, giving considerably less attention to relations of inequality attributable to gender, sexuality, social class, and physical handicap. This is not necessarily the case with those approaches labeled transformative, social reconstructionist, or social action inasmuch as these approaches tend to be premised on more complex theories of social inequality than the more traditional approaches.

Although much of the literature prior to the early 1990s evaluates the theories and rationales behind multicultural education, a number of studies since the mid-1990s have observed and analyzed the actual implementation of a variety of multicultural educational initiatives. These more recent studies are important for what they confirm about the pitfalls and blindnesses, as well as the successes, of the approaches to multicultural educational reform as outlined by Sleeter, Grant, and Banks. It is to these later studies that I turn now to examine the ideological underpinnings of different multicultural educational approaches.

Both Polly Ulichny and Brian Jacob have demonstrated (in separate articles analyzing the implementation of the same multicultural program) that when multicultural educational initiatives are put into place with an unexamined concept of culture, such initiatives can lead to the erroneous and harmful perception that some people are "more cultural" than others. The program that Ulichny and Jacob participated in was set up as a mini-school within a high school located in a mixed-income neighborhood in a large deindustrialized northeastern city. According to Polly Ulichny, who served as the university-based facilitator and documentor of the initiative, the school's student population was "majority-minority" and consisted of 49 percent black (U.S. born and immigrants from Africa and the Caribbean), 36 percent Latina/o (U.S. born and immigrants from the Caribbean and Central America), 12 percent white (U.S. born and immigrants from the Middle East and Eastern Europe), and 3 percent Asian (U.S. born and immigrants from Laos and the People's Republic of China) (336). What the researchers discovered was that because educators had failed to precede the implementation of the program with an examination of the concept of culture — and then to incorporate the study of that concept into the curriculum — the multicultural initiative they participated in had the unanticipated and undesired effect of worsening tensions between different cultural and linguistic groups.

According to Brian Jacob, the conflict which resulted from the implementation of the program was understood primarily as an African American and Latina/o conflict — as a struggle over social power involving whose music and whose style would prevail during school functions.[16] He argues, however, that the conflict was actually more complex — that there was an underlying and often overlooked monolingual/bilingual tension (360). He suggests that the way in which the concept of culture was discussed in the program affected the relationship between monolingual U.S.-born students and immigrant bilingual students: "By emphasizing

16. Jacob spent 240 hours as a participant-observer, conducted fourteen individual interviews with teachers and administrators, and did ten focus-group interviews with a total of twenty-six students.

primary cultural characteristics such as language, food, and country of origin, the construction of culture in the program embraced bilingual immigrant groups while alienating monolingual African-American students" (359). Jacob notes that both students and teachers who participated in the program saw "culture" as being synonymous with difference from the white, Anglo norm. They thus naturalized the culture of the white students and tended to speak of difference quantitatively as the degree of difference from this norm (359–60). This led to the idea that some students were "more cultural" than others. The problem was compounded by the perception, held by African American and non–African American students alike, that the culture of African Americans had been effectively destroyed by the historical experience of slavery. This left African American students feeling as though they lacked a valuable asset: a cultural heritage, complete with country of origin, national language, national anthem, national flag, and national cuisine, that could be displayed and celebrated. Thus, while white students were able to feel comfortably postcultural (or normal), African American students in this situation were made to feel acultural (and as such neither normal nor special). Jacob suggests that any solution to the problem he identifies must involve a "focus on the way culture is itself discussed in multicultural education" (372). Both Ulichny and Jacob conclude their essays by stressing the importance of emphasizing similarities, as well as differences, among diverse groups of students, and of incorporating into the curriculum a critical analysis of contemporary social and political issues (Ulichny, "Cultures in Conflict" 358–59; Jacob, "Defining Culture" 372–74).

Other researchers have also stressed the importance of incorporating an analysis of larger social forces into educational reform initiatives. Observing efforts to detrack a racially mixed school in Los Angeles, Amy Stuart Wells and Irene Serna discuss how efforts to enact policies consonant with the principles of transformative or reconstructionist multicultural education, such as detracking reform, can be derailed by the efforts of "local elite" parents whose children enjoy privileged status in a tracked system. Drawing upon the theoretical concepts employed by Pierre Bourdieu, Wells and Serna argue that the resistance of elite parents to detracking "cannot be understood separately from the 'sociodicy' or ideology employed to legitimize the privileged place elites and their children hold in the educational system" (100). Such parents, they argue, are primarily concerned about the cultural capital conferred upon their children by virtue of being tracked into "advanced" classes: "In all of the schools we studied, the most interesting aspect of elites' opposition to detracking is that they based their resistance on the symbolic mixing of high 'deserving' and low 'undeserving' students, rather than on information about what actually happens in detracked classrooms" (103). Following Bourdieu, Wells and Serna suggest that when "symbols of domination are rationalized" — that is, when the sorting of "deserving" and "undeserving" students into different tracks is justified on the basis of evaluative instruments that remain biased toward the subjective experience and ways of knowing of elite students — then "the *entitlement* of the upper strata [of society] is legitimized," and the sociocultural form of domination found in free, industrial societies where more coercive methods of domination are not allowed is seen as natural (104). Underlying elite parents' rhetoric of "deserving" versus "undeserving" students is the necessity to "mask" the degree to which their children owe their privileged position in the educational system more to their families' economic and cultural capital than to their objective merit or intellectual ability (104). Wells and Serna further note that by mobilizing the construct of the "deserving minority" student who embraces "American" values and is therefore entitled to receive rewards from the educational system, elite parents are simultaneously able to disavow their cultural chauvinism and to legitimize the existing and unequal racial order (100–101). After detailing four practices actually employed by elite parents in ten different locales to undermine and co-opt meaningful detracking reform, Wells and Serna remind educators and policymakers that, if they hope to be successful, they must be mindful of the cultural logic behind political opposition to multicultural educational reform efforts.

Kathe Jervis, in an ethnographic study of an alternative public middle school in New York that has a stated commitment to maintaining a "diverse community" for the purpose of "educat[ing] children for life in a democratic society," documents the difficulty that even well-meaning white liberal teachers often have in confronting the reality of racial inequality in U.S. society. Noting that racial tensions in the school and questions about racial dynamics articulated (often in strangled ways) by students (especially students of color) often were ignored or unaddressed by the school's predominantly white faculty, Jervis was particularly struck by how often she herself, as a white staff member, had registered in her notes racially tinged interactions among students, and between students and teachers, while failing to comprehend the full meaning of what she was recording (547). After retrospectively reconsidering the meanings of the events she had witnessed through her altered theoretical perspective, she suggests that the failure of educators to critically examine the interaction between and among students and teachers in light of current social relations of inequality (such as those posed by race) will reproduce those relations and contribute to the further alienation of individuals situated differentially within the racial landscape (573–75).

The difficulty even well-intentioned teachers have with confronting issues of racism within the school is further illustrated by Natalie Adams, who describes a white teacher's use of a literary text by a black author in a middle school classroom fifteen miles from a large city in the deep south. Adams tells us that in 1992, English teachers at the school instituted a multicultural literature-based English curriculum in the belief that their (mostly white) students would gain an appreciation of and tolerance for cultural and ethnic diversity by reading and discussing novels that centered on the experiences of nonwhites (29). The effort, however, was a failure: the teacher Adams observed was disappointed because class discussions about the book did not spark meaningful and honest discussions about racism in today's society; the white students felt reluctant to speak freely for fear of offending their black peers; and the black students were upset because they were not allowed to express the anger the book provoked in them. The initiative failed, Adams explains, because the teacher had put into place a multicultural educational effort without "critically analyzing the complex dynamics of race, power, and structured inequality within the institution of schooling itself" (30). In her efforts to maintain a "safe" classroom environment, the teacher had kept the discussions teacher centered and teacher directed: she determined how much time would be spent in discussion, who could speak and when, what questions were appropriate, and what answers were right or acceptable (31). Moreover, Adams documents the teacher's tendency to shut down any question or response that threatened to pull the discussion of racism outside the bounds of fiction and into the realm of everyday experience. Calling this the "not in my backyard syndrome," Adams reinforces the point made previously by Ulichny, Jacob, Jervis, and Wells and Serna that "multicultural" initiatives which fail to address how racism, classism, and sexism inform the lives of students, both in the classroom and in the larger society, may ultimately do more harm than good. She suggests that such initiatives thwart the stated goals of multicultural education and are tantamount to "one more form of tokenism" (38).

Anne Meis Knupfer's attempt to put critical pedagogical theory into practice in one Southern inner-city elementary school classroom illustrates the failure of some educational researchers to critically examine the interaction between researchers, students, and teachers in light of current social relations of inequality. Knupfer is a university researcher and an advocate of critical pedagogical theory who is committed to the goal of breaking down established structures of power by giving voice to and validating the identities and experiences of historically marginalized communities. With this goal in mind, she brings into the classroom elements of "popular culture" such as "Nintendo, computer games, comics, music videos, jump rope, and rap songs" for the purpose of teaching literacy (236). However, Knupfer's efforts to implement her plan are hampered both by the students' questioning of her use of nontraditional educational materials and by the resistance of the African American elementary school teacher she works with. In the essay that she writes about the project, she evaluates her experience and imagines what she could do differently the next time. However, despite Knupfer's sincere efforts to be self-critical, she fails to rethink her theoretical presuppositions and substantially revise her pedagogical practices in light of the unequal social relations in which she is implicated. Because she does not fully comprehend how she is herself implicated in the complex dynamics of race, power, and structured inequality within the institution of the school, she is finally unable to achieve the goal to which she is committed.

Knupfer's first difficulty is that even though she recognizes her position of relative privilege as a university researcher in relation to the African American elementary school teacher she works with, she fails to understand the implications of this privilege for her own behavior.[17] She notes, for instance, that if she were to do it over again she would "co-construct lessons with the teacher (*despite the fact that [the teacher] relished this free time to work on other class-related activities*)" (235, emphasis added). Knupfer does not recognize the teacher's real need for self-determination with respect to allocating her time. Her further statements reveal that her plan to co-construct lessons with the teacher is designed primarily to reinforce her own authority and increase her own comfort: "the co-construction of lessons might not completely reduce the tension of power and authority between teacher and researcher. However, it is more likely that teachers will engage in critical pedagogical practices if they partake in their ownership. Together, we would consider building critical pedagogical practices into the existing curriculum" (235). What her statements reveal is that Knupfer is willing to work "together" with the teacher — but only as long as the teacher follows

---

17. It is perhaps significant that though she notes the race of the teacher and the students with whom she works, Knupfer fails to identify her own racial background.

Knupfer's lead. Harmony will be restored when the teacher comes to understand the superiority of Knupfer's pedagogical approach.

Moreover, despite Knupfer's acknowledgment that the African American students she works with "may have questioned why their street knowledge and popular culture had to be legitimated in the classroom, particularly by someone from the outside," she fails to rethink her conviction that teachers should bring forms of popular narrative into the classroom for the purpose of teaching literacy (235). As noted, one of the primary goals of critical pedagogy is to break down structures of power by validating the identities and experiences of historically marginalized communities — hence Knupfer's insistence that teachers must incorporate elements of "popular culture" into the curriculum. Her unexamined assumption is that forms of popular culture, including rap songs and jump rope ditties, adequately represent the views and identities of inner-city African American children and their teachers. What she fails to ask, and then listen to, is how the African American students and teachers she works with view themselves, how *they* understand their relation to a larger society, and what *they* think are some of the best strategies for remedying current relations of inequality. By deciding ahead of time what pedagogical strategies and curricular materials are most appropriate for inner-city African American children, Knupfer subverts her own stated commitments and participates in what the educational researcher Lisa Delpit has identified as "the silenced dialogue."

In her important essay "The Silenced Dialogue: Power and Pedagogy in Educating Other People's Children," Delpit demonstrates how educators' failures to consider the consequences of their own social locations contributes to the silencing of the least powerful groups in any educational situation. She notes that elite educators (elite by virtue of their race, class, gender, and/or institutional affiliation) who consider themselves politically liberal or radical are often uncomfortable with the implications of their own privilege — a situation which leads them to disavow their own implication in what she calls the "culture of power." This disavowal can have serious consequences regarding these educators' ability to understand how certain educational prescriptives function to reproduce the status quo. In particular, Delpit explains how uncritical efforts to affirm the languages and cultures of non-dominant groups can have the practical effect of withholding from those groups the "codes of power" by which members of a society gain access to its goods and resources. Noting that there are codes or rules for participating in power in any given society, and that the rules of the culture of power are a reflection of the rules of the culture of those who have power, Delpit suggests that when culturally non-dominant students are told explicitly the rules of the culture of power, they more easily acquire the linguistic forms, communicative strategies, and manners of presentation that will allow them to successfully negotiate the larger society in which they live (282–84). Delpit's argument provides a framework for understanding the phenomenon of the "deserving minority" student in Wells and Serna's study. Such a student, by embracing the "American" values of the "local elites," effectively masters the "codes" of the "culture of power."

One of the implications of Delpit's argument is that although uncritical affirmation of non-dominant students' cultures may result in a temporary boost in self-esteem for the members of marginalized groups, it will not help them get past the numerous gatekeeping points they will eventually face. Delpit thus helps us understand that unless students are taught how to be culturally and linguistically acceptable to the people (those participants in the culture of power) who hold the keys to the students' economic well-being, culturally non-dominant students may fail to gain access to higher education, employment, adequate housing, and other forms of institutional opportunities.

Delpit's point, and my own, is not that members of culturally or linguistically marginalized cultures should be forced to assimilate to the dominant culture, or even that their ways of speaking and interacting should not be affirmed and valued. Rather, she stresses the need for educators to take responsibility for teaching culturally non-dominant children the rules of the culture of power *at the same time* that they work to change unequal structures of power that unfairly denigrate some cultures while exalting others. The only way to do this, she insists, is by devising educational curriculum and strategies in consultation with adults who share non-dominant children's cultures. They are the ones, she contends, who are in the best position to understand the importance of valuing one's home culture while confronting the urgency of learning how to operate within a culture (of power) that is not one's own. According to Delpit,

> The dilemma is not really in the debate over instructional methodology, but rather in communicating across cultures and in addressing some of the more fundamental issues of power, of whose voice gets to be heard in determining what is best for poor children and children of color. Will Black teachers and parents continue to be silenced by the very forces that claim to "give voice" to our children? Such an outcome would be tragic, for both groups truly have something to say to one another. . . . But both sides do need to be able to listen, and I contend that it is those with the most power, those in the majority, who must take the greater responsibility for initiating the process. (297)

Patricia Gándara's research on the educational mobility of low-income Chicana/os provides crucial support for some of Delpit's key points. In a book that is unique for its focus on what "went right" for her research subjects, Gándara charts and analyzes the educational successes of fifty high-achieving Chicanos and Chicanas who received a Ph.D., M.D., or J.D. from a highly regarded American university of national stature during the 1960s and 1970s. Her conclusions about why these low-income Chicana/os succeeded lend credence to Delpit's contention that minority students do best when they learn the codes of power while continuing to value their home culture. Gándara notes, for example, that when Chicana/o students have extensive exposure to middle-class and white students, they adapt more easily to widely differing situations, and move more easily between different cultures. At the same time, she shows that positive stories and myths about their cultural and ancestral origins are important for helping low-income Chicana/o students believe that they have the potential to succeed. Moreover, although she suggests that a "hard work/education-as-a-mobility-strategy ethic" is crucial to Chicana/o students' success, she also stresses the positive role that structured opportunity, in the form of financial aid and special recruitment efforts geared toward minorities, can play. What Gándara's study convincingly demonstrates is that school success is located in the interplay between individual effort and structural forces, and that it is in educators' and policymakers' power to create the institutional structures that facilitate individuals' success in school.

Delpit's article and Gándara's research together raise a number of important practical and theoretical considerations. Among them are the need for educators of the dominant culture to understand the political, economic, and epistemic consequences of their own social locations; and the need for those people to listen, in a serious and engaged way, to members of non-dominant cultures who identify and give voice to *alternative* perspectives regarding what sorts of educational reforms might be most beneficial to minority students.

The work of the educational researcher Linda Van Hamme suggests some further ways we might achieve the goals set out by Delpit and Gándara. According to Van Hamme, educators of American Indian children face the challenge of assisting in the "maintenance of bonds to traditional and contemporary American Indian cultures while also providing preparation for successful participation in a culturally diverse, modern technological society" (21). Rather than seeing a contradiction between these two goals, Van Hamme sees them as mutually reinforcing.

She notes that educational initiatives that respect children's cultures *and* that teach them how to negotiate within a culture of power that is not their own can "promote academic achievement by providing cultural relevance and a rationale for accepting school" while helping them to develop "an accurate understanding of relationships with the larger society" (21). Drawing on a rich bibliography of research on Indian education, Van Hamme argues that multicultural education that both draws on the values and the symbolism of students' day-to-day lives and provides students with an accurate account of the history of Indian removal, education, and achievement in this country helps them to better understand where they fit into the larger American society. Such an understanding, in turn, enables Indian students to more successfully negotiate the larger society while maintaining their own cultural identities. Van Hamme thus implicitly affirms Jacob's and Ulichny's insight that an examination of the meaning of "culture" is central to the success of multicultural educational initiatives.

Van Hamme makes two particularly important points. First, "Indian cultures, like all other cultures, are dynamic and continuously changing" (22). Defining culture as "the beliefs, characteristics, activities, fundamental values and outlooks, preferred ways of living, and aspects of personal identity that are shared by a group," Van Hamme reminds us that all cultures evolve over time, and that they do so largely as the result of the "intermingling and mutual influence between diverse cultures" (25). Second, Van Hamme suggests that "students from all cultural backgrounds need to be aware that acculturation has not been a one-way street," noting that American Indians have contributed in wide-ranging and significant ways to the larger society (31). Non–American Indian students who do not learn about the histories of American Indians, her argument implies, are missing out on crucial information. When, for example, non–American Indian students do not know that our country's form of government was at least partially inspired by the centuries-old functioning democracy of the Iroquois Confederacy, they lack important information about the origins of American democracy, and they develop a skewed vision of the contributions non-European cultures have made to the formation of our society (31).[18] This, in turn, can prevent them from being able to use history effectively as a context for understanding and talking about contemporary social relations. American Indian and

18. For more on the influence of the Iroquois Confederacy on our democratic institutions see Van Hamme; Loewen, esp. 110–12.

non–American Indians alike will be unable to construct what John Wills refers to as a "usable past."

In an ethnographic study of the multicultural educational efforts of three teachers at a predominantly white middle school in southern California, Wills examines the negative epistemic effects of a curriculum biased in favor of white Americans. He argues that white students, as much as students of color, are ill-served by a curriculum that perpetuates existing narratives of U.S. history which overemphasize events important to European Americans and underreport or ignore historical events central to the lives of African Americans, Native Americans, Asian Americans, and Latina/os. Through a close examination of the educational dynamics of one middle school classroom, Wills shows that "multicultural" textbooks and lesson plans that include the voices of historical figures of color within prevailing Eurocentric narratives of U.S. history often fail to provide students with what he calls a "usable past" (369–78, 385–86). Because they discuss historical persons of color only in those moments where their presence has significantly impacted white Americans — such that African Americans are discussed only in relation to the Civil War or the Civil Rights movement, Asian Americans are discussed only in relation to the building of the railroads, and Native Americans are remembered only as the friends of the early English colonists — such narratives convey the inaccurate impression that persons of color have been virtually absent in other times and places in U.S. history. It is a practice, Wills argues, that has the unintended consequence of undermining *all* students' ability to use history as a resource for thinking about contemporary race relations.

Many "multicultural" textbooks, Wills demonstrates, exhibit a "politics of speaking" by virtue of which historical figures of color speak in voices that affirm, rather than challenge, white Americans' conception of this country as one that generally extends to all its citizens the basic political and civil liberties and freedoms embodied in the Declaration of Independence and the Constitution (380–83). When, as often happens, black chattel slavery is presented as the result of a *moral* failing on the part of some (long-dead) individuals, rather than as an integral part of the *political* and *financial* economies of antebellum American society — when, in other words, slavery is presented as an aberration from the successful achievement of American ideals of liberty and justice, rather than as an important part of an ongoing struggle to realize those ideals — then all students fail to develop an adequate understanding of the role racial discrimination and economic exploitation have played in the shaping of

American society (383–85). Reminding us that history is not simply a found reality, but rather a culturally and socially constructed reality, Wills urges educators to rethink their presentation of U.S. history. Inasmuch as history is "a resource that is both enabling and constraining for students as citizens," Wills argues that only a "multiperspectival, truly multicultural history" of the United States has the potential to provide *all* students with the tools that they will need to deal effectively as active citizens with issues of structural (and especially racial) inequality (386).

In an attempt to imagine what such a "multiperspectival, truly multicultural" education might look like, I propose below eight postpositivist realist principles that I believe should be central to the pedagogical practice of educators and researchers who are interested in promoting a truly democratic and culturally diverse society. In developing these principles, I have drawn upon the insights and lessons contained in the empirical studies I cite above.

REALIST PROPOSALS FOR LEARNING HOW TO LEARN FROM OTHERS

1.

The study of culture as a concept should be an integral part of a multicultural curriculum. This means that educators will need a more complex conception of culture than the one presupposed by many current multicultural educational initiatives. "Culture" should not be understood merely as that which expresses a foreign national heritage (complete with anthem, cuisine, language, music, and food), or as something that designates the artistic and social practices of the socioeconomic elite in our own society. Rather, "cultures" should be understood as sets of practices involving habits of interaction, communicative codes, norms of behavior, and artistic expressions — all of which express in distinct ways relatively coherent systems of meanings and values. Because cultures involve habits of interaction, they provide their practitioners with guidelines for how to interact with others, with the animate and inanimate world around them, and even with themselves. Even so, cultures are never fully coherent or absolutely stable. Because individual members of a culture are capable of changing their practices, it is likely that there will be contradictory practices within any given cultural formation. Moreover, whole cultures can and do change as people alter their cultural practices. As a result, cultures will always be capable of being undermined and changed — partly as a result of internal contradictions and partly through human agency.

Understanding culture in this way can help students and teachers to see that certain groups are not "culturally deprived," while others are exceptionally "cultural." It will also help provide educators and their students with the conceptual tools they need to understand how and why their daily interaction is affected by their differing cultural practices. When students and teachers together talk about their own cultures as *learned* habits of interaction and *preferred* ways of living, they can more easily accept the legitimacy of others' cultural practices and understand the propensity for all cultures to undergo change; they can participate in the process of denaturalizing, while simultaneously affirming as important their own as well as others' cultures. Such an approach to culture will make students and educators less likely, for example, to bemoan the "loss" of "authentic" Indian culture and more likely to recognize the value of the contemporary cultural practices of present-day American Indians. The African Americans who participated in the multicultural project studied by Ulichny and Jacob might be relieved to know that they are not without culture (acultural), while white students might be surprised to find out that they are not beyond culture (postcultural). In all cases, the outcome is potentially enabling: when we recognize *all* cultures as preferred ways of living in the world, not only will we see *all* persons as cultural beings, but we acknowledge the possibility that any of us are capable of changing our ways. When we realize that our identities and life chances are not wholly determined by our cultures of origins or the social context within which we grew up, we enliven the possibility that we can learn about and adopt ways of living in the world that are more conducive to human flourishing than those we may have grown up with.

Finally, understanding culture in this way will help clarify the value of cultural diversity. As I noted in chapter three, cultures are important not only for the way they orient us to the world, but as an essential form of moral inquiry. In his discussion of multiculturalism as epistemic cooperation, Satya Mohanty notes that "cultural practices — ways of living, of creating, of choosing to value one thing over another in our daily lives" effectively serve as epistemic and moral experiments in humans' ongoing search for successful ways of living in the world (*Literary Theory* 240–42). Cultures are behavioral laboratories that are more or less suited to the conditions under which they come into being. To the extent that we are interested in working toward a non-colonial, non-oppressive society, we would want to pay attention to other cultures precisely because some of their practices may be more conducive to human flourishing than some of our own.

2.

Educators need to have a more precise understanding of the relationship between culture and identity. My argument for this proposal begins from the postpositivist realist premise that paying attention to certain kinds of identities, such as racial or gender identities, can help us to identify and interrogate significant social and cultural formations. As I argue throughout this book, certain kinds of identities are epistemically valuable because they refer outward, in more and less perfect ways, to the social world within which they emerge. Racial identities, for example, are socially significant because they *refer* to the sociocultural construct of "race," *and* (this is crucial) race is highly correlative to income level, social status, and economic opportunity in our society. Because some kinds of identities have this referential relationship to the social world, they are the starting point through which, and in relation to which, we interpret the world around us.

Once educators have accepted the premise that certain kinds of identities do in fact have a referential relationship to the world, they should always bear in mind the partiality and imperfectness of that reference. This will allow them to understand that identities can be variable without thereby compelling them to conclude that identities are not "real." After all, it is not necessary for every person of Mexican American heritage with the phenotypic features we associate with that group of people to participate in practices recognizable by themselves or others as particular to "Chicano culture" in order for us to decide that (1) such a cultural formation exists; (2) it exists in particular relations to other American cultures; and (3) an analysis of those relations can tell us something true about the kind of society we live in. It is enough that a significant number of such people in U.S. society do. Similarly, it is not necessary that every human being who has a vagina experience that biological fact in exactly the same way in order for us to assert that there is a social formation, generally referred to as "gender," that structures relationships between persons in our society in socially significant ways.

In practice, educators who work in multicultural settings will need to continually evaluate the extent to which the identities of their students are correlated with certain cultural values and practices — even as they avoid assuming that all students who appear to be members of a particular group think, feel, and identify the same way. The dangers are these: if educators perceive the connection between identity and culture to be more secure than it actually is, they risk saddling a reluctant student with the burden of speaking for, embodying, or representing an entire group or culture. If, on the other hand, they see the connection as being too elastic, they may insist on personalizing an individual student's experience (or text that they are teaching), and lose an opportunity to meaningfully contextualize that experience (or text) within a larger cultural or sociological framework.

3.

Educators need to acknowledge that the concept of "value" is always determined with respect to a particular reference group. When considering the value of assimilation, we need to remember that different cultures are not equally valuable to all people in the same way. Indeed, we cannot speak about the "value" of any given culture (or its daily practices and artistic productions) without specifying at least these two things: for whom and to whom is the culture about which we are speaking valuable?

Precisely because cultures are expressions and sedimentations of lived human relations, it makes no sense to speak in absolute terms about cultural value. Any evaluation of a cultural practice or cultural production must take into consideration the context of its emergence. For example, one culture may produce artwork that is more sophisticated and more technically refined than another. This will have more to do with the existence and continuity of an artistic and intellectual tradition, the amount and quality of interaction between different working artists, and the technological capacity of the society in which the artists work than it will have to do with the individual "talent" of the persons involved in making the art, or the "superiority" of the culture from which the artists come. Artistic traditions, opportunities for interaction, and technological capacities are, to a large degree, products of historical chance. Today we may be actively participating in an evolving artistic tradition, but if tomorrow our country is invaded by marauders from the north (or across the ocean) such that we are cut off from other artists and intellectual traditions or lose the capacity for manufacturing the materials we use in our work, our "development" as artists may slow down or even cease. If, as in the case of the Aztec empire, our libraries are burned and our intellectual tradition is demolished (that is, our priests are all killed or forced to convert), we may eventually be seen as having had no artistic tradition in the first place. The artwork that does survive will be seen as "primitive" — as chiefly functional or expressive of some primal urge of an unknown and untutored artisan. Moreover, because that artwork lies outside the hegemonic (in this case "Western") tradition, it will be judged to be of less importance, and hence less "value," than the artworks that belong to that tradition. What will have been overlooked in this too-hasty judgment is a careful consideration of the precise nature of "value."

When a hegemonic culture confuses what *it* finds valuable with the concept of value as such, it fails to acknowledge the way different cultural practices or artifacts are valuable in different ways for different people. When we do not carefully consider for whom and to whom a culture or a cultural practice is valuable, we can easily conclude that something foreign to us has no inherent value. After all, an Aztec artistic tradition may have little apparent value for Europeans, except as a foil against which they can judge the "superiority" of their own art. It may, on the other hand, have an immense value for descendants of the Aztecs, for whom it organizes and provides conceptual depth to contemporary cultural and symbolic practices by providing a crucial link to the past. Any judgment of the value of the artwork produced by a particular culture, or of the culture itself, must take into account the context in which it was produced as well as the political, ideological, decorative, and aesthetic functions it serves in the society in which it is being judged.

Aside from the question of value per se, a person's culture may have value for her precisely because it is hers: it provides her with habits of interaction and orients her as she goes about the business of living in the world. Her culture teaches her how to act in everyday circumstances, informs her most intimate habits, and tells her where she fits into the world. Moreover, were it to be suddenly or inexplicably wrested from her, she would experience a sense of disequilibrium and discomfort. The world, as she knows it, will have been turned upside down and inside out. This is the phenomenon we refer to when we talk about "culture shock."[19]

In acknowledging the very real value a person's culture of origin may have for orienting her in the world, we must nevertheless guard against the tendency to assume that she might not derive some equally real benefits from gradual and voluntary cultural change. Gradual and voluntary

19. For a discussion of the value of cultural membership, see Kymlicka, *Liberalism*, esp. chaps. 7–9; Kymlicka, *Multicultural Citizenship*, esp. chaps. 5 and 6; Moses.

cultural change may be beneficial to her for two reasons: (1) other cultures may be more conducive to her personal human flourishing than her own culture; and (2) cultures are not always co-extensive with the societies in which they exist. The very definition of a multicultural society presupposes the existence of several (possibly overlapping but nevertheless) distinct cultures. In any given multicultural society, then, we might have occasion to judge one culture as being more valuable than another for helping us to thrive in that society. If, for instance, I have learned always to put myself first; to "look out for number one"; to consider myself in purely individualist terms; and to consult only my own counsel when making a decision that affects others, then I may have a great deal of difficulty in a society where the majority of people do not value these qualities. I may be considered impudent, selfish, immature, and antisocial. I may, as a consequence, suffer significant social ostracism that may impair my ability to fulfill my material and emotional needs. If, on the other hand, I have been taught to subordinate my own desires to the desires of others; if, out of politeness, I step back when others try to push by; if I refrain from speaking out in class so as not to appear to be self-important; and if I deprecate myself so as not to appear prideful, then I may be taken advantage of or simply ignored in a society that sees such behavior as a genuine reflection of lack of worth. This may similarly negatively affect my ability to fulfill my material and emotional needs. When we realize the value of learning the "codes" of the "culture of power," we may be inclined to advise members of culturally non-dominant groups to "assimilate" to the dominant culture. This is the insight, I believe, that the neoconservative minorities whose writings I examined in chapter three see themselves as offering to the groups with which they are identified. Moreover, this insight is at least partially consistent with what Delpit, Van Hamme, and Gándara have concluded in their separate discussions of the best ways to educate African American, American Indian, and Chicana/o children. In their own ways, they have all argued that to the extent that educators want minority students to "do well" in the larger society, those students will need to learn the rules and protocol for succeeding in that society.

These multicultural educators would depart from the neoconservative minorities in that they do not believe the "culture of power" is necessarily consistent with the pinnacle of human achievement. They would also strongly disagree with the assumption that when students learn the codes of the culture of power they necessarily suffer a complete and total loss of their own cultures of origin. Gándara, for example, documents the persistence of both biculturalism and bilingualism among the Chicanas and Chicanos who are highly successful in school, and demonstrates that "additive acculturation" and "additive bilingualism" are major factors in their academic and professional success.[20] Moreover, as both Van Hamme and Juan Flores point out in their separate discussions about processes of acculturation, cultural change is never unidirectional.[21] The behavioral and expressive practices of culturally non-dominant peoples in the United States have had much more of a formative influence on so-called "American culture" than many Americans realize. Moreover, the mere fact that a culture is hegemonic does not prove that it is conducive to human flourishing. History teaches us that hegemony quite frequently goes hand-in-hand with oppression. Consequently, progressive educators who are working to help minority students negotiate the hegemonic culture of the larger society must never confuse the need to help them "do well" in a culture of power that they were not initially socialized into with the idea that the dominant culture is always better and that the cultural change they undergo is necessarily cultural progress. Rather, we must help students to become critical practitioners of culture. Only in this way can they become more self-conscious about the options available to them as they work toward a better understanding of the implications of their own preferred ways of living in the world.

4.

The goal of multicultural education should be to create the conditions in which students feel empowered to work toward identifying those aspects of different cultures that are most conducive to human flourishing. The tendency of people to be ethnocentric, to naturalize their own cultural practices, and to believe in the superiority of their own preferred ways of living makes the project of identifying those aspects of different cultures that are most conducive to human flourishing very difficult. Moreover, the resistance many postmodernist academics have to acknowledging the existence of any kind of human universal makes such a project politically suspect in the eyes of many "radical" intellectuals. After all, to speak of "human flourishing" requires that we have some basic conception of human capabilities and needs, some idea of what is universal or funda-

20. See Gándara, esp. 76–22, 88–89.
21. See Flores, " 'Qué assimilated,' " as well as my discussion of his work in chapter three.

mental to our species. Nevertheless, I contend a multiperspectival, truly multicultural education should enable students to work toward this goal. I argue this for three reasons. First, if we want to prevent the kind of balkanization that Jacob and Ulichny witnessed in the multicultural program they participated in, we will need to focus on what is common to humans of diverse cultures as well as on what is different. The multicultural initiative Ulichny and Jacob participated in shows that when students are not encouraged to see others as bearing crucial similarities to themselves, tensions among different racial and ethnic groups worsen. More importantly, the most oppressive regimes in human history have attempted to dehumanize their victims as a strategy for justifying their victims' exploitation or elimination.[22] Conversely, the most effective anticolonial and human rights movements over the last four centuries have succeeded largely by insisting that all people have certain basic and universal needs and capabilities that should not be denied to any member of the human species — regardless of how "different" they may seem. As I argued in chapter three, rather than assuming that the concept of the human universal is inherently oppressive, progressive intellectuals need to have a conception of universal humanity that is not culturally elaborated. This will allow us to see "others" as cultural beings who are in some ways like and in other ways unlike ourselves.

Second, some amount of cultural sharing is desirable for productive human interaction. As I argued in chapter three, productive human interaction is predicated on the ability to communicate effectively. Furthermore, the ability to communicate effectively is facilitated when people share linguistic codes and/or fundamental values. Cultural change, as such, should not be seen as wholly negative. Cultural change is an inevitable and even desirable aspect of human life. What is negative, and what does stifle human flourishing, is the kind of forced unidirectional cultural change that occurs when a hegemonic society approaches its cultural "others" in an ethnocentric way.

Finally, if we take seriously the idea that some cultures may provide models for ways of living in the world that are more conducive to human flourishing than some others, then we will want to learn from them in order to consider whether we want to change our own cultural practices. We might learn, for example, that children who are expected to assume

---

22. Two examples that come quickly to mind would be the American government's treatment of slaves under the system of black chattel slavery and the German Third Reich's treatment of Jews during the Holocaust.

real responsibility earlier in life than most middle-class American children are expected to grow up on average to be more resourceful adults. Or we might discover that cultures that promote the formation of large extended kinship families have fewer instances of child abuse or neglect than cultures who valorize the smaller nuclear family. Or we might find that cultures where meditation or meditative exercise is commonly practiced are more likely to produce calmer, healthier, and happier adults than cultures in which self-reflection and relaxation are viewed as a waste of time. It is not certain what we will learn. We might, for instance, find that some of our own cultural practices, such as the current trend among American fathers to become more involved in the daily care of their children, are beneficial to human flourishing and should be retained or encouraged.

One of our most important tasks as multicultural educators, then, would be to resist the human tendency to view the world ethnocentrically. We need to remember that our own preferred ways of living in the world are not necessarily "the best" ways to be. Nor should we assume that the hegemonic culture, the current "culture of power" in the United States, is co-extensive with a common culture toward which all members of our society should strive. To do so would be to abandon the democratic project, to foster narrow-mindedness, and, quite possibly, to participate in cultural oppression. The educational researcher Michael Apple reminds us:

> A common culture can never be the general extension to everyone of what a minority mean and believe. Rather, and crucially, it requires not the stipulation of lists and concepts that make us all "culturally literate," *but the creation of the conditions necessary for all people to participate in the creation and re-creation of meanings and values.* It requires a democratic process in which all people — not simply those who are the intellectual guardians of the "western tradition" — can be involved in the deliberations over what is important. It should go without saying that this necessitates the removal of the very real material obstacles — unequal power, wealth, time for reflection — that stand in the way of such participation. (xiii)

Although I am in substantial agreement with what Apple says in the above passage, I am also aware that educators cannot remove those very real material obstacles he alludes to prior to stepping into the classroom. What educators can do, however, is strive to create the conditions within the school and classroom that can make our colleagues and students more sensitive to the epistemic value of learning from cultural "others."

5.

Students and teachers alike should strive to approach cultural others with what I call, borrowing from Donald Davidson, a Principle of Charity.[23] In order for us to learn from cultural others, we must begin with the assumption that they are rational, that their world makes sense, and that there is a substantial range of agreement between their beliefs and our own. We should do this because even though we realize that cultures are not fully coherent, and that not every aspect of every culture is reasonable or beneficial to human flourishing, we have no way of knowing ahead of time which aspects are reasonable or beneficial and which are not. Furthermore, without assuming some shared areas of agreement against which we can identify areas of disagreement, we will be unable to proceed with any kind of interpretive or translative project. Because humans do not enter into an interpretive situation devoid of presuppositions, and because *any* process of discovery depends on how what is presented to us fits into our prior theoretical frameworks, the only way we can begin to understand an other is to try to puzzle out how what he or she says or thinks accords or does not accord with our own.[24] The first step in trying to understand an other thus inevitably involves an assimilation of the other's logic or speech into our own.[25] Granting to others the Principle of Charity is thus not something we do because we are "charitable" people, but something we do because doing so is the condition of possibility for cross-cultural understanding.[26] Lisa Delpit sets out some guidelines for multicultural educators that sound very much like what I am suggesting.

> We must keep the perspective that people are experts on their own lives. There are certainly aspects of the outside world of which they may not be aware, but they can be the only authentic chroniclers of their own experience. We must not be too quick to deny their interpretations, or accuse them

23. See Davidson, "The Structure and Content of Truth"; Davidson, "On the Very Idea of a Conceptual Scheme"; Davidson, "Thought and Talk."

24. For a cogent account of how our fore-understandings affect the acquisition of knowledge, see Benhabib, esp. 148–77.

25. Alcoff points out that "when we do not know what [a] person means to say — that is, if we cannot effect an assimilation — then we are unable to determine whether we agree with them or not" (*Real Knowing* 93).

26. For a helpful discussion of Donald Davidson's Principle of Charity see Alcoff, *Real Knowing*, esp. 81–114. For a discussion of how to adjudicate between competing rationalities see Mohanty, *Literary Theory*, esp. 130–42.

of "false consciousness." We must believe that people are rational beings, and therefore always act rationally. We may not understand their rationales, but that in no way militates against the existence of these rationales or reduces our responsibility to attempt to apprehend them. (297)

In attempting to understand the cultural practices and rationales of cultural others, we must remember that because cultures are constantly changing, there are bound to be contradictory practices within any given cultural formation. There are also likely to be remnants of cultural practices that once made a great deal of sense, but which have now ceased to serve their original function. What may have once served to promote the physical survival or spiritual well-being of a people may now be nothing more than empty ritual. The existence, therefore, of seemingly "irrational" practices does not indicate that the people who practice them are themselves irrational. All it means is that we do not yet understand the meanings or logic behind those practices. This should be viewed as our failing, and not the failing of the people whose practices we fail to understand. Furthermore, it is important to remember that we, as much as anyone else, are likely to engage in "irrational" cultural practices. Why, after all, do most Americans "bless" those who have just sneezed? There once *was* a reason, and the fact that most Americans no longer believe that persons who sneeze are at risk of being invaded by an evil spirit does not prevent them from passing on to their children this nonsensical cultural practice. When considering the necessity of granting to others the assumption that they too are rational beings, we would do well to remember that "our" culture, as much as "theirs," may be shown to have seemingly nonsensical or unreasonable aspects.

Because of the possibility that "they" may have something to teach "us," and because our own cultural practices may be unreasonable or counter to human flourishing, our cultural assumptions, as well as theirs, must be subject to scrutiny. If we are serious about intellectual and moral growth, we must be willing to question our own theoretical frameworks in the face of contradictory beliefs or evidence. Questioning our own beliefs should be seen as a starting point, however, and not as an end in itself. Embedded in the postpositivist realist approach I have been elaborating in this book is the belief that we cannot (and should not) try to avoid all moral or epistemic judgment. We must not rush to judgment, but unless we eventually arrive at some sort of judgment, we will not work through the hermeneutic process of interpretation. Unless we effect the translation, unless we decide what a given statement or cultural practice means both to others and to ourselves, we will not fuse our horizon (in the Gadamerian sense) with the horizon of the other, and we will lose the opportunity to challenge and possibly change our own preconceptions.[27] In Delpit's words, "We must learn to be vulnerable enough to allow our own world to turn upside down in order to allow the realities of others to edge themselves into our consciousness" (197). Under this view, the ongoing dialectical process of questioning and adjudicating a range of beliefs and values is central to the process of intellectual and moral growth.

6.

The curriculum should be structured to give greater emphasis to the cultures and views of non-dominant groups. One of the consequences of the fact that the dominant culture tends to naturalize social relations is that cultural critics who wish to arrive at a more objective understanding of society will need to give members of marginalized groups a disproportionate share of "air time." This will be for epistemic, more than ethical, reasons. The point here is not to "compensate" those who have been previously denied a place in the conversation, but rather to facilitate the emergence of alternative perspectives and accounts. We need to remember that in order to maintain its hegemony, the culture of power must make its dominance appear natural — must convince everyone that what is, is what should be. This is why the alternative perspectives of members of subordinated cultures within a larger society will have the potential to teach all of us more about the relations of power in a society than the perspectives of the members of the dominant culture in that same society.[28] Just as John Wills argues that white students, as well as students of color, need a truly multiperspectival, multicultural historical education in order to be able to construct a "usable past," I am arguing that culturally dominant, as well as culturally non-dominant, people need to pay close attention to the views and perspectives of those persons who are marginalized within society. Because the marginalized person's condition of subordination will be at odds with her human need and capacity for self-

27. For a helpful discussion of Gadamer's philosophical hermeneutics, see Alcoff, *Real Knowing*, chap. 1.

28. I should emphasize that I am affirming the value of *alternative* perspectives, not simply the views of members of racial minority groups whose perspectives reflect that of the dominant culture.

determination, she will be the one most likely to encounter the contradictions inherent in a social formation that claims to extend to all its members the promise of equality even as it keeps some persons in subordination to others. How well she understands those contradictions will depend on the theoretical framework she employs. But, as I have argued thus far, experiences of oppression create the necessary (if not sufficient) conditions for the achievement of an epistemically privileged position. Therefore, to the extent that we are interested in working for a better world, we will pay particular attention to the experiences of people from subordinated cultures. We will understand the value their alternative perspectives and accounts can have for revealing the deep economic, social, and political structures of the society within which they are subordinated.

Moreover, inasmuch as we understand cultures to be fields of moral inquiry, we will see subordinated cultures as containing a potential resource of alternative ways of living in and relating to the world. But because those cultures are by definition subordinated, we will not "naturally" learn about them through the normal channels of cultural transmission. Therefore, we will have to work harder if we want to understand their ways of knowing and being. We will, in other words, have to pay more attention and spend more time learning about them than we will have to spend on the dominant culture, precisely because we are not constantly exposed to subordinated cultures through the everyday ideological state and social apparatuses.

7.

Educators should incorporate into their pedagogical strategies an awareness of the power dynamics of the classroom, attending to the ways in which such dynamics reflect or refract the relations of inequality in the larger society. In order to be able to give greater emphasis to the cultures and alternative perspectives of non-dominant groups, we need to be aware of the dynamics of power and the relations of inequality within which we are operating at any given moment. This will require that teachers as well as educational researchers develop an awareness of the consequences of their own social locations. They will need to denaturalize current social relations by acknowledging the existence of gender, racial, social, and economic inequality in this country and discussing current racist, sexist, and homophobic practices. They will have to help their students become aware of how they themselves fit into those relations, and invite them to imagine how they can alter their own practices in ways that might productively affect those relations. This, of course, will not be easy. As Jervis demonstrates, it is often very difficult for liberal white teachers to accept the reality that, by virtue of their race, they frequently occupy a place of privilege relative to the students they teach. As Natalie Adams shows, even teachers with the best of intentions who fail to make the connection between past exploitation on the basis of race and current social structures while attempting to discuss issues of race risk worsening, rather than ameliorating, racial tensions. As Knupfer illustrates, even the most "liberatory" of pedagogical practices can have oppressive effects when the "liberator" fails to engage in a self-critical dialogue with the people she is intending to educate.[29] And, as Wells and Serna demonstrate, educational policymakers who fail to understand how what they do is connected to larger social structures may find themselves ill-equipped to deal with the resistance of local elites to the educational reforms they try to implement.

8.

Educators must recognize conflict as inevitable and necessary, as a potentially creative, not always destructive, force. Educators who are uncomfortable with the idea of conflict must remember that as long as societies are structured by relations of inequality, conflict is inevitable. Furthermore, to the extent that people take their values seriously, they will experience their engagement with doctrines that provide incompatible guidance as deeply upsetting and profoundly painful — as conflict. Within the postpositivist realist framework, cross-cultural engagement and even conflict is not seen as something to be avoided, but rather as something that is absolutely necessary for epistemic and moral growth. Unless we engage with other belief systems seriously enough to be forced to call into question our own views and beliefs, such growth will cease to occur. Inasmuch as the conflict that arises as a result of inequality is understood to be a potentially productive and creative force, we need to learn to work through it rather than attempting to cover it over or trying to avoid it. As I argued in chapter one, only through engagement (which may take the form of conflict) with others who have different ways of approaching the world can we become aware of other "preferred ways of living" in the world. As ethnocentric beings, humans need to be seriously

29. For a discussion about the importance of dialogue to truly liberatory education, see Freire, esp. chaps. 3 and 4.

challenged in order for growth to occur. The task of educators is to learn to work through, but not manage or suppress, conflict.

One way to test the theoretical framework underlying the realist approach to multicultural education is to see how it responds to the moral conundrum underlying all sincere commitments to cultural pluralism — what Dwight Boyd has called the "dilemma of diversity," which is predicated on the co-existence of two epistemologically contradictory beliefs: (1) that "any number of comprehensive doctrines about how humans ought to lead their lives may be held by equally reasonable people, even though these doctrines can and do provide fundamentally incompatible guidance"; and (2) that there is a need "for some perspective that can provide legitimating, normative leverage across this diversity in the face of practical questions requiring common action, such as educational prescriptions" (614). The dilemma comes into clear focus when we morally prescribe that everyone ought to treat each other in a way that will support and maintain cultural diversity while at the same time denying that there is a moral point of view common to the cultures of everyone who might be subjected to this prescriptive (616). After grouping current approaches to multicultural education into three increasingly sophisticated theoretical perspectives, Boyd suggests that each perspective has the real effect of leaving the prescriptive preferences of the dominant view in control. He concludes that the dilemma of diversity should be seen as a "sign-post" or "heuristic device" against which we measure the various approaches to multicultural education. He does not himself formulate an approach that would be more theoretically or practically adequate than the ones he criticizes.

I would like to suggest that Boyd fails to formulate an adequate response to the problem he so elegantly articulates because he understands the two sides of the dilemma in excessively rigid terms. On one side of the dilemma, he figures cultures as "comprehensive" yet "incompatible" doctrines held by "equally reasonable" people. By conceiving of culture in this way, he does not allow for the possibility that some aspects of some cultures (including our own) may be unreasonable. On the other side of the dilemma, he presumes that any "legitimating, normative leverage" we might use to mediate between cultures must transcend or come from outside those cultures. As such, he fails to consider the ways in which useful educational prescriptives might be discovered within the dynamic processes involved in cross-cultural communication.

While a postpositivist realist approach to cultural diversity does not magically resolve the dilemma Boyd identifies, it does help us formulate a theoretically adequate way of approaching the multicultural challenges we face. The postpositivist realist does not subscribe to the idea that a legitimating or mediating perspective exists outside or in advance of any process of cross-cultural communication. At the same time, she does not give up the idea that any such mediating perspective might, at some point, exist. Instead, she sees this perspective as an achievement arrived at through cross-cultural human interaction and the conflict that sometimes arises as a result of that interaction. In the search for educational prescriptives, the realist acknowledges that all cultural practices are socially constructed and contingent, but not — and this is the central realist thesis — in an entirely arbitrary way. Because we are all biologically limited and temporally situated beings, the cultural practices through which we become human selves will be constrained (but not determined) by the physical laws to which all humans beings are subject. It is not hard to imagine, therefore, that different human cultures would share at least *some* cultural practices. Thus, the educational prescriptives we propose can be evaluated in light of the basic cultural commonalities we discover in the process of cross-cultural communication. In this way, the educational prescriptives we discover will not transcend our limited perspectives, but will be imbued with and come into being through them.

The postpositivist realist approach to objectivity responds to Boyd's most troubling objection concerning current approaches to multiculturalism: that existing theoretical perspectives on multiculturalism have the real effect of leaving the prescriptive preferences of the dominant view in control. According to the framework I have been defending, the epistemic norm of objectivity requires that we privilege the perspectives of members of *non-dominant* groups. Because humans cannot do away with their conceptual frameworks, and because the dominant perspective is likely to prevail if we ignore power dynamics and pretend that the playing field is level, Boyd is right when he says that the "universal" values we discover are more than likely to reflect the values of the dominant culture. This is why in order to create a situation of epistemic balance we will need to *privilege* the views of marginalized people. Only in this way can we ensure that we get enough information to produce more objective knowledge.

Finally, the realist acknowledges that the search for the best way to educate our nation's children is an ongoing one. Because she is working with a postpositivist conception of objectivity, she understands that the educational prescriptives she arrives at today cannot be absolute and that they may be subject to revision as she receives more information and/or revises her theoretical framework. This does not mean, however, that she chooses her pedagogical methods in an arbitrary way or that she believes that all methodologies are equally valuable for promoting a more democratic and culturally diverse society. Because she understands that cultures and identities refer outward to causally significant social structures, she will continually refine her pedagogical practice in light of the empirical studies that demonstrate the epistemic and political effects of different approaches to education.

If progressive social thinkers want schools to benefit society as a whole, then we must take the project of multicultural education seriously. A curriculum and pedagogy that self-consciously or un-self-consciously privileges the experiences and values of the dominant members of society rarely helps, and in many cases actually harms, those members of society whose lives and experiences have been or continue to be subordinated within that social order. This is fundamentally an ethical issue and involves the self-conception of American society as a whole. To the extent that we wish to foster a just and democratic society, we must take seriously the situation of marginalized groups who are underserved or actively harmed by an educational system that devalues their cultures.

Furthermore, if schools are to serve as a vehicle through which we promote the creation of a better world, we must insist that schools be actively involved in training students and teachers to interact in culturally sensitive ways with peoples whose cultural traditions differ from theirs. As I have argued throughout the book, the justification for this is epistemic as well as ethical. An educational approach that privileges the hegemonic culture actually presents an inaccurate conception of the world — a conception that is harmful to dominant and minority cultures alike. It fails to reveal the conflicts and contradictions that attend the formation of any given social order. By naturalizing and reifying existing relations of power, it forecloses a critical examination of the society we live in and gives us a distorted picture of the world and of the people in it. Thus, if we believe that one of the purposes of education is to teach us the truth about the world we live in, we will argue for a postpositivist realist examination of a plurality of perspectives in both curricular offerings and pedagogical strategies. Only by remaining open to the habits of interaction and ways of relating to the world that other cultures offer can any of us fairly evaluate "our" way of being as one worth preserving and perpetuating.

CHAPTER 5

Reading as a Realist

*Expanded Literacy in Helena María
Viramontes's* Under the Feet of Jesus

The great secret is that class matters, very much, in this society
dizzy with the illusion of classlessness. Writing about class is
to write about power relationships as they really are, in their
nakedness, and so to write about how this system actually
works.

Martín Espada, Zapata's Disciple

In a book that is about the relationship between identity, interpretation,
and agency, it is perhaps fitting that I conclude with a reading of a novel
that is centrally concerned with these same issues. In *Under the Feet of
Jesus,* Helena María Viramontes develops an expanded notion of literacy
that figures "reading" as a skill involving a human agent's total engagement with the world. In the process, the novel poses, and proposes
answers to, a number of questions about how, what, and why people
should read. Some of the questions the novel asks are: How do people
learn to read? What kinds of texts do they read? What are the processes
by which people become better readers? And finally, what are the connections among interpretation, understanding, and agency? As she develops it in this novel, Viramontes's expanded notion of literacy posits a
person's ability to "read" as a precondition for effective human agency.

Before I proceed with my argument, I want to situate the novel within
a literary and critical context. I do so both in the interest of clarifying my
theoretical intervention and to explain why I compare it to the novels
that I do. I contend that this novel should be placed within the tradition
of American social realism, and that it is more usefully compared to novels like William Faulkner's *The Sound and the Fury,* John Steinbeck's *The
Grapes of Wrath,* and Tomás Rivera's *... y no se lo tragó la tierra,*

among others, than to works by other Chicana writers such as Sandra
Cisneros, Gloria Anzaldúa, or Ana Castillo. The reasons for this placement should become clearer throughout the course of this chapter; here I
simply note that when critics conceive of canons too narrowly, very good
novels can be seriously misread, or at least, underread. Although this
criticism is meant to be directed, as well, toward "Americanists" who
ignore the substantial body of writings by Chicana/os and other U.S.
Latina/os in their conceptualization of "American literature," I focus
here on the problem of reading works written by Chicanas, such as
Viramontes, solely in relation to works written by other Chicana/os,
women of color, or women more generally.[1] While such interpretive practices are generally sound, in some cases they do a disservice to the text
under consideration by limiting the range of interpretive frameworks
that will be brought to bear on a work of literature.

Paradoxically, it is the concern with the activity of reading in *Under the
Feet of Jesus* that makes this novel difficult to read within contemporary
critical paradigms set forth by Chicana and women of color literary criticism. Up until this point, Chicana and women of color literary criticism
have tended to privilege tropes and themes other than that of reading —
tropes and themes such as coming to voice, talking back, breaking down
boundaries, crossing borders, making what was hidden visible, and resisting the patriarchal repression of female sexuality.[2] While these tropes and

1. This problem becomes acute when, for example, a woman of Mexican American
descent writes a novel with a theme that is not overtly, or even arguably, "ethnic." Cecile
Pineda is a notable example. For more on the literary reception of Pineda's work, see
Gonzalez, *The Postmodern Turn*, chap. 6.

2. Two common tropes of feminist literature and criticism, including work produced by
Chicanas, have been those of coming to voice and breaking down the boundaries between
the public and the private. Think, for example, of Carol Gilligan's groundbreaking book, *In
a Different Voice*. Debra Castillo and bell hooks both have books entitled *Talking Back*.
Gloria Anzaldúa's book *Borderlands/La Frontera* breaks boundaries on a generic level,
privileges border crossing on a thematic level, and includes an essay entitled "How to Tame
a Wild Tongue," in which she asserts her right to speak in Spanglish, Caló, and Chicano
Spanish. Sandra Cisneros's collection of short stories is aptly titled *Woman Hollering Creek*,
and Maxine Hong Kingston's *The Woman Warrior* is very much concerned with the young
protagonist's ability to find her voice. The subtitle of Cherríe Moraga's book *Loving in the
War Years*, "lo que nunca pasó por sus labios," carries dual implications of coming to voice
and making visible a female homosexuality that has been repressed by a patriarchal society.
Moraga's *Waiting in the Wings* serves the purpose of making visible queer motherhood,
while Sandra Cisneros's two books of poetry, *Loose Woman* and *My Wicked Wicked Ways*,
contain poems that thematize female sexuality, sometimes in exhibitionistic ways, in an
attempt to resist patriarchal control of female agency. A 1998 graduate student conference on Latina feminism at Berkeley, entitled "Oppositional Wetness," a 2000 Latina/o
studies conference on Latina/o queer theory at the University of Michigan, entitled "Sin

themes have represented important critical interventions within the fields of literary criticism and cultural studies and continue to be appropriate to a large body of cultural productions by Chicanas, they are not adequate for all works by Chicanas nor, I contend, for this novel in particular. Although there are aspects of *Under the Feet of Jesus* that fit into these critical paradigms, the novel as a whole is not easily assimilated to them.[3] Viramontes's challenging novel thus presents its critics with an opportunity to expand the range of interpretative concerns usually brought to bear on literature written by Chicanas. It does so by calling for a theory of interpretation that foregrounds the material aspects of the interpretive process itself. I demonstrate in this chapter that the novel implies a postpositivist realist approach to identity and interpretation on at least three different levels. On the metaphorical level, Viramontes analogizes words to tools to figure the act of interpretation as a materialist engagement with the world. On a structural level, she employs the narrative strategy of focalization to emphasize the epistemic status of identity. Finally, on a thematic level, the novel documents Estrella's transformation of consciousness and her personal empowerment by tracing the process through which she becomes a better reader of her social world.

WORDS AS TOOLS: VIRAMONTES'S EXPANDED NOTION OF LITERACY

When Estrella, the young protagonist of *Under the Feet of Jesus,* first comes across the red tool chest of her mother's new boyfriend, she

---

Vergüenzas," and the artwork on the cover of Carla Trujillo's edited volume *Living Chicana Theory* also participate in the logic of resistance through exhibitionistic sexual display. Chicano cultural critics have also found the tropes of coming to voice and crossing borders especially powerful and appropriate to their projects. Alfred Arteaga's edited collection is entitled *An Other Tongue: Nation and Ethnicity in the Linguistic Borderlands,* while Carl Gutiérrez-Jones titled his book *Rethinking the Borderlands.* Finally, José David Saldívar has co-edited an anthology with Héctor Calderón entitled *Criticism in the Borderlands* and titled his single-author book *Border Matters.* This list is not intended to be exhaustive; I include it simply to illustrate the pervasiveness of these tropes within these fields of study.

3. See, for example, Lawless. Although her essay contains many useful insights on the novel, she errs by reading the novel in terms of the commonly privileged tropes of "home" and "borders." Her decision to read the novel through these tropes leads her to some strange conclusions, such as that Petra, in an act of female resistance to male patriarchy, moves her cooking and other domestic activities "outside the walls of the house to expand domestic intimacy into the public world: she makes the inside become outside" (374–75). I suspect that Petra's behavior in these instances is conditioned more by material necessity than by some sort of impulse, conscious or not, to resist patriarchy: she cooks at the grill and bathes her children outside because the shack they live in has no kitchen or bathroom.

becomes "silent with rage" (24). Part of her anger undoubtedly derives from the chest's placement — "like a suitcase near the door" — and the threat of semi-permanent residency that such a placement implies (24). But mostly Estrella is angry because she does not know what the chest or the tools inside of it are for. The "jumbled steel inside the box, the iron bars and things with handles, the funny shaped objects" all seem to Estrella to be "as confusing as the alphabet she could not decipher. . . . The curves and tails of the tools made no sense and the shapes were as meaningless to her as chalky lines on the blackboard" (24–25). Estrella's anger, we learn, stems from her conviction that the people who have the knowledge that she wants will refuse to share it with her. It is a conviction born of experience — of years of encountering teachers more concerned about the cleanliness of her body than the curiosity of her intellect. This migrant child, whose mother has taken up with a man who is "not her father" after that father abandoned the family, slams the lid shut on the tool chest and remains silent for days (3). It is not until Perfecto Flores, the "man who came with his tool chest and stayed," opens the box and begins to teach Estrella the names and functions of the tools, that she begins to understand the meanings of the things she has seen (25). As Perfecto names the tools and demonstrates their useful functions, they begin to take on shape and significance. It is only after this process of instruction, a process during which Perfecto "barters" his knowledge for her voice, that Estrella learns how to read.

The link between tools and language that Viramontes dramatizes in this scene is central to the expanded notion of literacy that she develops in the novel. Viramontes sets up a series of associations that make explicit the connection between communication, interpretation, and agency. The metaphor of the "tool" figures the connection: language as a tool of communication; a tool as something that has transformative potential; language as a tool that has the power to transform the world. It is a metaphor that recalls the notion of "complete literacy," which Luis Rodríguez develops in his autobiography *Always Running, La Vida Loca: Gang Days in L.A.* In his preface to that book, Rodríguez defines "complete literacy" as the "ability to participate competently and confidently in any level of society one chooses" (9).[4] It is a conception of literacy that is not confined to reading printed texts, but encompasses the

---

4. Because participating competently in society at any level involves a range of cultural as well as cognitive skills, Rodríguez's notion may be (in practice) unattainable. Nevertheless, it is suggestive and offers us an ideal with which we can work.

totality of a human being's active engagement with the world. In his autobiography, Rodríguez examines the link between interpretation and agency by recounting the process by which he comes to discern, interpret, and then *resist* the structural forces that undergird the lack of choices he faces as a young Chicano growing up in Los Angeles. By reflecting on his experiences as a member of a gang, by reading the works of writers like Piri Thomas and Malcolm X, and by participating in a marxist reading group, Rodríguez gains insight into the social processes by which people like himself are interpellated into delinquency and criminality. His autobiography and his current work on behalf of juvenile justice are efforts to combat those processes. For Rodríguez, then, "complete literacy" is intimately tied to a human agent's ability to act in and on the world.

Similarly, Viramontes figures literacy as a skill involving a human agent's total engagement with the world.[5] It is worth noting that when Perfecto teaches Estrella the meanings of the tools, he does so by showing her how to *use* them. Immediately following the scene involving the tool box is another in which Perfecto and Estrella work together to manipulate their living space in order to make it more habitable for the family. The scene clearly demonstrates that Estrella's cooperation is necessary for Perfecto's ability to accomplish the task efficiently. It begins when Perfecto, who is kneeling on the floor to plug a hole, calls Estrella in from outside to help him.

—I'm not your papa. But you're getting me old with your . . .
—Where did you put the lantern?
—Stay away from the barn, hear me?
—You're right. You're not my papa.
—That should do it.

Although reluctant at first, Estrella helped him up from his knees by cupping her hand under his elbow. The room was now clean and safe to spread the blankets. They held a sky-blue sheet between them to divide the rooms. He held one corner, she another, and he nailed one corner, passed the hammer to her, and she did the other. He hammered a thick nail near the entrance and plucked off his hat and hung it. He then placed a bucket in the corner for the weak bladders of the twins who refused to go outdoors in the night.

—It will be good to sleep laying down, he said, dragging his feet outside.

5. By developing their expanded notions of literacy, Rodríguez and Viramontes are evoking an older meaning of the Latin verb *legere,* from which is derived the Spanish verb *leer* (to read). According to literary critic Walter Mignolo, one of the original meanings of *legere* was "to discern." He argues that with the rise of alphabetic writing the meaning of the verb began to be applied more exclusively to the idea of discerning the letters of the

—Where did you put the lantern? she asked again, following close
behind. (27–28)

The smoothness with which the sheet is hung and the lack of any verbal
communication about how to hang it demonstrate how accustomed
Estrella and Perfecto have become to working together. Their coordi-
nated movements imply a mutual attentiveness (Perfecto does not need to
ask Estrella to help him up) and a recognition of the needs and abilities of
the other (Perfecto does not doubt Estrella's ability to wield the hammer).
What is even more remarkable about their silent cooperation is that it
takes place within a relationship that is otherwise characterized by
resentment ("You're right. You're not my papa"). However Estrella and
Perfecto might feel about each other, they recognize their mutual interdependence. By portraying the process of learning to read as similar to
the communicative process by which an apprentice is instructed in the
use of tools, Viramontes portrays the acquisition of knowledge as necessarily intersubjective and tied to the material effects that words (as tools)
have on the world.

Embedded within Viramontes's expanded notion of literacy is a thesis
about the nature of language. *Under the Feet of Jesus* figures words as
more or less powerful to the extent that they refer outward, beyond language as such, to actions or objects in the world.[6] Where words lack a
more or less determinate referent they are figured simply as noise.
Estrella's father, for instance, never delivers on his promise to return to
the family from Mexico. His promises are meaningless; his words fail to
correspond to lived behavior. Not surprisingly, he is portrayed as someone who uses language carelessly, whose "words clanked like loose
empty cans in a bag" (16). In this, he provides a contrast to Perfecto,
whose refrain, "trust me," keeps Petra, Estrella's mother, from worrying
overmuch that he will leave her. Although we as readers who are privy to
Perfecto's thoughts understand much more clearly than Petra does how

---

alphabet in a text (105). Moreover, if one accepts Mignolo's compelling argument that the
Spaniards and the Mexicans during the encounter had "not only different material ways of
encoding and transmitting knowledge but also, as is natural — different concepts of the
activities of reading and writing," then Viramontes and Rodríguez are returning to a conception of "reading" that is in accord with the way their Amerindian forebears would have
understood the concept. See Mignolo, esp. chap. 2.

6. The conception of reference that I am working with is not one of perfect correspondence. Rather, I am working with the notion of partial denotation developed by philosophical realists such as Field and R. Boyd.

badly Perfecto wants to leave, we also understand why Petra's last impulse in the novel is to believe in his ability to fix things (169). She responds to Perfecto this way because he has always backed up his words with action. He is, as they say, a man of his word.

Estrella's friend Maxine is another character in the novel who often uses words carelessly. As someone who "rattle[s] on like a broken wheel on a shopping cart," she provides an important foil for Estrella, who is represented as reticent, as careful with her speech (34). However, Maxine's meaningless and annoying chatter becomes both meaningful and destructive when she touches on an issue related to Estrella's life. My point is that when Maxine's words start to refer, they cease to be noise and become words that can wound. The incident that ends the two girls' friendship begins one evening when Maxine asks Estrella why her papa is "so old." When Estrella explains that Perfecto is "not [her] papa," Maxine responds by asking why Estrella "let [her] grandpa fuck [her] ma fo'?" Such activity, Maxine explains, "makes for one-legged babies" (34). Estrella's enraged answer that Petra "isn't fucking him" merely causes Maxine to press the matter further.

> — And how'd you know that?
> — 'Cause he's not my papa.
> — Jesus Henry Christ! Maxine replied incredulously. She began to laugh, her giggles bubbling like welling water when the irrigation pipe was twisted on. Sweet toast, don't you know nothin'?
> — Shut your trap!
> — They ain't dry-humping. (35)

Maxine's careless, but accurate, remarks about Petra and Perfecto have the effect of forcing Estrella to see her family from a different perspective. She is forced to realize that people she has been taught to look down on have been simultaneously judging her family and finding them wanting. More importantly, Maxine's remarks compel Estrella to confront the truth of Petra's sexuality and her unsanctified relationship with Perfecto, the man who is "not [Estrella's] papa." Because Maxine's words refer to a verifiable aspect of Estrella's life — the relative truth or falsity of which is discoverable — they are meaningful. They have the power to wound.

Another passage in which words are figured as tools with the ability to injure involves Estrella's experience with an uncomprehending and uncaring school system. When Estrella's teacher, Mrs. Horn, "asked her how come her mama never gave her a bath," Estrella realizes, for the first time, that "words could become as excruciating as rusted nails piercing the heels of her bare feet" (25). Before then, "it had never occurred to

Estrella that she was dirty, that the wet towel wiped on her resistant face each morning, the vigorous brushing and tight braids her mother neatly weaved were not enough for Mrs. Horn" (25). As with the incident involving Maxine, Mrs. Horn's words have the power to hurt Estrella because they refer to something verifiable in Estrella's life. Although Mrs. Horn's interpretation of Estrella's situation is unkind and biased, her observation that Estrella does not bathe as often as Mrs. Horn would like is accurate. Mrs. Horn's words are powerful precisely because they communicate to Estrella some more or less determinate content that Estrella must recognize as at least partially true. Unfortunately, as a young girl, Estrella lacks the interpretive framework within which to understand the racism and classism behind Mrs. Horn's accusation. Consequently, Mrs. Horn's interpretation of Estrella's empirically verifiable situation goes unchallenged, and the damage to Estrella's psyche is done.

On one level, the novel's thesis about language is unremarkable. Most people would readily agree that words have meaning only to the extent that they refer to something. It is a thesis that becomes controversial only in the context of structuralist and poststructuralist debates about the nature of language. In the wake of theorists such as Saussure, de Man, and Derrida, postmodernist literary critics have been loath to admit that language, as a system of signs, has a referential relationship to anything beyond itself. While the postmodernist turn spawned by poststructuralism has crucially informed many cultural critics' understanding of the constructed nature of our social world, some critics have argued that it has also had a debilitating effect on the academic left's ability to theorize and justify progressive social action.[7] In an article about the problems in theories of working-class representation, Peter Hitchcock argues that, at the very least, constructionist theories of representation can be distracting: "For the constructionist, the lure here is ironically the role of the deconstructionist, for the artful play of the signifier can become a full-time occupation, and what [Stuart] Hall calls 'the work of representation' offers to be simultaneously meaning's primary mode of production and its ultimate abyss: this 'workday' never ends" (22). Hitchcock worries that when too much attention is given to the productivity of language, the givenness of class as a socioeconomic category begins to disappear from view (22).

7. See, for example, Benhabib; Calhoun; Eagleton; Lazarus; McGowan; Mohanty, *Literary Theory*; Moya and Hames-García; Norris.

At stake for Hitchcock, and for Viramontes, is the "aboutness" of working-class representation. Although neither would deny the constitutive role of language in how people understand and experience the social world, both are concerned with retaining a role for the referent in meaning-making practices of representation and interpretation. Viramontes has a message she wants to convey, and although her medium is a linguistic one, her message refers to something outside her medium. As I have argued above, Viramontes approaches the problem at least partly through a novelistic meditation on the nature of language. In *Under the Feet of Jesus,* the power of language resides in the contextually determined meaning that becomes actualized in the process of human communication. Words in this novel are figured as noise until they serve the function of transmitting some (more or less determinate) meaning from one human consciousness to another.

The link between meaning and reference is perhaps most clearly figured in the character of Estrella. As I noted above, Estrella is not much of a talker.[8] She distrusts casual conversation and is quick to criticize words that do not correspond to action.[9] Notably, when Estrella does talk, her words have all the more impact. When, near the end of the novel, Estrella thanks Perfecto for driving Alejo (a fellow camp worker who is dying of pesticide poisoning) to the hospital, he is deeply affected.

> Perfecto sat behind the steering wheel, the warm hum of engine under his feet. He had given this country his all, and in this land that used his bones for kindling, in this land that never once in the thirty years he lived and worked, never once said thank you, this young woman who could be his granddaughter had said the words with such honest gratitude, he was struck by how deeply these words touched him. (155)

This passage illustrates that words can heal as well as wound. When Estrella says "thank you," her utterance is performative; it performs the act that it names. Moreover, her utterance is productive; it creates in

8. Lawless astutely observes that characters in this novel are as likely to communicate through gestures as with words (371). Lawless interprets this to mean that the characters are still struggling to build a home for themselves "within different sedimentary layers of language," but I would argue instead that the characters' use of gestural language figures the insufficiency of words that are unconnected to actions and objects in the world (362). Talk is just noise unless it impels a human agent to do or feel something that will help change the material conditions of her life.

9. When Petra remarks that "for the pay we get, [the growers] are lucky we don't burn the orchards down," Estrella rebukes her by saying, "No sense talking tough unless you do it" (45).

Perfecto a feeling of goodwill. But significantly, her words are not *in themselves* productive or performative. They have the effect that they do because they successfully convey to Perfecto, within the continuing context of his communicative interaction with Estrella, her feeling of "honest gratitude."

Before I conclude my discussion of Viramontes's expanded notion of literacy, I want to return to the passage with which I began this section in order to focus on the way in which Perfecto interacts with Estrella. In what turns out to be the first instance in the novel that we see him barter his valuable skills for necessary goods and services, Perfecto barters his knowledge for Estrella's voice — and her help. Throughout the novel, barter is represented as a social relation that requires both parties to an exchange to take into account the unique needs, desires, and capabilities of the other. For example, when Perfecto approaches Estrella about tearing down the old barn, he does not order her to help him. Instead, he appeals to what he knows is Estrella's considerable love for her mother. He explains that he has asked her to help him because to split the money with someone else would mean "less for [her] mama" (74). Later, when Estrella finally does assent to Perfecto's request, she renegotiates the terms, asking him for something that she wants more than money for her mother. Importantly, she asks for something that she knows that Perfecto will be able to give her. When Alejo becomes very ill, Estrella wants to help him but does not have the resources to do so on her own. So, she barters her labor to Perfecto in exchange for his promise to drive Alejo to the doctor. In their exchanges with one another, Perfecto and Estrella each "read" the other — that is, they attempt to discern the concrete needs, desires, and capabilities of the other in order to work out an acceptable and fair exchange. Each must recognize the particularity, the "otherness," of the other, even as they view the other in relation to the self. What is missing from representations of barter in this novel is the element of exploitation. As such, barter represents an alternative to relations of capitalist exchange that otherwise structure the world of migrant laborers. Thus, Viramontes represents barter both as a form of mutual recognition and as an ideal form of communicative interaction — one that stands in opposition to coercive and exploitative forms of human exchange.

The expanded notion of literacy that Viramontes develops in this novel is thus embodied, intersubjective, and egalitarian. It is embodied because Estrella's ability to read the world develops as a result of practical activity; it is intersubjective because what Estrella knows depends on

her communicative interaction with others; and it is egalitarian because
the knowledge Estrella gains is acquired through non-exploitative relations of human exchange. As with any notion of literacy, interpretive
consciousness — or the ability to read symbols and discern patterns in
order to abstract a general meaning from a literary or social text — is crucial to Viramontes's expanded notion of literacy. But what is noteworthy
about her conception of literacy is that one's ability to "read" is not separable from the material conditions through which one's interpretive
consciousness comes into being in the first place. Moreover, as I will
argue in more detail further on, one's ability to read well is tied to one's
ability to empathetically identify with others. Viramontes's expanded
notion of literacy is thus more than a pious statement about the importance of learning to read; rather, it is an implicitly postpositivist realist
vision of social justice. Her vision of how humans can become better
"readers" is intimately wedded to her moral vision of how humans most
effectively interact with one another.

"THE HUMP AND TEAR OF THE STITCHED PAVEMENT": FOCALIZATION AND THE PARTIALITY OF PERSPECTIVE

Earlier, I asserted that Viramontes employs a narrative structure in *Under
the Feet of Jesus* that demonstrates the epistemic status of identity. In this
section, I discuss precisely how this works. Through the use of variable
character-bound focalization, Viramontes demonstrates the partiality of
individual perspective. In the process, she reveals how social location and
social ideologies influence characters' identities and, by extension, their
understandings of the world. Although all novels — indeed, all acts of
representation — are focalized, Viramontes's signature use of variable
character-bound focalization is unique in the way it attempts to call into
existence an ideal reader for the novel. She employs a narrative structure,
I argue, that is designed to reproduce in her ideal reader a transformation
of consciousness similar to the one Estrella undergoes.

   Focalization is a term that was introduced by the French literary critic
Gérard Genette in 1972 to make clearer the distinction in a narrative
"between the question *who is the character whose point of view orients
the narrative perspective?* and the very different question *who is the narrator? —* or more simply, the question *who sees?* and the question *who
speaks?*" (186). The distinction, Genette points out, is one that is not
adequately limned in narrative theories that attempt to describe narrative
perspective in terms of "point of view" (186–89). Since it was intro-

duced, the concept of focalization has been usefully elaborated by the literary critics Mieke Bal and Shlomith Rimmon-Kenan, among others. The reader interested in learning more about the concept of focalization should consult the works by these scholars. For the purpose of clarifying my argument, I will present below a brief description of the major components of this concept.

Focalization refers to the mediation (the prism, perspective, or angle of vision) through which a story is presented by a narrator in the text. As such, it describes a relationship between the " 'vision,' the agent that sees, and that which is seen" (Bal 104). In such a relationship, we can distinguish between the *focalizer,* the point from which the elements are viewed, and the *focalized object(s),* or the element(s) viewed. A focalizer can correspond to a character, in which case the individual perspective of that character orients the narrative. In such a case the focalization is said to be *internal* to the story. The focalizer can also be an anonymous agent situated outside the story. The focalization is then said to be *external.* It is important for understanding the concept of focalization to remember that the focalizer and the narrator can, but need not, be the same. It is quite possible, for example, to have a third-person narrator that presents the perspective of one or more characters in the story. It is also possible for the narrator and the focalizer to converge. The case of the so-called "ominiscient narrator" is an example of external focalization in which the narrator and the focalizer are one and the same; both are located outside the story (Bal 104–10).

Rimmon-Kenan points out that all focalization involves perceptual, psychological, and ideological facets. The perceptual facet has to do with sense perception and is determined by the coordinates of space and time. A character-focalizer, for example, can orient the narrative only toward those objects that she has smelled, seen, touched, tasted, or heard (or heard about). Moreover, her "vision" will necessarily be affected by such material factors as her stature and physical location. The psychological facet has to do with the focalizer's emotional state and cognitive capacity. A character-focalizer who is ill, upset, depressed, worried, or tired will perceive the world very differently from one who is enthusiastic, joyful, happy, or well rested. Additionally, a character's age and level of experience will influence how she perceives events or objects that are unfamiliar. Finally, the ideological facet has to do with a character's general system of viewing the world conceptually. How a given character interprets any event will be influenced by the social ideologies she is presented as having grown up with. These ideologies, which are constitutive of her fictionalized identity, not only determine where she fits into society and how she should relate to others, but also color her perceptions of the world. I shall have more to say about each of these three facets in the course of describing how focalization works in the novel under consideration.

Although *Under the Feet of Jesus* is narrated in the third person, its focalization is neither omniscient nor stable. Rather, the narrative perspective shifts among four main characters so that the world portrayed literally changes character — often from one paragraph to the next. Although all the characters in the novel occupy the "same" physical world, they experience and perceive it very differently. So, for example, when the members of Estrella's family arrive together at the shack that will be their new home, they each look around and see very different things: where Perfecto sees utility, and Petra sees danger, Estrella, younger and less jaded than both, sees adventure and possibility. The "furniture" of the world they occupy and perceive simultaneously thus changes according to who is doing the perceiving: Perfecto looks at crates and sees an altar for Petra's religious statues; Petra looks at her children's bare feet and sees the threat of scorpions; Estrella looks at a row of eucalyptus trees and sees dancing girls fanning their feathers (8–9).[10] The novel's variable character-bound focalization thus emphasizes the partiality of perspective even as it pulls together different perspectives and juxtaposes them so that the reader is placed in a privileged position vis-à-vis the characters. The reader is frequently allowed to see the same world, the same event, through several different characters' eyes.[11] Because of this, the reader comes to understand that how each character interprets the world is largely determined by her social location (the particular nexus of race, class, gender, and sexuality in which a given character exists in the world) and by her understanding of her place in the larger society (whom she identifies with or against, what her experiences have been, what social ideologies she has grown up with, and what pos-

---

10. For more on the realist conception of the universe as an empty room that is "furnished" by people's conceptual choices, see Alcoff, *Real Knowing,* esp. 169–70.

11. Bal writes, "Character-bound focalization (CF) can vary, can shift from one character to another. In such cases, we may be given a good picture of the origin of a conflict. We are shown how differently the various characters view the same facts. . . . Nevertheless, there usually is never a doubt in our minds which character should receive the most attention and sympathy. On the grounds of distribution, for instance the fact that a character focalizes the first and/or the last chapter, we label it the hero(ine) of the book" (105). Thus, even though the narrative is focalized in turn by Estrella, Alejo, Petra, and Perfecto, we know Estrella is the protagonist because she focalizes the beginning and end of the novel.

sibilities she imagines for herself in the future).[12] In short, how each character interprets the world is largely determined by her identity.

Viramontes's use of variable character-bound focalization calls to mind William Faulkner's use of this narrative technique in *The Sound and the Fury*. Like Viramontes, Faulkner employs four different focalizers. Unlike Viramontes, however, he segregates the focalizers into four different sections of the text. The novel is divided into four sections (each of which takes place on a different day), the first three of which are focalized and narrated by different members of the Compson family, an aristocratic Southern family whose fortunes have declined concurrently with the demise of the old South. Each of the three character-focalizers focalizes and narrates his own actions as well as the actions of others within his immediate purview. The first section is focalized by Benjy, the "idiot" Compson whose cognitive capacities are quite limited. Because Benjy's capacity for organization and analysis is extremely limited, he focalizes much that he does not himself understand. Moreover, because Benjy confuses past and present, his section does not obey the constraints of chronological time; as a result, his is a difficult section to read. The second and third sections are focalized and narrated by Quentin and Jason Compson, respectively. Both sections obey the constraints of chronological time and are differentiated from each other by the characters and worldviews of Quentin and Jason. The fourth and last section, significantly, is focalized not by a character but a by a narrator who is external to the story. The use of external focalization in the last section allows Faulkner more authorial control over the climax and the denouement of the novel. By making the last focalizer external to the story, Faulkner is able to move the narrative quickly from one locale to another and to invoke a simultaneity that his previous use of multiple, but segregated, character-bound focalization had not allowed.[13] It also allows the

12. See, for example, how differently Estrella, Alejo, and Gumecindo interpret the sound made when the door of the old barn swings open. For Estrella, who sees the barn door open, it "squeaks worse than the brakes of Perfecto's wagon" (10). For Alejo, who hears the sound from afar without seeing what caused it, the sound is suggestive of "cats fighting" (10). Gumecindo, meanwhile, hears the sound and thinks of La Llorona, the wailing women of Chicana/o and Mexican mythology (10). For more on the myth of La Llorona, see chapter two, note 9. Another example involves the breaking of Petra's statue of Jesus Christ. We see the incident first from Petra's perspective (167) and then again from Estrella's perspective (170).

13. In the last section, as Dilsey serves lunch to Benjy and Luster, she notes that Jason is not coming home. This provides the cue for Faulkner to note that Jason "was twenty miles away at that time" (317). The narrative focus then shifts to Jason until the narrator tells us,

narrator to "stand back," as it were, and narrate the last section in a manner conducive to a satisfactory dramatic resolution of the story. By employing an external, near-omniscient narrator-focalizer with the power both to report on the characters' actions, thoughts, and feelings and to provide analyses of them, Faulkner empowers himself as author to guide the reader's final interpretation of the novel.[14]

The focalization in the final section of *The Sound and the Fury* is further distinguished from the other three sections in that its principal focalized object is Dilsey, the elderly black servant whose labor and loyalty have served to keep the Compson family together as a (dys)functional unit. Curiously, however, despite the fact that the narrative follows Dilsey around, focalizing her actions, she is never herself the focalizer of the narrative. Nor does the narrative intrude into her thoughts and feelings as it does into the thoughts and feelings of the principal Compson characters. Consequently, the reader, who is watching Dilsey along with the narrator, often does not know why she does what she does until something happens in the story that reveals her probable motivations.[15] Effectively, this means that Dilsey, as an exemplar of the working class or the marginalized in Faulkner's novel, is the "object," but never the "subject," of her own and other characters' representations. While the exter-

---

"He wasn't thinking of home, where Ben and Luster were eating cold dinner at the kitchen table" (329). At that point, the narrative focus transfers to Benjy and Luster and remains on them until the conclusion of the novel — despite the fact that Jason shows up briefly near the end.

14. The following passage is representative of the near-omniscient status of the final, external narrator: "Jason got in and started the engine and drove off. He went into second gear, the engine spluttering and gasping, and he raced the engine, jamming the throttle down and snapping the choke in and out savagely. . . . He thought how he'd find a church at last and take a team and of the owner coming out, shouting at him and of himself striking the man down. . . . Of his niece he did not think at all, nor the arbitrary valuation of the money. Neither of them had had entity or individuality for him for ten years; together they merely symbolized the job in the bank of which he had been deprived before he ever got it" (321).

15. Note how in the following passage the reader cannot understand why Dilsey goes outside until Luster enters the scene and Dilsey asks him where he has been. Only then can the reader surmise that she has gone looking for him: "She returned to the kitchen. She looked into the stove, then she drew her apron over her head and donned the overcoat and opened the outer door and looked up and down the yard. The weather drove upon her flesh, harsh and minute, but the scene was empty of all else that moved. She descended the steps, gingerly, as if for silence, and went around the corner of the kitchen. As she did so Luster emerged quickly and innocently from the cellar door. Dilsey stopped: 'What you up to?' she said" (288). Compare this passage to the one cited in the previous footnote, which focalizes Jason Compson. In that passage, the narrator gets into Jason's head and we understand why he acts as he does while he is in the process of doing it.

nal narrator who focalizes Dilsey is sympathetic to her, so that the reader
is encouraged to recognize the aches, pains, and trials of her life (most of
which are caused by the Compson family), Dilsey herself, as a representative of the working class, is never provided the opportunity to present
her own perspective on the events and people who shape her life.

The question of what character is, or is not, allowed to orient the narrative in a novel is not an innocent one. As Bal has stated, focalization is
"the most important, most penetrating, and most subtle means of manipulation" available to an author of a narrative text (116). She notes that a
character who is allowed to focalize the narrative has the "advantage as
a party in [a] conflict. [Focalization] can give the reader insight into its
feelings and thoughts, while the other character cannot communicate
anything" (110). Focalization thus sets up a situation of inequality in a
text that influences the sentiments of the reader. Consequently, we should
not pass over too quickly the question of why Dilsey, as one of four main
characters in *The Sound and the Fury*, is the only one who does not act as
focalizer. What is noteworthy about Faulkner's departure in the last section of the novel from the pattern of focalization he sets up in the first
three sections is his apparent inability, or unwillingness, to view the
world from the perspective of a black female servant. Such a departure is
even more marked in light of his willingness, and apparent ability, to
allow Benjy, the "idiot" Compson, to orient the perspective of the narrative in the first section of the novel. We might want to ask: What mechanisms of silencing and erasure along lines of race, gender, and class—
consciously or unconsciously employed—are taking place in the narrative of this otherwise quite extraordinary novel?

I have devoted so much space to the question of focalization in *The
Sound and the Fury* both because it is a canonical example of the use of
that literary device and to emphasize the contribution to an American literary canon that novels like Viramontes's can make. Viramontes's novel,
after all, is focalized entirely from the perspective of Mexican-origin
migrant farmworkers. It is certainly not the first novel to center on the
lives and struggles of working-class people; John Steinbeck's 1939 novel
The Grapes of Wrath, for example, also treats the lives of migrant farmworkers. But Viramontes's novel can be distinguished from Steinbeck's in
two important ways. First, Viramontes's novel treats *Mexican-origin*
farmworkers. Second, Viramontes does not employ an external narrator-
focalizer to guide her reader's interpretation of the novel. In *The Grapes
of Wrath,* Steinbeck included fifteen "inner," "intercalary," or "general"

chapters that are narrated by an external narrator-focalizer. The short inner chapters, which are interspersed with the longer chapters focused on the lives of the Joad family, provide explicit political, historical, and symbolic interpretations of the larger forces and events that shape the family members' lives. Steinbeck himself was quite conscious of the effect he wanted the inner chapters to have. In a February 1953 letter to an enthusiastic undergraduate critic, Steinbeck explained that "their basic purpose was to hit the reader below the belt. With the rhythms and symbols of poetry one can get into a reader — open him up and while he is open — introduce things on a [sic] intellectual level which he would not or could not receive unless he were opened up" (Dircks 91). Although Steinbeck initially received a great deal of criticism from literary critics for the overt political message of the chapters, the chapters apparently had the effect on readers that he wanted them to have.[16] His willingness to guide his readers' interpretation of the novel in a way that might seem heavy-handed was ultimately very successful.[17]

I mention Steinbeck's "psychological trick" partly to distinguish it from the kind of manipulation Viramontes achieves through her variable character-bound focalization.[18] More precisely, however, I want to emphasize the difficulty Viramontes's narrative strategy presents to readers who are accustomed to having their interpretations of a novel guided in a more or less explicit way. Viramontes does not hit her reader over the head with the political message of her novel; indeed, her prose has more often been described as "lush" and "poetic" than as polemical.[19] Instead, through the use of variable character-bound focalization, Viramontes challenges her reader to become a better, more sensitive, interpreter of the social world represented in the text. By allowing the four main characters to take turns orienting the narrative perspective, Viramontes encourages her reader to empathetically identify, in turn, with each of the character-focalizers and to undertake, without intervention or help from an external narrator-focalizer, the hard work of order-

16. See Dircks; Emory; Howarth; Owens and Torres.

17. The novel, which was released in March 1939, was a huge commercial success, and was translated into ten different European languages. By April, it was selling 2,500 copies a day. By May, it had reached the top of the best-seller list. In 1982, the *New York Times* reported that it was the "second-best-selling novel ever in paperback in America, with 14,600,000 copies printed" (Wyatt 3).

18. Steinbeck himself refers to the use of the inner chapters as a "psychological trick" (Dircks 91).

19. See Miner; Chambers.

ing the events and synthesizing the characters' disparate perspectives.[20] Only by creating the conditions through which an ideal reader can dialectically transform her consciousness — and, in the process, reproduce Estrella's transformation of consciousness — does Viramontes unobtrusively guide her reader's interpretation of the novel.

I turn now to a scene in *Under the Feet of Jesus* that demonstrates the epistemic effects of social location by focalizing a familiar object — a highway — from a perspective unfamiliar to most middle-class readers of novels. Petra (after her husband's desertion but before Perfecto's arrival) faces the challenge of transporting her five children on foot across a busy highway in order to buy the food they need to survive. The scene is inserted into the novel immediately after a passage in which Perfecto contemplates leaving the family. Its placement highlights how difficult it is to be a working-class woman alone with children.

> Petra knew the capricious black lines on a map did little to reveal the hump and tear of the stitched pavement which ascended to the morning sun and through the trees and no trees, and became a swollen main street and then a loose road once again outside the hamlets that appeared as splat dots on paper. They had travelled by foot, in and out of the orchards, until they reached the main highway and Petra could feel the heat pulsating from the asphalt. The oil of the pavement mirrored like puddles of fresh rainwater though it hadn't rained in months. The family stood in file on the thistle belt of road and rested.
>
> Under the strutting powerlines, Estrella sat on her haunches. The floral fabric of her dress was thin from repeated washes and the reddish blue violets paled against the searing sunlight. She sunk her white thumbnail into the pavement and slowly sliced a sliver on the melted tar. Not far across the highway, the rickety store stood as desirous as a drink of water. (103)

Petra, who focalizes the above passage, conveys how different a highway looks, feels, and smells from the perspective of someone who must travel it by foot as opposed to someone who travels it by car. The highway, which for people with cars is an aid to rapid transit, is for Petra, in her present circumstances, a physical barrier she must surmount to get food for her family. The tar, which provides a smooth surface for automobiles to travel on, is for Petra and her children a concentrator of solar heat and a source of unpleasant smells.

In the scene immediately following the one recounted above, Petra

20. Lawless notes the interpretive demands placed on the reader of this novel and observes that "the narrative demands an active role from the reader, we must make an effort not to become lost amongst the different time locations framed by blank spaces" (368).

encounters a man who stops to fuel his vehicle at the gas station. This encounter is important for what it shows about the way social ideologies condition human experience. While Petra and her children are standing in the hot sun, looking across the highway and waiting for the heavy traffic to abate, a lime green Bermuda rolls off the road and under the awning of the store's single gas pump. Petra, after having succeeded in getting half her family across the road, looks at the car and notes the whiteness of its plush carpet and the plumpness of its seats as she watches the driver buff its chrome with a blue paper towel. She envies both the car and its driver. He is, she imagines, someone for whom payday always comes at the end of the week, and who "knows" things such as "where the schools and where the stores [are]" (105). However, Petra cannot dwell for long on either the car or its driver. Her boys have not crossed the road because they have been frightened by the memory of a snake that had been crushed "so perfectly" by the tire of a huge semi that they "couldn't even scrape the slithered body off the pavement with a butterknife" (106). Because she is tired and frustrated, Petra screams at her sons and threatens them with bodily harm if they do not hurry across. As she yells, she captures the man's attention.

> The Bermuda man looked at her over the hood of his lime green car, and the sun reflected wavy green on his face. Petra wore mismatched clothes and had chosen the clothes for their blues because blue was a cool color against the hot tempered sun and that was why she was dressed the way she was and she hoped he would stop staring. The man crumpled up the blue of his towel into a ball and tossed it on the ground and the twins watched it slowly unfold. (106)

The scene recounted above illustrates the asymmetry in social relations between people who occupy different locations in a hierarchical economic system. Notice that Petra's envy of the man takes the form of attributing to him knowledge that she does not herself possess. Moreover, she becomes self-conscious when he looks at her: the functionality of her clothing does not protect her from internalizing the middle-class expectation that she should be dressed in an aesthetically pleasing way. Evidently, the asymmetry in economic relations is reinforced by ideological narratives that reinforce the relation of inequality. Petra does not look down on the man; rather, she feels inadequate in his presence. Moreover, although she knows things he might not, such as what it is like to be a woman abandoned with her children, or what the highway looks like to someone who travels it by foot, she imagines *him* as someone who "knows" things. In contrast, it is unlikely that the

Bermuda man either envies Petra or attributes to her any admirable faculties that he himself does not possess. Although the novel does not allow the Bermuda man to focalize the narrative, we can discern his attitude both as it is reflected in Petra's consciousness of his stare and in the carelessness with which he tosses away the blue towel. The juxtaposition of Petra's mismatched blue clothes (chosen so that she might be able to withstand the heat) with the blue paper towel that the Bermuda man uses and carelessly discards resonates with meaning. At a metaphorical level, this juxtaposition suggests that, from the Bermuda man's perspective, Petra (like the towel) is to be used and then cast aside. The man exhibits no obvious malice toward Petra, and he may not be consciously aware that he exists in any kind of economic relation to her at all. But it is precisely in the carelessness of his toss that we can locate the depth of his disregard. He no more cares who will pick up the towel than he knows who will pick the vegetables that he buys at the supermarket.

I do not mean that the Bermuda man is meant to represent an evil person — or even someone who consciously embraces an exploitative socioeconomic system. Nor do I mean to suggest that his character cannot, in principle, understand his economic relation to Petra. Rather, my argument is that the Bermuda man functions in the novel as a stand-in for the middle-class American whose social location inhibits his apprehension of the real economic relations in which he exists. The possibility that Petra may have something to teach the Bermuda man about the world they both live in would probably not occur to him. Because, presumably, such a man does not come into regular contact with migrant farmworkers, at some conscious everyday level he could imagine that the agricultural products he consumes simply come from the grocery store. Although he might well "know" that they are picked by someone or something out in a field somewhere, the socially produced blindness he would have developed as a result of his individual experience might not have given him the imaginative resources by which he could adequately reconstruct that process. And because the Bermuda man lives a comfortable existence — because he speeds through the world on plump white seats in a shiny green car — he might well lack the motivation to transcend the limitations of his own partial perspective. The isolation his relative wealth provides would thus perpetuate his socially produced blindness and facilitate his unconscious disregard for Petra's and other farmworkers' well-being.

Viramontes imparts significance to the Bermuda man's disregard for Petra and her family by giving him a cameo role in a novel that powerfully champions the cause of social and economic justice for migrant farmworkers. The setting of the scene at a gas station, the oily appearance of the road, and the sliver of tar that Estrella slices off with her thumbnail as she waits to cross the highway all point to one of the central tropes of the novel — fuel and its origins. The trope of fuel is pivotal to this novel in at least the following two ways: (1) it introduces the principle of permutation (the process whereby one thing is changed into another), and (2) it provides a metaphor for the situation of migrant farmworkers. As the people who pick the vegetables that we find washed and wrapped for our purchasing convenience in the produce sections of our supermarkets, migrant farmworkers literally provide the "fuel" that keeps our bodies going. Despite the fact that farmworkers' labor literally provides the "energy" that keeps middle- and upper-class Americans from "running out of gas," however, migrant farmworkers are some of the most vilified members of our society. Although migrant farmworkers and their families labor to keep us fed and clean up after us, they are often viewed by those in positions of power and privilege as "outsiders" to American society. Because their first language is often not English, and because members of their families are frequently new arrivals to the United States, they are periodically scapegoated as the people responsible for downturns in the economy. Moreover, because their labor is either invisible to or seen as illegitimate by a middle-class American population that begrudges the tax dollars used to educate and medicate their children, they have been targeted by legislation such as California's Proposition 187.[21] By depicting what is normally invisible to American consumers — that is, the effect on a migrant farmworker family of the systematic economic exploitation to which they are subjected — the scene at the gas station implicitly calls for a reconsideration of their place within American society.

My claim that Viramontes intends to contest farmworkers' outsider status is further demonstrated by the first of two eponymous moments in the novel. The first moment brings together the related themes of citi-

21. California's Proposition 187, which was passed in 1994 by California voters by a majority of almost 60 percent, was intended to make undocumented residents ineligible for public social services, public health care services (except for emergency care, under federal law), and public school education at elementary, secondary, and postsecondary levels; to require various state and local agencies to report persons who are suspected undocumented residents to the California attorney general and the United States Immigration and Naturalization Service; to mandate the California attorney general to transmit reports to the Immigration and Naturalization Service and maintain records of such reports; and to make it a felony to manufacture, distribute, sell, or use false citizenship or residence documents. As noted in chapter four, note 8, the core provisions of the proposition were never implemented.

zenship, belonging, and entitlement, which concern so many Latina/o immigrants and their descendants. One night, after Estrella is startled by the lights of a baseball park, mistaking them for the lights of the border patrol, Petra warns Estrella not to let *la migra* pull her into the green vans. She speaks to Estrella of her *earned* right ("Don't let them make you feel you did a crime for picking the vegetables they'll be eating for dinner.") as well as her *birthright* to be in this country, and reminds Estrella that her own U.S. birth certificate is "under the feet of [Petra's statue of] Jesus" (63). It is in this context that we must consider Viramontes's decision to focalize Petra's encounter with the Bermuda man from Petra's perspective. Unlike Faulkner, who reproduces the situation of inequality that Dilsey finds herself in by denying her the power to act as the subject of her own narrative, Viramontes attempts to undermine existing relations of inequality by manipulating the narrative perspective so that the reader must view the world from Petra's marginalized perspective. In the process, Viramontes creates the possibility that her readers will, vicariously at least, enlarge the realm of their class-bound experience and mitigate the partiality of their own perspectives.

Partiality of perspective, as I noted in my initial discussion of focalization, involves perceptual, psychological, and ideological facets. An individual who wishes to become a better reader of her social world, then, must first recognize and then examine for adequacy the ideological as well as the perceptual and psychological biases that structure her own perspective. While we cannot hope to apprehend the world free of mediating theories and biases, we can strive toward less distorted understandings of our social world. One of the central tenets of postpositivist realism is that not all ideologies are equally illuminating. As I have argued throughout this book, some in fact serve to obscure real social and economic relations. To the extent that a reader of a social text can recognize distorting social narratives, then, she has a better chance of coming to a more objective understanding of her social world. Something of this sort is what Estrella is able to do after Maxine rudely alerts her to the possibility that there may be an alternative, and perhaps more accurate, interpretation of the text of her mother's life. The incident that ends Estrella's and Maxine's friendship, which I discussed briefly in the first section of this chapter and to which I return now, brings to light some of the obstacles, in the form of social ideologies, that Estrella needs to overcome in order to become a better "reader" of her social world.

Ironically, it is only because Estrella can read at all that she and

Maxine become friends. Estrella is at first reluctant to answer Maxine's friendly hail because Petra has taught Estrella to look down on the Devridges — whose family members have been arrested for theft and who sun-dry without "shame" a pee-stained mattress on the front porch every morning. But because Maxine is waving a glossy comic book featuring a picture of Millie the Model, Estrella is persuaded to disregard her mother's warnings and approach Maxine's porch. Estrella quickly learns that Maxine owns a crate full of comic books, none of which she can read. Maxine's hailing of Estrella is thus motivated by the hope that Estrella can read them to her. Estrella, meanwhile, is starved for reading material. She has been reading "over and over" the catechism chapbook given to her by her godmother and other found reading material: newspapers thrown in trash cans at filling stations, oatmeal instructions, and billboard signs (31). Most of what Estrella reads advertises products — like Clorox, Swanson's TV Dinners, and Coppertone — which she has no reason to use and no means to buy. Estrella's primary reading material is thus produced by and for a consumer culture from which she is excluded: bleach is irrelevant to someone who owns no linens; TV dinners are useless to someone who has no oven; and suntan lotion sounds like a cruel joke to someone who is already brown and for whom the sun is associated not with leisure time and lolling on the beach, but with sunstroke and an unquenchable thirst. So, when Maxine offers to barter access to her comic books in exchange for Estrella's willingness to read them to her, the girls form a fast friendship. Sharing, over the course of a tomato-picking season, the adventures of Millie the Model and her photographer boyfriend Clicker, Estrella and Maxine bond over the promise of the idealized heterosexual romance narrated through the comics.

This is the context within which Maxine makes her careless remarks about Estrella's mother. Maxine's assertion that Petra is "fucking" Perfecto is difficult for Estrella to accept. Estrella, after all, has been socialized into Mexican Catholic norms of morality and respectability. As far as Estrella is concerned, her mother cannot be having sex with Perfecto because they are not married. Petra, Estrella reasons, is still married to her father. Good Catholic women do not have sex outside of marriage; they remain married to and true to their husbands. Furthermore, mothers (according to Estrella's naive Catholic worldview) are not sexual beings; rather, they are self-abnegating madonnas who engage in sexual relations only for the purpose of reproduction. From Estrella's perspective, Petra is both her mother and a good woman; therefore, she cannot be having sex with Perfecto. Such are the distorted notions and values by which the young Estrella lives.

Meanwhile, the relative material security that Perfecto's labor has provided for the family since his arrival, and the real value of his companionship to Petra's sense of well-being, has gone unnoticed by Estrella. In a crucial way, the real exigencies and moral dilemmas her family faces have less ideological relevance for Estrella than do the norms of respectability and Catholic religious values that she has internalized as a result of growing up as a working-class Mexican Catholic child in the United States.[22] As part of a normal process of socialization and identification, Estrella has incorporated into her identity certain social ideologies that have blinded her to the lived realities of her existence. Moreover, Estrella has been as blind to these social ideologies as she has been to Petra's sexuality. Only after Maxine's remarks jolt Estrella into seeing herself from an another perspective does she realize that there are other ways of viewing her mother's situation. Only when she realizes that her views about her mother can be contested does she worry about whether what she has known all along to be true is in fact true.

Maxine's remarks and her accompanying laughter do more than simply challenge Estrella's sense of reality. They also oblige Estrella to see herself and her mother, with whom she strongly identifies, as outsiders to the norms of bourgeois acceptability and, more disturbingly, as inhabitants of a freak show capable of producing one-legged babies or children with no mouths. These visions provoke in her a violent reaction. In an instant, Estrella's contradictory feelings about having been abandoned by her father (and so forever excluded from bourgeois respectability and Catholic piety), about occupying a position of economic marginality, and about having been betrayed by a mother whose sexuality exposes them both to ridicule, come rushing to the fore. All of Estrella's anger, hurt, and fear become concentrated on Maxine, and she pulls "Maxine's stringy sandy hair with such pure hatred it startled even her. For a moment she felt as if she could kill the white girl" (35). The fight is eventually broken up by Maxine's mother; it ends before either girl is seriously injured, but not before the friendship is permanently destroyed.

Why does Estrella turn on Maxine with such ferocity? First, at some level Estrella knows that what Maxine has said is likely to be true. Her anger at Maxine is thus, to some degree, displaced anger at herself for

22. A real moral dilemma explored in the novel, but one which I do not treat in detail in this chapter, involves Perfecto's decision to remain with, or abandon, the family.

not knowing better. More important, however, Maxine has become narratively associated — through her race, her ownership of the magazines, her infatuation with Clicker, the yellow color of her toes, and her corncob dress — with the comic book character Millie the Model, who is described as having "bold yellow hair" (30). Through a series of metonymic associations, Estrella, as the primary focalizer of Maxine, links Maxine to a consumer culture in which young women have the luxury of weeping over the faithlessness of men and where the possibility of a failed romance is purportedly the biggest concern a woman with breasts like "perfect smiles on her chest" will have (30).[23] When Estrella attacks Maxine, she expresses not only the anger she feels as a result of her father's abandonment, but also the ambivalent rage she feels toward the consumer culture which Maxine, as a white girl, momentarily represents. Like many girls her age, Estrella wants to be able to buy things, have fun, and be attractive to boys. But her exclusion, by virtue of her race and class, from that consumer culture gives rise to a volatile mixture of resentment and desire that erupts in her attack on Maxine.[24] The irony, of course, is that Maxine, by virtue of her socioeconomic class, is as much outside that consumer culture as Estrella.

23. The focalization of Maxine is actually what Bal would describe as "complex." Bal points out that various focalization levels can be distinguished in most narratives. When an external focalizer on the first level of focalization delegates focalization to an internal focalizer on the second level of focalization, we say that the character-focalization is embedded within the all-encompassing view of the external focalizer (110–15). Because my interest in this chapter is in how the different character-focalizers in this novel view the world, and not in developing or elaborating a theory of focalization, I have chosen not to spend a great deal of time distinguishing between different levels of focalization in this novel. Nevertheless, acknowledging the existence of an external focalizer that more frequently than not yields focalization to one of the four character-focalizers helps us to make sense of passages such as the one describing Estrella's fight with Maxine (35). Portions of the fight are described in such a way that Estrella, as a participant, could not have perceived them. And since Petra, Perfecto, and Alejo do not witness the fight, we must assume the existence of an external focalizer. Significantly, though, the bulk of *Under the Feet of Jesus* is focalized by one of the four main characters; the appearance of an external focalizer is infrequent.

24. The attack on Maxine brings to mind another passage in the novel in which Estrella dances with the Quaker oatmeal container in an attempt to distract the twins from their hunger. In that passage, Estrella "headlock[s] the Quaker man's paperboard head," "drum[s] the top of his low crown hat," "slap[s] the round puffy man's double chins," and "beat[s] his wavy long hair the silky color of creamy hot oats." Metaphorically, the Quaker man, with "chubby pink cheeks," "double chins," and "hair the silky color of creamy hot oats" on a "red white and blue" cylinder, stands in for a complacent and well-fed American populace oblivious to the hunger and despair of its most economically disadvantaged members. The violence of the terms describing Estrella's actions suggests the anger that fuels the amusement she concocts for her siblings (18–19).

That Estrella's anger and hatred is not really directed against Maxine as an individual, but rather against the consumer culture and social ideologies that Maxine momentarily stands in for is made clear by Estrella's bewilderment the moment the fight is broken up. Estrella holds no grudge against Maxine and wants only to pick up the friendship where it left off. But it is too late. Shortly after the fight is over, Big Mac the foreman visits Perfecto and Petra to tell them that they must leave the camp. The family is forced to pack up and leave without collecting wages for the last few days of work. The experience is instructive for Estrella, and it clears the way for her to let go of some her illusions in order to better understand the actual social relations in which she, her mother, and Perfecto exist — an understanding that proves necessary for Estrella's eventual ability to transcend her own particular perspective by entering into an empathetic identification with Petra and Perfecto. As a result of the incident with Maxine, Estrella loses a friend, but becomes a more discerning reader of her social world.

FROM BONES TO FUEL: PERMUTATION AND THE DYNAMICS OF ECONOMIC EXPLOITATION

Estrella's increasing ability to "read" her social world is depicted in the novel not simply as a process of accumulating ever-increasing amounts of information but also and primarily as a process of learning to distinguish between more and less illuminating theories of the social world. Part of that process necessarily involves choosing the right metaphors or tropes by which she can organize the various bits of information she receives. Estrella seizes on the trope of fuel, and the process by which it comes into being, to help her understand the dynamics of economic exploitation in which she and others like her are caught.

The trope of fuel is first introduced in connection with Alejo, the young man who becomes infatuated with Estrella at the beginning of the novel. For Alejo, migrant farm labor is not a way of life; rather, it is a way of earning some extra money during the summer to help his grandmother, who is raising him, with expenses. Unlike Estrella, Alejo attends high school during the school year in Edinburg, Texas, and plans to attend college, where he hopes to study geology. It is Alejo who introduces Estrella to the principle of permutation (the process whereby one thing is changed into another). He does so inadvertently when, as part of his seduction of her, he shares with her his fascination with the geologic processes through which tar oil pits come into existence. One day during lunch, as they lie together under the shade of a truck in order to escape the brutal effects of the sun, Alejo tells Estrella about the tar oil pits. "Ever heard of tar pits? he asked. . . . Millions of years ago, the dead animals and plants fell to the bottom of the sea. . . . Bones and rocks and leaves. Falling. Slowly. . . . The bones lay in the seabed for millions of years. That's how it was. Makes sense don't it, bones becoming tar oil?" (87). Estrella, who is trying not to think about the closeness of Alejo's body, eventually asks, "Tar oil? You say tar oil, huh?" He answers, "Once, when I picked peaches, I heard screams. It reminded me of the animals stuck in the tar pits." Estrella then asks, "Did people? Did people ever get stuck?" To which Alejo responds, "Only one, . . . in the La Brea tar pits, they found some human bones. A young girl" (88). This brief exchange, and Estrella's concern for the people whose bones, because they had the misfortune to get "stuck," might be turned into oil, is crucial to her subsequent ability to abstract from her own situation some general principles which will allow her to more adequately interpret the socioeconomic system in which she lives. Before I turn to Estrella's transformation of consciousness, however, I want to look at another passage in which the metaphor of the tar pits plays a prominent role.

The first time we see Alejo, he is in the orchard with his cousin Gumecindo filching peaches which they intend to sell during the weekend for extra cash. It is from his perch in a peach tree that Alejo first spies on and becomes infatuated with Estrella. The fact that Alejo and Gumecindo need this extra money raises the question of just compensation for migrant farm labor, even as the consequence Alejo suffers for his actions introduces into his mind considerations of sin and punishment. In a subsequent scene, the two young men are once again out picking peaches when a biplane approaches to fumigate the orchards. Because the plane has arrived one week ahead of schedule, Alejo and Gumecindo are caught off-guard. Unable to get out of the tree in time, Alejo is drenched in the poisonous spray of the pesticides. The scent of the poison (like ocean salt and beached kelp) and Alejo's experience of drowning in sand evokes the image of the seabed on which organic matter is slowly transformed into oil and tar (77). This image, in turn, suggests that Alejo might yet become one of the people who gets "stuck" in the metaphorical tar pit — that his very bones might be sacrificed to the social and economic mobility of others. The specter of this possibility becomes more apparent when the biplane approaches for a second sweep. Alejo closes his eyes and imagines sinking into the tar pits.

> He thought first of his feet sinking, sinking to his knee joints, swallowing his waist and torso, the pressure of tar squeezing his chest and crushing his ribs. Engulfing his skin up to his chin, his mouth, his nose, bubbled air. Black bubbles erasing him. Finally the eyes. Blankness. Thousands of bones, the bleached white marrow of bones. Splintered bone pieced together by wire to make a whole, surfaced bone. No fingerprint or history, bone. No lava stone. No story or family, bone. (78)

As the poison invades his system, Alejo feels what it might be like to be erased by black bubbles of tar that squeeze his chest, crush his ribs and reduce him to bone. It is an experience that affects his sense of self and initiates a possible transformation of his identity. Whereas previously Alejo had believed himself to be a "solid mass of boulder thrust out of the earth and not some particle lost in infinite and cosmic space" and had assumed that he would "not only [become] a part of earth's history, but would exist as the boulders did, for eternity" (52), now, faced with the shock of the poison to his system, he confronts the possibility that he may become — like the girl who was trapped in the La Brea tar pits — a nameless, faceless, history-less sacrifice to the mobility (through the profits ensured by corporate agribusiness) of others: "no fingerprint or history, bone. No lava stone. No story or family, bone" (78).

Part of what is at stake for Viramontes in this fictional representation of a migrant farmworker community is the risk that life stories like Alejo's might have no historical meaning. The full recognition by others of Alejo's humanity (both as an individual and as a representative of the thousands of other farmworkers who labor and die in relative obscurity) depends, to some extent, on how well his needs, desires, abilities, and experiences are represented in the social world. Just as creating a personal narrative is a way of constructing a sense of self, so is learning about an individual's history a way of recognizing that person's membership in a human community. But because historical meaning is a human construct, its existence is tenuous and subject to erasure. The danger is that in the absence of a complete and accurate historical record, some humans risk becoming nothing more than organic material that may be useful for someone's else's purposes.

The climactic scene in the novel, which is brought about by Alejo's poisoning, brings together the themes of communication, interpretation, and agency introduced in the tool box passage that I began with. Unsure how to handle Alejo's illness, Alejo's very young and panicked cousin places him in Petra's care. Not only does this place further strain on the already-taxed resources of an increasingly infirm Perfecto and a newly-pregnant Petra, but it forces Estrella to act on behalf of someone (Alejo) whose inability to understand and appreciate the difficulty of her particular situation is wearying to her. Perfecto and Petra both do what they can for Alejo, but their capabilities simply do not extend to curing pesticide poisoning. Finally, Estrella barters her labor by agreeing to help Perfecto tear down the old barn in exchange for his promise to drive Alejo to the migrant camp's medical clinic. On the way to the clinic they get stuck in a mud sinkhole created by a broken water pipe, and by the time they finally arrive, Estrella and her family are hot, dirty, and exhausted. To make things worse, instead of a modern clinic, what they find when they arrive is a "heap of aluminum foil," an impatient nurse, and a rusted-out ambulance with no tires.

The inauspicious appearance of the clinic does not bode well for the quality of medical care Alejo is likely to receive. In fact, the nurse, who has been preparing to leave work, is visibly annoyed by the family's late arrival. She checks her watch more than once, mutters to herself, and separates herself from the family's predicament by adopting a bureaucratic demeanor toward them. Before attempting to assess the situation, before even informing them that there is no doctor on the premises, the nurse rips a fresh sheet of paper out of a tablet, picks up a pen, and begins filling out her forms. Her eventual diagnosis, for which she charges them $10, is that Alejo is too sick for her to treat. Having dispatched what she understands as her responsibility to the family, she advises them to take Alejo twenty miles further away to the hospital in Corazón.

By this time, after having spent their gas trying to get out of the sinkhole and having paid the nurse their last $9.07, they have no gas, no money, and a dying man on their hands. The nurse, however, is concerned only with getting them out of the clinic so that she can lock up. She waves away Estrella's repeated efforts to barter Perfecto's labor in exchange for the "services" she has rendered — even as she maintains her self-image of generosity by patronizingly accepting their last $9.07 in lieu of the $10 she charges them. It is unclear whether she even hears Estrella tell her that the money is all they have, for her bureaucratic mode of interaction does not require her to actually listen to them. After giving them a carbon-copy receipt and clicking off the fan, the nurse stands impatiently waiting for the family to leave. Her behavior in this scene speaks clearly: their problems are not worth her time.

The problem that Estrella and her family confront in this situation is that of being heard.[25] Although Estrella speaks to the nurse, and the nurse responds to her, there is a profound failure of communication. It is a failure rooted in the nurse's refusal of empathetic identification. Because the nurse refuses to recognize Estrella and her family as similar, in some crucially human ways, to herself, she feels relieved of the responsibility to act in a way that might alleviate Alejo's situation. As a result, she can dismiss Estrella's attempts to change the terms of their interaction. She can refuse to consider seriously Perfecto's offer to fix the toilet, or re-cement the poles, or sand and paint the wall in lieu of the cash she demands. The nurse's resistance to bartering with Estrella thus signals her inability to "read" the family, to discern their concrete and particular needs, desires, and capabilities in order to work out an acceptable and fair exchange. Because she cannot or will not see the family's predicament from something even approximating their own perspective, she is unable to conceive the existence of a relation to them outside one of abstracted commodity exchange. Her socially produced blindness thus prevents her from recognizing the potential value to herself of the family's labor — either in their capacity as producers of her food or as potential parties to a fair exchange of value. Like the Bermuda man before her, the clinic nurse remains in a relation of exploitation, rather than of equality, to Estrella and her family.

Estrella's response to the nurse's refusal to hear her is to give up on words and resort to action. First, however, she engages in an act of "reading" that allows her to better understand her situation. Once the nurse declines any responsibility for Alejo's situation, the full weight of his predicament falls on Estrella's shoulders — primarily because she is the only one willing or able to accept it. Standing in the clinic, dismissed by the nurse, the thirteen-year-old Estrella looks around the room and deliberates on what appears to be an impossible situation.

25. The Mexican feminist Rosario Castellanos writes of the necessary relationship between mutual recognition and the act of "speaking with": "The meaning of a word is its addressee: the other being who hears it, understands it, and who, when he answers, converts his questioner into a listener and understander, establishing in this way the relationship that is only possible between beings who consider themselves and deal with each other as equals. And that is only fruitful between those who wish each other to be free" ("Language as an Instrument of Domination" 253). Black feminist bell hooks suggests that black women have had to struggle to be listened to. In her experience, black women have always spoken, but their speech was frequently understood as the type of speech that could be disregarded. "Dialogue," hooks tells us, "is the sharing of speech and recognition" (*Talking Back* 6). It takes place, in other words, between those who recognize and acknowledge each other as equals.

Estrella thought for a moment as the heat condensed into sweat which trickled between her breasts in the trailer room when the nurse clicked off the fan. She tried to make her mind work, tried to imagine them back on the road with an empty gas tank and wallet and Alejo too sick to talk. She stared at Perfecto's tired face. The wrinkles on his face etched deeper with the sweat and soil and jagged sun. Was this the same panic the mother went through? There was no bartering this time. If only the nurse would consent. Estrella knew she couldn't get him home, but the hospital was only twenty miles. A simple nod, a break. If only God could help.

Estrella stared at her mother's resentfulness, at whom, what, she didn't know. They were not asking for charity, not begging for money. She stared at Alejo's forehead. All that was left of his fall was a darkened scar. They would all work, including the boys if they had to, to pay for the visit, to pay for gas. Alejo was sick and the nine dollars was gas money. (147–48)

It is at this point that Estrella begins to transcend her individual perspective and transform her understanding of her place in the world. As she looks around the room, Estrella imaginatively projects herself into the lives of the others in the room. She stares at Perfecto's tired face, sees his desire for escape, and intuits her mother's panic at the threat of another abandonment. She stares at her mother's resentfulness and feels the injustice of being charged for the privilege of being told what they already knew. She looks at Alejo, remembers his earlier lesson about the tar oil, and extracts from it the principle of permutation in order to understand by analogy the dynamics of her family's disadvantaged economic situation.

She remembered the tar pits. Energy money, the fossilized bones of energy matter. How bones made oil and oil made gasoline. The oil was made from their bones, and it was their bones that kept the nurse's car from not halting on some highway, kept her on her way to Daisyfield to pick up her boys at six. It was their bones that kept the air conditioning in the cars humming, that kept them moving on the long dotted line on the map. Their bones. Why couldn't the nurse see that? Estrella had figured it out: the nurse owed *them* as much as they owed her. (148)

By looking around at the people in the room and imagining what they are thinking and how they are feeling, Estrella engages in a process of empathetic identification. By imaginatively projecting herself into the thoughts and feelings of the people she lives among, she does what the nurse could not and transcends her own particular perspective. She merges and incorporates the others' diverse perspectives into her analysis (or "reading") of the situation and experiences a transformation of consciousness that provides her with a more objective understanding than she previously had of her own and her family's situation of exploitation.

Estrella's materialist analysis of the situation prompts her realization that her family's socially necessary labor has been systematically undercompensated. She looks at the nurse and realizes that her own family and people like them provide the unacknowledged and undercompensated human labor that allows the nurse to live her relatively privileged life. After coming to this realization, Estrella makes one last effort to barter with the nurse. She gives the nurse one more chance to interact with the family in a non-exploitative way. But the nurse once again refuses empathetic identification with Estrella and her family: "this time, the nurse didn't even look up as she filed the folder away" (148).

Estrella's activity of synthesizing the various perspectives of the people she lives among in this climactic scene powerfully evokes the last chapter of Tomás Rivera's remarkable novel . . . *y no se lo tragó la tierra*. In that chapter, Rivera brings together all the different voices that have animated his novel, juxtaposing and then filtering them through the consciousness of the young boy who serves as the "chronotopic point . . . around which the collective subjective experiences of [his] Texas-Mexican farmworkers coalesce" (R. Saldívar 75). Although at the beginning of the novel the young boy inhabits a state of existential confusion, by the end he succeeds in ordering the events of his life and synthesizing the perspectives of the others with whom he lives into a more or less coherent and intelligible whole. The young boy's quest for understanding is rewarded, and he has not only regained the year he thought he had lost, but he has also acquired a sense of his own agency.

> Se dio cuenta de que en realidad no había perdido nada. Había encontrado. Encontrar y reencontrar y juntar. Relacionar esto con esto, eso con aquello, todo con todo. Eso era. Eso era todo. Y le dio más gusto. Luego cuando llegó a la casa se fue al árbol que estaba en el solar. Se subió. En el horizonte encontró una palma y se imaginó que ahí estaba alguien trepado viéndolo a él. Y hasta levantó el brazo y lo movió para atrás y para adelante para que viera que él sabía que estaba allí. (75)

> (He realized that in reality he hadn't lost anything. He had made a discovery. To discover and rediscover and piece things together. This to this, that to that, all with all. That was it. That was everything. He was thrilled. When he got home he went straight to the tree that was in the yard. He climbed it. He saw a palm tree on the horizon. He imagined someone perched on top, gazing across at him. He even raised one arm and waved it back and forth so that the other could see that he knew he was there.)[26] (152, emphasis added)

26. The English translation, by Evangelina Vigil-Piñon, appears in the bilingual version of the novel.

Although Rivera's novel differs from Viramontes's in a number of significant ways — for example, in its insistence on the necessity of temporarily
withdrawing from the world in order to gain a perspective on it
("Apenas estando uno solo puede juntar a todos. Yo creo que es lo que
necesitaba más que todo. Necesitaba esconderme para poder compren-
der muchas cosas" [75])[27] — it is similar to Viramontes's novel in some
other very important ways. Both novels focalize the social world from
the perspectives of Mexican-origin farmworkers. Both novels center
around a young person who models the process of coming to a more adequate understanding of the world he or she lives in. Both juxtapose, in
achronological narratives, a variety of farmworkers' subjective experiences that a careful reader must order and synthesize before they can be
understood as an intelligible whole. And finally, both posit the activity of
interpretation as a necessary precondition to effective agency.[28] Rivera's
novel, however, ends just as the young boy comes to his understanding.
His wave is the physical act that symbolizes his newfound will and prefigures what might be a more revolutionary act in the as-yet-unfulfilled
future.[29] Viramontes's novel, by contrast, carries us past Estrella's
moment of understanding to a moment of physical, even violent, resistance to economic exploitation.

Estrella's response to the nurse's refusal to empathize with the family's
predicament is remarkable both for how uncharacteristic it is of her and
for how decisive it is. In an epiphany-like moment, Estrella gives up on
God, turns and walks out of the clinic, returns to the car, grabs Perfecto's
crowbar, and walks back into the clinic, where she demands that the
nurse give them back their money. It is crucial to note that although
Estrella is driven to desperation, hers is a deliberative, not desperate, act.
When she demands the money, when she slams the crowbar down on the
desk, shattering the pictures of the nurse's children and sending pencils

27. "Only by being alone can you bring everybody together. That's what I needed to do,
hide, so that I could come to understand a lot of things" (151).

28. Both also powerfully contest a Catholic worldview, although I have chosen not to
dwell on the religious aspects of Viramontes's novel in this chapter. I plan to address this
issue in a separate article tentatively titled "'Standing on the Verge of Faith': Religious
Imagery and Secular Humanism in the Fiction of Helena María Viramontes." That essay
will look at the way in which Viramontes's fiction employs religious imagery to undermine
conventional Catholic religious beliefs and to construct a secular humanist faith that runs
counter to postmodernist skepticism. For essays that treat Rivera's rejection of religious idealism, see R. Saldívar, *Chicano Narrative,* esp. 77–84; J. D. Saldívar, *Dialectics of Our
America,* esp. 60–61.

29. For Rivera's own statement on the connection between interpretation and agency in
his novel, see his essay "Remembering, Discovery, Volition."

flying to the floor, Estrella remains in control of her faculties (149). The extremity of her family's situation has brought into focus for Estrella the contradictions of their existence and has allowed her to see beyond these contradictions to the deeper causal forces that sustain an exploitative socioeconomic system. She has transformed her understanding of her relation to such people as the nurse who are situated differently within that shared socioeconomic system and has come to understand something important about the exploitation to which her family been subjected. As a result, she begins to exist in a different relation to that system than she has in the past. She has transformed her thinking dialectically and, in the process, begins to become a different person: "She did not feel like herself holding the money. She felt like two Estrellas. One was a silent phantom who obediently marked a circle with a stick around the bungalow as the mother had requested, while the other held the crowbar and the money. The money felt wet and ugly and sweaty like the swamp between her legs" (150). Note that the entire experience for Estrella is figured in explicitly embodied, relational, and gendered terms: she feels the sweat trickle between her breasts as she tries to think; she imagines herself doing something for her mother; she holds in one hand Perfecto's crowbar (the primary symbol of literacy and agency in this novel); and she holds in the other hand the money, that symbol of abstracted commodity exchange that feels as "wet and ugly and sweaty" as the swamp between her legs.

Estrella's ability to abstract from her own situation some general principles about the socioeconomic system she lives in is premised on her increased ability to interpret correctly, or "read," her world. Importantly, that ability has been accrued both through physical labor in the fields and in the home and through embodied and empathetic identification with others around her. The knowledge that she gains as a result of her ability to "read" her world is thus historically and materially situated and fundamentally social. The notion of expanded literacy Viramontes develops in *Under the Feet of Jesus* thus helps to reveal both the social and material bases of individually arrived-at knowledge.

As before, Viramontes stages this scene in a way that encourages the reader to identify with Estrella and her family. The nurse functions as a symbolic figure whose epistemic and moral blindness — her see, hear, and know no evil attitude — is put on display for the reader as a cautionary tale. Moreover, because Viramontes does not allow the nurse to focalize the narrative, the reader is discouraged from identifying with the nurse; she remains a one-dimensional yet all-too-real character. It is in part by guiding her readers' processes of identification through the narrative technique of focalization that Viramontes powerfully contests the outsider status typically accorded to migrant farmworkers. By encouraging her readers to enter into a relationship of empathetic identification with Estrella and her family and by exposing them to the moral and epistemic blindness of those Americans who would view migrant farmworkers as outsiders to American society, Viramontes implicitly invites her readers to transcend their own particular perspectives, to complicate their own previous understandings of the world, and to reach for a less partial, more objective understanding of the exploitative economic system in which we all participate. In this relatively unobtrusive way, Viramontes guides our interpretations of her novel and creates the narrative conditions meant to reproduce in the reader the transformation of consciousness Estrella undergoes.

"SHINY AS NEW LOVE": THE POWER AND LIMITS OF INDIVIDUAL TRANSFORMATION

Although the long-term consequences of Estrella's action are never revealed in the novel, her actions benefit Alejo and the family in the short term. Estrella recovers their money, and the family successfully transports Alejo to the hospital in Corazón. Along the way, however, Estrella has a conversation with Alejo that illustrates why identity must be considered in any account of the production of knowledge. Only by paying careful attention to the epistemic effects of identity can we theorize the *individual* nature of socially based knowledge.

On the way to the hospital in Corazón, Alejo, who appears moments away from death, wants to know whether Estrella has physically harmed the nurse. At first, Estrella tries to turn his concern toward a consideration of why the nurse had refused to identify with his predicament. But Alejo is persistent, and his questions eventually provoke Estrella's anger.

> —Did you hurt her?
> —Sweet Jesus, what do you think? Her anger flared. Does it matter now?
> —For what? he whispered.
> —For what? Estrella asked. For what? For nine dollars and seven cents! Alejo did not understand her sarcasm. He seemed not to understand anything.
> —Don't make it so easy for them. The fevers had drained him. He couldn't keep warm enough, and he trembled. Estrella continued to wipe his forehead with the handkerchief, but he grabbed her hand slightly and held it. His eyes welled and became glassy. I'm not worth it Star. Not me.

— What a thing to say, she replied, forcing her hand away from between his cold fingers. (151–52)

The novel juxtaposes Estrella's disappointment with Alejo's lack of understanding with her sudden recollection of the discouragement she once felt at seeing a thing of beauty too easily destroyed. Immediately after pulling her hand from his, she remembers having once been struck by the unexpected brilliance of an incandescent mosaic of red, green, and yellow bell peppers built in the shape of a pyramid in a ranch store that she had visited with her mother. But she also remembers that before she was able bring it to Petra's attention, a woman walked into the store and "toppled the peak by removing the top single red one, shiny as new love" (152–53). The ease with which a thing of beauty can be destroyed or, in this case, an epistemic gain can be refused is then metaphorically tied to the ease with which one can "kick a can on the road" (153). Thus, although Estrella still very much cares for Alejo, her disappointment with his lack of understanding is palpable.

— That's a stupid thing to say, Estrella replied, not able to disguise the tone of disappointment. She forgave him because he was sick. *You* don't make it so easy for *them*. (153)

Alejo's lack of understanding and his condemnation of Estrella's actions make evident the *individual* nature of Estrella's socially constituted knowledge. Although Estrella drew on Alejo's teaching and on the teachings of her mother and Perfecto in the course of her reflections, her "reading" of the situation — which includes as one of its elements a more objective understanding of the socioeconomic system they all live in — remains within the bounds of her own interpretive consciousness. The reasons why Estrella is the only one who comes to this better understanding are complex, and are related to the fact that each character exists in a slightly different social location — each of which brings with it differing concerns and interests. As a mother, Petra is most concerned with the day-to-day upkeep and well-being of her family, while Perfecto, as an elderly person, is most interested in finding respite from the hard work and responsibility that he no longer feels able to shoulder. They both correctly perceive that Estrella's violent actions have the potential to disrupt, at least temporarily, their abilities to fulfill these interests. While we might want Perfecto and Petra to acknowledge what Estrella has come to understand and to set aside their own particular concerns in the larger interest of taking political action designed to change the system that exploits them, we can do so only if we ignore the very material dimension of their encumbered human selves. We must remember that, of the three, Estrella is the only one who is young, healthy, and relatively unencumbered. She bears no parental responsibility for the emotionally and physically needy children with whom she lives. In addition, she is young and quite strong. It is far easier for her than it is for Perfecto to imagine that she has a future and that the quality of that future might be something to be concerned about, something worth fighting for. As hard-working as he is, Perfecto is looking primarily for a respite; he wants only to go home and rest a little before meeting what he senses is his imminent death.

Alejo, meanwhile, is still caught within the bourgeois sensibility that prompted him to steal peaches in order to set himself and his cousin up as independent entrepreneurs. Even on the brink of death, Alejo still believes in the American dream. He still believes that if he works hard, studies diligently, and follows the rules of those in power, he can "seize the chance and make something of [himself] in this great and true country" (54). For Alejo, cheating within the system (i.e., stealing the peaches) is permissible for getting ahead, but resisting with violence the rules created by those who benefit from that exploitative economic order ("Can't you see they want us to act like that?") is not. While Estrella has come to understand that there is more than one way to kill or do violence to someone ("Can't you see they want to take your heart?"), Alejo holds fast to a set of values that considers armed resistance to the capitalist economic system as the only real "criminal" behavior (153).

Alejo's inability to comprehend the rationale behind Estrella's action reminds us how difficult it is for individuals to transcend the cherished social ideologies by which they organize their lives. Alejo's sense of self and his understanding of his place in the world have been intimately formed through at least two very powerful social ideologies. The first, as noted above, is that of the American Dream, with its promise of equal opportunity for all regardless of circumstances of birth. The second is Mexican Catholicism, with its heavy emphasis on sin and retribution. Because Alejo believes that his poisoning represents divine retribution for his thievery, he is at some level prepared to play the part of the martyr who sacrifices his life ("I'm not worth it Star. Not me.").[30] For Alejo to

---

30. The association of Alejo with Christ is made firmer by the fact that Alejo is literally "crucified" by the shadow of the plane that sprays the pesticide: "Alejo had not guessed the biplane was so close until its gray shadow crossed over him like a crucifix" (76).

accept what Estrella has done as legitimate would require a reorientation of the way he sees the world. He would have to see himself as standing in a different relation both to the U.S. socioeconomic system and to God than he currently does. Such an achievement would require a profound transformation of Alejo's identity. It would require him to consider and accept an alternative explanation for the meanings behind his recent experiences. But to ask Alejo to transform his identity as he lays dying might be to ask too much. And it is precisely because Estrella under-stands this that she is able to forgive him.

The fictional situation Viramontes presents here illustrates the theo-retical point Susan Babbitt makes in her claim for the epistemic signifi-cance of non-propositional knowledge.

> In many cases supplying people with information that would be useful to them in individual deliberations is not a matter of providing increased access to propositional truths; instead, it is a matter of the bringing about of dif-ferent, more appropriate, social and political situations. . . . [I]n order for some situations to be understood, it is not just new concepts that need to be introduced but new relations, and new relations sometimes constitute epis-temic standards according to which concepts can be more properly evaluat-ed and applied. ("Feminism and Objective Interests" 257)

Estrella understands that she cannot simply tell Alejo what she has learned (that is, she cannot simply provide him access to her proposi-tional truths) because she knows that he will not understand what she is saying; the conceptual framework he would need to accept her actions as justified is too much at odds with his bourgeois sensibility and his Mexican Catholic morality. Moreover, she realizes that she is in no posi-tion to bring about the conditions that would enable him to understand why she behaved the way she did. This is why, despite the disappoint-ment she feels, she is able to forgive him.

However empowering Estrella's decisive action during the climax of the novel might appear, the novel refuses an unambiguously happy end-ing. We never find out, for instance, whether Perfecto will stay with the family, whether Alejo will survive the poisoning, or whether Estrella will escape the legal charges that might result as a consequence of her actions at the clinic. Nor are we assured that the rest of Estrella's family will ever fully understand the rationale behind Estrella's actions. Because of this, we cannot assume that they will join together with her and other farm-workers and activists to form a collective that will resist, with violence or through strikes, the economic exploitation they face. Indeed, this novel — written during the late 1980s and early 1990s and published in 1995, well after the fragmentation of the new social movements in this country and the crumbling of the communist economies of the Eastern bloc — does not opt for a utopian depiction of a mass uprising by farmworkers intent on destroying their capitalist oppressors.

What the novel does offer is a hopeful, if tentative, conclusion regarding Estrella's enhanced ability to transform the conditions of her own life. But like the effervescent beauty of the "top red single [bell pepper], shiny as new love," carelessly toppled by the woman in the ranch store, the epistemic gains that attend individual growth are tenuous at best. As long as an insight remains confined to an individual consciousness, it will be as easy for others to refuse as it is to "kick a can in the road." In other words, what Estrella has come to understand about the socioeconomic system she lives in will not become knowledge in the true sense of the word until she successfully shares it with others — that is, when it becomes a social, and not simply an individual, understanding.

The novel thus implicitly warns the activist or academic interested in theorizing possibilities for social change that she cannot ignore the epistemic consequences of identity. Not all farmworkers can be expected to think the same way. The activist interested in building an effective long-term coalition must do more than simply provide accurate information about the injustices people face. Indeed, she must also work to foster the conditions that will enable people to recognize and understand the larger social and economic forces that constrain and enable the choices they can make. Rather than bemoaning the fact that all people do not think alike, or that different people will need different circumstances in order to transform their thinking about the world, the real lesson of this novel might be that enacting social change is a complex and multifaceted process that will involve, among other things, a great deal of what feminists have long called "consciousness-raising."

I end this book with a reading of Helena María Viramontes's novel *Under the Feet of Jesus* in part because it so effectively demonstrates both the individual and social character of knowledge. It stresses the social constitution of knowledge even as it recognizes that knowledge manifests in and through the interpretive consciousness of individual people. It thus theorizes an epistemological position that is neither objectivist (true knowledge is unmediated by interests or ideology) nor subjectivist (knowledge is a reflection of power and bias). It refuses both the vulgarly marxist position that those who do not understand the nature of reality are simply mystified and in need of enlightenment and the skeptically postmodernist position that holds that reality is an effect, but never a ground, of discursive formations. Rather, the novel dramatizes what I have described elsewhere in this book as a postpositivist realist approach to understanding and knowledge. By juxtaposing differing perspectives on the same social world, it suggests that individuals can have better and worse understandings of that world and that their understandings are unavoidably mediated through their identities. Through its emphasis on Estrella's ability to learn about her world both by engaging in physical labor and by interrogating social situations, this novel underscores the causal influence the world has on what humans know. Finally, by dramatizing Estrella's transformation of consciousness, it posits an adequate understanding of the social world as a necessary precursor to effective social action. It thus illustrates the link I have been drawing throughout this book between the epistemic status of identity, the interpretation of experience, and the conditions of possibility for effective human agency.

Bibliography

Acuña, Rodolfo. *Occupied America: A History of Chicanos.* 3rd ed. New York: HarperCollins, 1988.

Adams, David Wallace. "Fundamental Considerations: The Deep Meaning of Native American Schooling, 1880–1900." *Harvard Educational Review* 58.1 (1988): 1–28.

Adams, Natalie G. "What Does It Mean? Exploring the Myths of Multicultural Education." *Urban Education* 30.1 (1995): 27–39.

Alarcón, Norma. "Chicana Feminism: In the Tracks of 'the' Native Woman." *Cultural Studies* 4.3 (1990): 248–56.

———. "Chicana's Feminist Literature: A Re-vision through Malintzin/or Malintzin: Putting Flesh Back on the Object." In *This Bridge Called My Back: Writings by Radical Women of Color,* 2d ed., ed. Cherríe Moraga and Gloria Anzaldúa, 182–90. New York: Kitchen Table Women of Color Press, 1983.

———. "Conjugating Subjects: The Heteroglossia of Essence and Resistance." In *An Other Tongue: Nation and Ethnicity in the Linguistic Borderlands,* ed. Alfred Arteaga, 125–38. Durham: Duke University Press, 1994.

———. "La Prieta." In *This Bridge Called My Back,* ed. Cherríe Moraga and Gloria Alzaldna, 198–209.

———. "Interview with Cherríe Moraga." *Third Woman* 3.1–2 (1986): 127–34.

———. "Making 'Familia' from Scratch: Split Subjectivities in the Work of Helena María Viramontes and Cherríe Moraga." In *Chicana Creativity and Criticism: Charting New Frontiers in American Literature,* ed. María Herrera-Sobek and Helena María Viramontes, 147–59. Houston: Arte Público Press, 1988.

———. "The Theoretical Subject(s) of *This Bridge Called My Back* and Anglo-American Feminism." In *Criticism in the Borderlands: Studies in Chicano Lit-*

erature, Culture, and Ideology, ed. Héctor Calderón and José David Saldívar, 28–39. Durham: Duke University Press, 1991.

———. "Traddutora, traditora: A Paradigmatic Figure of Chicana Feminism." *Cultural Critique* 13 (Fall 1989): 57–87.

———. "Tropology of Hunger: The 'Miseducation' of Richard Rodriguez." In *The Ethnic Canon: Histories, Institutions, and Interventions,* ed. David Palumbo-Liu, 140–52. Minneapolis: University of Minnesota Press, 1995.

Alcoff, Linda [Martín]. "Cultural Feminism versus Post-structuralism: The Identity Crisis in Feminist Theory." *Signs* 13.3 (1988): 405–36.

———. "The Elimination of Experience in Feminist Theory." Paper presented at Women's Studies Symposium, Cornell University, 23 February 1995.

———. "The Politics of Postmodern Feminism, Revisited." *Cultural Critique* 36 (Spring 1997): 5–27.

———. *Real Knowing.* Ithaca: Cornell University Press, 1996.

———. "Who's Afraid of Identity Politics?" In *Reclaiming Identity: Realist Theory and the Predicament of Postmodernism,* ed. Paula M. L. Moya and Michael R. Hames-García, 312–44. Berkeley: University of California Press, 2000.

Alcoff, Linda, and Elizabeth Potter, eds. *Feminist Epistemologies.* New York: Routledge, 1993.

Alexander, M. Jacqui, and Chandra Talpade Mohanty. "Introduction: Genealogies, Legacies, Movements." In *Feminist Genealogies, Colonial Legacies, Democratic Futures,* xiii–xlii. New York: Routledge, 1997.

Anderson, Perry. *The Origins of Postmodernity.* New York: Verso, 1998.

Anzaldúa, Gloria. *Borderlands/La Frontera: The New Mestiza.* San Francisco: Spinsters/Aunt Lute Books, 1987.

———, ed. *Making Face, Making Soul/Haciendo Caras: Creative and Critical Perspectives by Women of Color.* San Francisco: Aunt Lute Books, 1990.

Appiah, K. Anthony. "Race, Culture, Identity: Misunderstood Connections." In *Color Conscious: The Political Morality of Race,* ed. K. Anthony Appiah and Amy Gutmann, 30–105. Princeton: Princeton University Press, 1996.

Apple, Michael W. *Ideology and Curriculum.* 2d ed. New York: Routledge, 1990.

Arteaga, Alfred, ed. *An Other Tongue: Nation and Ethnicity in the Linguistic Borderlands.* Durham: Duke University Press, 1994.

Babbitt, Susan E. "Feminism and Objective Interests: The Role of Transformation Experiences in Rational Deliberation." In *Feminist Epistemologies,* ed. Linda Alcoff and Elizabeth Potter, 245–64. New York: Routledge, 1993.

———. "Identity, Knowledge, and Toni Morrison's *Beloved:* Questions about Understanding Racism." *Hypatia* 9.3 (1994): 1–18.

Bal, Mieke. *Narratology: Introduction to the Theory of Narrative.* Trans. Christine van Boheemen. Toronto: University of Toronto Press, 1985.

Banks, James A. "Integrating the Curriculum with Ethnic Content: Approaches and Guidelines." In *Multicultural Education: Issues and Perspectives,* ed. James A. Banks and Cherry A. McGee Banks, 189–207. Boston: Allyn and Bacon, 1989.

Barad, Karen. "Meeting the Universe Halfway: Realism and Social Construction without Contradiction." In *Feminism, Science, and the Philosophy of Science,* ed. Lynn Hankinson Nelson and Jack Nelson, 161–94. Dordrecht: Kluwer, 1996.

Baye, Betty Winston. "Jim Crow Redux." *Louisville Courier-Journal,* 9 April 1998, metro ed., sec. forum: 11A.

Benhabib, Seyla. *Situating the Self: Gender, Community, and Postmodernism in Contemporary Ethics.* New York: Routledge, 1992.

Benhabib, Seyla, Judith Butler, Drucilla Cornell, and Nancy Fraser. *Feminist Contentions: A Philosophical Exchange.* New York: Routledge, 1995.

Bennett, William J. *Our Children and Our Country: Improving America's Schools and Affirming the Common Culture.* New York: Simon and Schuster, 1988.

———. "To Reclaim a Legacy: Report on the Humanities in Higher Education." Washington, D.C.: National Endowment for the Humanities, 1984.

Best, Steven, and Douglas Kellner, eds. *The Postmodern Turn.* New York: Guilford Press, 1997.

Bloom, Allan D. *The Closing of the American Mind.* New York: Simon and Schuster, 1987.

Boyd, Dwight. "Dominance Concealed through Diversity: Implications of Inadequate Perspectives on Cultural Pluralism." *Harvard Educational Review* 66.3 (1996): 609–30.

Boyd, Richard N. "How to Be a Moral Realist." In *Essays on Moral Realism,* ed. Geoffrey Sayre-McCord, 181–228. Ithaca: Cornell University Press, 1988.

———. "Metaphor and Theory Change: What Is a 'Metaphor' a Metaphor for?" In *Metaphor and Thought,* 2d ed., ed. Andrew Ortony, 481–532. Cambridge: Cambridge University Press, 1993.

Bulkin, Elly, Minnie Bruce Pratt, and Barbara Smith. *Yours in Struggle: Three Feminist Perspectives on Anti-Semitism and Racism.* Brooklyn, N.Y.: Long Haul Press, 1984.

Burdman, Pamela. "Sigh of Relief at UC over Minority Enrollment." *San Francisco Chronicle,* 21 May 1998, final ed.: A21.

Butler, Judith. *Bodies That Matter: On the Discursive Limits of "Sex."* New York: Routledge, 1993.

———. "Contingent Foundations: Feminism and the Question of 'Postmodernism.'" In *Feminists Theorize the Political,* ed. Judith Butler and Joan Scott, 3–21. New York: Routledge, 1992.

———. "For a Careful Reading." In *Feminist Contentions: A Philosophical Exchange,* by Seyla Benhabib, Judith Butler, Drucilla Cornell, and Nancy Fraser, 127–43. New York: Routledge, 1995.

———. *Gender Trouble: Feminism and the Subversion of Identity.* New York: Routledge, 1990.

———. *The Psychic Life of Power: Theories in Subjection.* Stanford: Stanford University Press, 1997.

Butler, Judith, and Joan Scott, eds. *Feminists Theorize the Political.* New York: Routledge, 1992.

Calderón, Héctor, and José David Saldívar, eds. *Criticism in the Borderlands:*

Studies in Chicano Literature, Culture, and Ideology. Durham: Duke University Press, 1991.

Calhoun, Craig. *Critical Social Theory: Culture, History, and the Challenge of Difference.* Cambridge, Mass.: Blackwell, 1995.

California Ballot Propositions Database. 1999. UC Hastings College of the Law. 4 April 2000: http://holmes.uchastings.edu:80/cgi-bin/starfinder/16935/calprop.txt.

Camia, Catalina. "House Rejects Move to Extend Affirmative Action Ban; Losing Side Vows to Continue Fight." *Dallas Morning News,* 7 May 1998, home final ed.: 12A.

Candelaria, Cordelia. "La Malinche, Feminist Prototype." *Frontiers: A Journal of Women Studies* 5.2 (1980): 1–6.

Cantor, George. "Grades-Only Plan Poses Problems for Universities." *Detroit News,* 8 March 1998: B4.

Carr, Raymond. *Puerto Rico: A Colonial Experiment.* New York: New York University Press, 1984.

Carter, Stephen. *Reflections of an Affirmative Action Baby.* New York: Basic Books, 1991.

Castellanos, Rosario. "Language as an Instrument of Domination." Trans. Maureen Ahern. In *A Rosario Castellanos Reader,* ed. Maureen Ahern, 250–53. Austin: University of Texas Press, 1988.

———. "Rosario Castellanos habla de Rosario Castellanos." (Suplemento Cultural) *Mujeres* (May 1969): 20–22. As cited in Thomas Washington, "The Narrative Works of Rosario Castellanos: In Search of History — Confrontations with Myth." Ph.D. diss., University of Minnesota, 1982.

Castillo, Debra A. *Talking Back: Toward a Latin American Feminist Literary Criticism.* Ithaca: Cornell University Press, 1992.

Cervantes, Lorna Dee. "You Cramp My Style, Baby." *El Fuego* 1.4 (1977): 38.

Chambers, Veronica. "Exploring Her World: Falling under the Spell of a Friend Named Estrella." Review of *Under the Feet of Jesus,* by Helena María Viramontes. *Los Angeles Times Book Review,* 17 September 1995, home ed.: 12.

Chao, Julie. "Ethnic Studies Spark Debate in California; Academics Howl as Regent Works to End Race-Based Programs." *San Francisco Examiner,* 21 June 1998, international ed., sec. B: 8A.

Chávez, John R. *The Lost Land: The Chicano Image of the Southwest.* Albuquerque: University of New Mexico Press, 1984.

Chávez, Linda. *Out of the Barrio: Toward a New Politics of Hispanic Assimilation.* New York: Basic Books, 1991.

Christian, Barbara. "The Race for Theory." *Cultural Critique* 6 (Spring 1987): 51–63. Rpt. in *Making Face, Making Soul/Haciendo Caras: Creative and Critical Perspectives by Women of Color,* ed. Gloria Anzaldúa, 335–45. San Francisco: Aunt Lute Books, 1990.

Cisneros, Sandra. *Loose Woman.* New York: Alfred A. Knopf, 1994.

———. *My Wicked Wicked Ways.* New York: Turtle Bay Books, 1992.

———. *Woman Hollering Creek and Other Stories.* New York: Random House, 1991.

Collier, Andrew. *Critical Realism: An Introduction to Roy Bhaskar's Philosophy*. New York: Verso, 1994.

Córdova, Teresa. "Roots and Resistance: The Emergent Writings of Twenty Years of Chicana Feminist Struggle." *Handbook of Hispanic Cultures in the United States: Sociology*, ed. Félix Padilla, 175–202. Houston: Arte Público Press and Instituto de Cooperación Iberoamericana, 1994.

Cotera, Marta. "Feminism: The Chicano and Anglo Version — A Historical Analysis." In *Chicana Feminist Thought: The Basic Historical Writings*, ed. Alma García, 223–31. New York: Routledge, 1997.

Davidson, Donald. "On the Very Idea of a Conceptual Scheme." In *Inquiries into Truth and Interpretation*, 183–98. Oxford: Clarendon Press, 1984.

———. "The Structure and Content of Truth." *Journal of Philosophy* 6 (1990): 279–328.

———. "Thought and Talk." In *Inquiries into Truth and Interpretation*, 155–70. Oxford: Clarendon Press, 1984.

Davis, Angela. "Reaping Fruit and Throwing Seed: Women of Color and Community-Building Practices." Paper presented at the Third Annual Undergraduate Women's Conference, State University of New York, Oneonta, 20 April 1996.

de Cardenas, Diana. "New UCLA Admissions Data Show 40 Percent of All Admitted Freshman to Enroll This Fall." *UC News Wire*. 3 April 2000. University of California. 23 August 2000: http://www.ucnewswire.org/articles/2000/apr/ucla%20admissions%20data%20show.htm.

———. "New UCLA Admissions Data Show Slight Increase in the Number of Underrepresented Students Admitted for Fall 2000." *UC News Wire*. 3 April 2000. University of California. 23 August 2000: http://www.ucnewswire.org/articles/2000/june/ucla%20admissions%20data%20show.htm.

del Castillo, Adelaida R. "Malintzin Tenepal: A Preliminary Look into a New Perspective." In *Essays on La Mujer*, ed. Rosaura Sánchez and Rosa Martinez Cruz, 124–49. Los Angeles: Chicano Studies Publications, UCLA, 1977.

Delpit, Lisa D. "The Silenced Dialogue: Power and Pedagogy in Educating Other People's Children." *Harvard Educational Review* 58.3 (1988): 280–98.

D'Emilio, John, and Estelle B. Freedman. *Intimate Matters: A History of Sexuality in America*. 2d ed. Chicago: University of Chicago Press, 1997.

Deutsch, Sarah. *No Separate Refuge: Culture, Class, and Gender on an Anglo-Hispanic Frontier in the American Southwest, 1880–1940*. New York: Oxford University Press, 1987.

Devitt, Michael, and Kim Sterelny. *Language and Reality: An Introduction to the Philosophy of Language*. 2d ed. Cambridge: MIT Press, 1999.

Díaz del Castillo, Bernal. *The Conquest of New Spain*. Trans. J. M. Cohen. Aylesbury, England: Penguin, 1963.

Dietz, James L. *Economic History of Puerto Rico: Institutional Change and Capitalist Development*. Princeton: Princeton University Press, 1986.

Dircks, Phyllis T. "Steinbeck's Statement on the Inner Chapters of *The Grapes of Wrath*." *Steinbeck Quarterly* 24.3–4 (1991): 87–94.

Eagleton, Terry. *The Illusions of Postmodernism*. London: Blackwell, 1996.

Emory, Doug. "Point of View and Narrative Voice in *The Grapes of Wrath*:

Steinbeck and Ford." In *Narrative Strategies: Original Essays in Film and Prose Fiction,* ed. Syndy M. Conger and Janice R. Welsch, 129–35. Macomb: Western Illinois University Press, 1980.

Epstein, Gady A. "Accountant Fires Opening Shots in Bid to Halt Affirmative Action." *Tampa Tribune,* 17 March 1998, final ed., sec. nation/world: 1.

Espada, Martín. "Zapata's Disciple and Perfect Brie." In *Zapata's Disciple: Essays,* 3–12. Cambridge: South End Press, 1998.

Faulkner, William. *The Sound and the Fury.* New York: Vintage, 1946.

Felski, Rita. "The Doxa of Difference." *Signs* 23.1 (1997): 1–21.

Field, Hartry. "Theory Change and the Indeterminacy of Reference." *Journal of Philosophy* 70 (16 August 1973): 462–81.

Flores, Juan. *Divided Borders: Essays on Puerto Rican Identity.* Houston: Arte Público Press, 1993.

———. " 'Qué assimilated, brother, yo soy asimilao': The Structuring of Puerto Rican Identity in the U.S." In *Divided Borders,* 182–95, 245. Houston: Arte Público Press, 1993.

Foner, Eric. "Who Is an American? The Imagined Community in American History." *The Centennial Review* 41.3 (1997): 425–38.

Foucault, Michel. *The Archaeology of Knowledge.* Trans. A. M. Sheridan Smith. New York: Pantheon Books, 1972.

———. "The Concern for Truth." Trans. Alan Sheridan. In *Politics, Philosophy, Culture: Interviews and Other Writings, 1977–1984,* ed. Lawrence D. Kritzman, 255–67. New York: Routledge, 1988.

———. "Truth and Power." Trans. Colin Gordon. In *Power/Knowledge: Selected Interviews and Other Writings, 1972–1977,* ed. Colin Gordon, 109–33. New York: Pantheon Books, 1980.

———. "Two Lectures." Trans. Kate Soper. In *Power/Knowledge: Selected Interviews and Other Writings, 1972–1977,* ed. Colin Gordon, 78–108. New York: Pantheon Books, 1980.

Fraser, Nancy. "Pragmatism, Feminism, and the Linguistic Turn." In *Feminist Contentions: A Philosophical Exchange,* by Seyla Benhabib, Judith Butler, Drucilla Cornell, and Nancy Fraser, 157–71. New York: Routledge, 1995.

Freire, Paulo. *Pedagogy of the Oppressed.* Trans. Myra Bergman Ramos. New York: Herder and Herder, 1970.

Fuss, Diana. *Essentially Speaking: Feminism, Nature, and Difference.* New York: Routledge, 1989.

Gándara, Patricia. *Over the Ivy Walls: The Educational Mobility of Low-Income Chicanos.* Albany: State University of New York Press, 1995.

García, Alma M. "The Development of Chicana Feminist Discourse, 1970–1980." *Gender and Society* 3.2 (1989): 217–38.

———, ed. *Chicana Feminist Thought: The Basic Historical Writings.* New York: Routledge, 1997.

Genette, Gérard. *Narrative Discourse: An Essay in Method.* Trans. Jane E. Lewin. Ithaca: Cornell University Press, 1980.

Gilligan, Carol. *In a Different Voice: Psychological Theory and Women's Development.* Cambridge: Harvard University Press, 1982.

Gilroy, Paul. *The Black Atlantic: Modernity and Double Consciousness.* Cambridge: Harvard University Press, 1993.

Gonzales, Sylvia. "La Chicana: Guadalupe or Malinche." In *Comparative Perspectives on Third World Women: The Impact of Race, Sex, and Class,* ed. Beverly Lindsay, 229–50. New York: Praeger, 1980.

Gonzalez, Marcial. "The Postmodern Turn in Chicana/o Cultural Studies: Toward a Dialectical Criticism." Ph.D. diss., Stanford University, 2000.

González, Nancie L. *The Spanish-Americans of New Mexico: A Heritage of Pride.* Albuquerque: University of New Mexico Press, 1967.

Gracia, Jorge J. E. *Hispanic/Latino Identity: A Philosophical Perspective.* Malden, Mass.: Blackwell, 2000.

Gutiérrez, Ramón A. "Community, Patriarchy and Individualism: The Politics of Chicano History and the Dream of Equality." *American Quarterly* 45.1 (1993): 44–72.

Gutiérrez, Ramón, and Genaro Padilla, eds. *Recovering the U.S. Hispanic Literary Heritage.* Vol. 1. Houston: Arte Público Press, 1993.

Gutiérrez-Jones, Carl. *Rethinking the Borderlands: Between Chicano Culture and Legal Discourse.* Berkeley: University of California Press, 1995.

Hames-García, Michael R. "Dr. Gonzo's Carnival: The Testimonial Satires of Oscar Zeta Acosta, Chicano Lawyer." *American Literature* 72.3 (2000): 463–93.

———. "Mestizos in Flux: (un)Closeting Race and Sexuality in Cherríe Moraga and Richard Rodriguez." In *Expanding Raza World Views: Sexuality and Regionalism: Selected Proceedings from the 22nd NACCS Conference,* ed. Adalijiza Sosa-Riddell, 26–38. National Association for Chicana and Chicano Studies, 1999.

———. "'Who are our own people?' Challenges for a Theory of Social Identity." In *Reclaiming Identity: Realist Theory and the Predicament of Postmodernism,* ed. Paula M. L. Moya and Michael R. Hames-García, 102–29. Berkeley: University of California Press, 2000.

Haraway, Donna. "A Manifesto for Cyborgs: Science, Technology, and Socialist Feminism in the 1980s." In *Feminism/Postmodernism,* ed. Linda J. Nicholson, 190–233. New York: Routledge, 1990.

Harding, Sandra. "Rethinking Standpoint Epistemology: 'What Is Strong Objectivity?' " In *Feminist Epistemologies,* ed. Linda Alcoff and Elizabeth Potter, 49–82. New York: Routledge, 1993.

———. *Whose Science? Whose Knowledge? Thinking from Women's Lives.* Ithaca: Cornell University Press, 1991.

Harris, Marvin. *Patterns of Race in the Americas.* New York: Norton, 1964.

Harvey, David. *The Condition of Postmodernity: An Enquiry into the Origins of Cultural Change.* New York: Blackwell, 1989.

Hau, Caroline S. "On Representing Others: Intellectuals, Pedagogy, and the Uses of Error." In *Reclaiming Identity: Realist Theory and the Predicament of Postmodernism,* ed. Paula M. L. Moya and Michael R. Hames-García, 133–70. Berkeley: University of California Press, 2000.

Hayward, Brad. "Drop in Blacks, Latinos Admitted to All of UC Less Than at

Cal, UCLA." *Sacramento Bee,* 3 April 1998, metro final ed., sec. main news: A4.

Hitchcock, Peter. "They Must Be Represented? Problems in Theories of Working-Class Representation." *PMLA* 115.1 (2000): 20–32.

Hogue, W. Lawrence. "An Unresolved Modern Experience: Richard Rodriguez's *Hunger of Memory.*" *The Americas Review* 20.1 (1992): 52–64.

Hollibaugh, Amber, and Cherríe Moraga. "What We're Rollin Around in Bed With: Sexual Silences in Feminism, a Conversation toward Ending Them." *Heresies* 12 (Spring 1981): 58–62.

Homans, Margaret. " 'Women of Color' Writers and Feminist Theory." *New Literary History* 25.1 (1994): 73–94.

hooks, bell. "Essentialism and Experience." *American Literary History* 3.1 (1991): 172–83.

———. *Talking Back: Thinking Feminist, Thinking Black.* Boston: South End Press, 1989.

Hoppe, Christy. "Early Figures Show Slight Increase in UT Minority Enrollment; Official Attributes Growth to New Admission Law." *Dallas Morning News,* 20 May 1998, home final ed.: 16A.

Howarth, William. "The Mother of Literature: Journalism and *The Grapes of Wrath.*" In *New Essays on "The Grapes of Wrath,"* ed. David Wyatt, 71–99. New York: Cambridge University Press, 1990.

"Initiative 200: Wrong Direction for this State." *Seattle Times,* 5 April 1998, Sunday final ed., sec. editorial: B6.

Jacob, Brian A. "Defining Culture in a Multicultural Environment: An Ethnography of Heritage High School." *American Journal of Education* 103.3 (1995): 339–76.

Jameson, Fredric. *Postmodernism, or, The Cultural Logic of Late Capitalism.* Durham: Duke University Press, 1991.

Jervis, Kathe. " 'How come there are no brothers on that list?': Hearing the Hard Questions All Children Ask." *Harvard Educational Review* 66.3 (1996): 546–76.

Kaestle, Carl F. "Ideology and American Educational History." *History of Education Quarterly* 22 (1982): 123–38.

———. *Pillars of the Republic: Common Schools and American Society, 1780–1860.* New York: Hill and Wang, 1983.

Katz, Michael B. *The Irony of Early School Reform: Educational Innovation in Mid-Nineteenth Century Massachusetts.* Boston: Beacon Press, 1970.

Kingston, Maxine Hong. *The Woman Warrior: Memoirs of a Girlhood among Ghosts.* New York: Vintage International, 1989.

Knupfer, Anne Meis. "Conflict Resolution or 'Convict Revolution'? The Problematics of Critical Pedagogy in the Classroom." *Urban Education* 30.2 (1995): 219–39.

Kymlicka, Will. *Liberalism, Community, and Culture.* New York: Oxford University Press, 1989.

———. *Multicultural Citizenship: A Liberal Theory of Minority Rights.* New York: Oxford University Press, 1995.

Laviera, Tato. "asimilao." In *AmeRícan.* Houston: Arte Público Press, 1985.

Lawless, Cecelia. "Helena María Viramontes' Homing Devices in *Under the Feet of Jesus.*" In *Homemaking: Women Writers and the Politics and Poetics of Home,* ed. Catherine Wiley and Fiona R. Barnes, 361–82. New York: Garland, 1996.

Lazarus, Neil. *Nationalism and Cultural Practice in the Postcolonial World.* Cambridge: Cambridge University Press, 1999.

Lempinen, Edward. "Connerly Calls for Review of UC Ethnic Studies." *San Francisco Chronicle,* 17 June 1998, final ed.: A17.

Lesher, Dave. "Deadlock on Prop. 187 Has Backers, Governor Fuming; Immigration: Wilson Seeks Rare Rebuke of Federal Judge, Claiming She Is Tying Up Measure Passed in 1994." *Los Angeles Times,* 8 November 1998, home ed., sec. A: 1.

Limón, José. *Dancing with the Devil: Society and Cultural Poetics in Mexican-American South Texas.* Madison: University of Wisconsin Press, 1994.

Loewen, James W. *Lies My Teacher Told Me: Everything Your American History Textbook Got Wrong.* New York: Simon and Schuster, 1996.

López, Sonia. "The Role of the Chicana within the Student Movement." In *Essays on La Mujer,* ed. Rosaura Sánchez and Rosa Martinez Cruz, 16–29. Los Angeles: Chicano Studies Publications, UCLA, 1977.

Lorde, Audre. "The Master's Tools Will Never Dismantle the Master's House." In *This Bridge Called My Back: Writings by Radical Women of Color,* 2d ed., ed. Cherríe Moraga and Gloria Anzaldúa, 98–101. New York: Kitchen Table Women of Color Press, 1983.

———. *Sister Outsider.* Freedom, Calif.: The Crossing Press, 1984.

Lucero-Trujillo, Marcela Christine. "Machismo Is Part of Our Culture." In *The Third Woman: Minority Women Writers of the United States,* ed. Dexter Fisher, 401–3. Boston: Houghton Mifflin, 1980.

Lugones, Maria. "Purity, Impurity, and Separation." *Signs* (Winter 1994): 458–79.

Marquez, Antonio C. "Richard Rodriguez's *Hunger of Memory* and the Poetics of Experience." *Arizona Quarterly* 40.2 (1984): 130–41.

Martin, Biddy. "Sexualities without Genders and Other Queer Utopias." *Diacritics* 24.2–3 (1994): 104–21.

McDonnell, Patrick J. "California and the West; Judge's Final Order Kills Key Points of Prop. 187; Courts: A Permanent Injunction Is Levied on the '94 Measure Targeting Illegal Immigrants' Use of Public Benefits." *Los Angeles Times,* 19 March 1998, home ed., sec. A: 3.

———. "Prop. 187 Found Unconstitutional by Federal Judge; Law: Decision Means Anti-Illegal Immigration Measure Won't Be Implemented, Barring Appeal. But Initiative's Supporters Condemn Outcome, Plan Plea to Higher Court." *Los Angeles Times,* 15 November 1997, home ed., sec. A: 1.

McGowan, John. *Postmodernism and Its Critics.* Ithaca: Cornell University Press, 1991.

Mignolo, Walter. *The Darker Side of the Renaissance: Literacy, Territoriality, and Colonization.* Ann Arbor: University of Michigan Press, 1995.

Miner, Valerie. "Hopes, Fears, and Secrets." Review of *Under the Feet of Jesus,* by Helena María Viramontes. *Women's Review of Books* 13.1 (1995): 19–20.

Mohanty, Chandra Talpade, Ann Russo, and Lourdes Torres, eds. *Third World Women and the Politics of Feminism.* Bloomington: Indiana University Press, 1991.

Mohanty, Satya P. "Can Our Values Be Objective? On Ethics, Aesthetics, and Progressive Politics." *New Literary History* 32. 4 (2001).

———. "The Epistemic Status of Cultural Identity: On *Beloved* and the Postcolonial Condition." *Cultural Critique* 24 (Spring 1993): 41–80.

———. *Literary Theory and the Claims of History: Postmodernism, Objectivity, Multicultural Politics.* Ithaca: Cornell University Press, 1997.

Moraga, Cherríe. *The Last Generation.* Boston: South End Press, 1993.

———. *Loving in the War Years: Lo que nunca pasó por sus labios.* Boston: South End Press, 1983.

———. *Waiting in the Wings: Portrait of a Queer Motherhood.* Ithaca: Firebrand Books, 1997.

Moraga, Cherríe, and Gloria Anzaldúa, eds. *This Bridge Called My Back: Writings by Radical Women of Color.* 2d ed. New York: Kitchen Table Women of Color Press, 1983.

Moses, Michele S. "The Relationship between Self-Determination, the Social Context of Choice, and Authenticity." In *Philosophy of Education, 2000,* ed. Lynda Stone, 294–302. Urbana-Champaign, IL: Philosophy of Education Society, 2001.

Moya, Paula M. L. "Why I Am Not Hispanic: An Argument with Jorge Gracia." *The American Philosophical Association Newsletter on Hispanic/Latino Issues in Philosophy* 00.2 (2001) 100–105.

Moya, Paula M. L., and Michael R. Hames-García, eds. *Reclaiming Identity: Realist Theory and the Predicament of Postmodernism.* Berkeley: University of California Press, 2000.

Muñoz, Carlos Jr. *Youth, Identity, Power: The Chicano Movement.* London: Verso, 1989.

National Commission on Excellence in Education. *A Nation at Risk: The Imperative for Educational Reform. A Report to the Nation and the Secretary of Education, United States Department of Education.* Washington, D.C.: National Commission on Excellence in Education, 1983.

"New UC Berkeley Admission Figures Show Modest Gain in Underrepresented Minority Students for Fall 1999." *UC News Wire.* 3 April 2000. University of California. 23 August 2000: http://www.ucnewswire.org/articles/99/03/ucb%20admissions/html.

Nguyen, Minh T. " 'It Matters to Get the Facts Straight': Joy Kogawa, Realism, and Objectivity of Values." In *Reclaiming Identity: Realist Theory and the Predicament of Postmodernism,* ed. Paula M. L. Moya and Michael R. Hames-García, 171–204. Berkeley: University of California Press, 2000.

Nicholson, Linda J., ed. *Feminism/Postmodernism.* New York: Routledge, 1990.

Nicholson, Linda J., and Steven Seidman, eds. *Social Postmodernism: Beyond Identity Politics.* Cambridge: Cambridge University Press, 1995.

Norris, Christopher. *Truth and the Ethics of Criticism*. Manchester: Manchester University Press, 1994.

Oboler, Suzanne. *Ethnic Labels, Latino Lives: Identity and the Politics of (Re)Presentation in the United States*. Minneapolis: University of Minnesota Press, 1995.

Omi, Michael, and Harold Winant. *Racial Formation in the United States: From the 1960s to the 1990s*. New York: Routledge, 1994.

Owens, Louis, and Hector Torres. "Dialogic Structure and Levels of Discourse in Steinbeck's *The Grapes of Wrath*." *Arizona Quarterly* 45.4 (1989): 75–94.

Padilla, Genaro. Introduction to *The Short Stories of Fray Angelico Chavez*, ed. Genaro Padilla, vii–xx. Albuquerque: University of New Mexico Press, 1987.

———. *My History, Not Yours: The Formation of Mexican American Autobiography*. Madison: University of Wisconsin Press, 1993.

Palumbo-Liu, David, ed. *The Ethnic Canon: Histories, Institutions, and Interventions*. Minneapolis: University of Minnesota Press, 1995.

Paz, Octavio. "The Sons of La Malinche." Trans. Lysander Kemp. *The Labyrinth of Solitude*, 65–88. New York: Grove Press, 1985.

Pederson, Rena. "Diversity and Assimilation." *Dallas Morning News*, 4 April 1995, Sunday final ed., sec. editorials: 2J.

Pesquera, Beatriz M., and Denise M. Segura. "There Is No Going Back: Chicanas and Feminism." In *Chicana Critical Issues*, ed. Norma Alarcón, Rafaela Castro, Emma Pérez, Beatriz Pesquera, Adaljiza Sosa Riddell, and Patricia Zavella, 95–115. Berkeley: Third Woman Press, 1993.

Phillips, Rachel. "Marina/Malinche: Masks and Shadows." In *Women in Hispanic Literature*, ed. Beth Miller, 97–114. Berkeley: University of California Press, 1983.

Postrel, Virginia, and Nick Gillespie. "On Borders and Belonging: A Conversation with Richard Rodriguez." *Utne Reader* (March/April 1995): 76–79.

Putnam, Hilary. "Explanation and Reference." In *Mind, Language, and Reality*, 196–214. New York: Cambridge University Press, 1975.

———. "The Meaning of 'Meaning.' " In *Mind, Language, and Reality*, 215–71. New York: Cambridge University Press, 1975.

———. *Mind, Language, and Reality*. New York: Cambridge University Press, 1975.

———. *Realism with a Human Face*. Cambridge: Harvard University Press, 1990.

———. *Reason, Truth, and History*. Cambridge: Cambridge University Press, 1981.

Ravitch, Diane. "Diversity and Democracy: Multicultural Education in America." *American Educator* 14.1 (1990): 16–20, 46–48.

Reagon, Bernice Johnson. "Coalition Politics: Turning the Century." In *Homegirls: A Black Feminist Anthology*, ed. Barbara Smith, 356–68. New York: Kitchen Table Women of Color Press, 1983.

Rimmon-Kenan, Shlomith. *Narrative Fiction: Contemporary Poetics*. London: Methuen, 1983.

Ristine, Jeff. "New Data Maintain Minority Dip in UC Freshman Admissions." *San Diego Union-Tribune*, 6 May 1998: A7.

————. "UC Figures on Minority Admissions Fine-Tuned; Systemwide, Picture Called Encouraging." *San Diego Union-Tribune*, 3 April 1998, first ed.: A1.

Rivera, Tomás. "Remembering, Discovery, and Volition in the Literary Imaginative Process." Trans. Gustavo Valadez. In *Tomás Rivera: The Complete Works*, ed. Julián Olivares, 365–70. Houston: Arte Público Press, 1975.

————. "Richard Rodriguez' *Hunger of Memory* as Humanistic Antithesis." *MELUS* 11.4 (1984): 5–13.

————. *. . . y no se lo tragó la tierra/. . . And the Earth Did Not Part*. Trans. Evangelina Vigil-Piñon. Houston: Arte Público Press, 1987.

Robinson, Clay. "UT Regents Right in Appealing Hopwood." *Houston Chronicle*, 17 May 1998, star ed., sec. outlook: 2.

Rodríguez, Luis J. *Always Running, La Vida Loca: Gang Days in L.A.* New York: Simon and Schuster, 1993.

Rodriguez, Richard. *Days of Obligation: An Argument with My Mexican Father.* New York: Penguin, 1992.

————. *Hunger of Memory: The Education of Richard Rodriguez.* New York: Bantam Books, 1983.

Roman, Leslie. "White Is a Color! White Defensiveness, Postmodernism, and Anti-racist Pedagogy." In *Race, Identity, and Representation in Education*, ed. Cameron McCarthy and Warren Crichlow, 71–88. New York: Routledge, 1993.

Roof, Judith. "Lesbians and Lyotard: Legitimation and the Politics of the Name." In *The Lesbian Postmodern*, ed. Laura Doan, 47–66. New York: Columbia University Press, 1994.

Rosaldo, Renato. *Culture and Truth: The Remaking of Social Analysis.* Boston: Beacon Press, 1989.

Ruíz, Vicki L. *From Out of the Shadows: Mexican Women in Twentieth-Century America.* New York: Oxford University Press, 1998.

Saldívar, José David. *Border Matters: Remapping American Cultural Studies.* Berkeley: University of California Press, 1997.

————. *The Dialectics of Our America: Genealogy, Cultural Critique, and Literary History.* Durham: Duke University Press, 1991.

Saldívar, Ramón. *Chicano Narrative: The Dialectics of Difference.* Madison: University of Wisconsin Press, 1990.

Saldívar-Hull, Sonia. *Feminism on the Border: Chicana Gender Politics and Literature.* Berkeley: University of California Press, 2000.

Sánchez, George J. *Becoming Mexican American: Ethnicity, Culture, and Identity in Chicano Los Angeles, 1900–1945.* New York: Oxford University Press, 1993.

Sánchez, Rene. "With Ban on Preferences, UC Will Enroll 12% Blacks, Hispanics." *Washington Post*, 21 May 1998, sec. A: A10.

Sánchez, Rosaura. "Calculated Musings: Richard Rodriguez's Metaphysics of Difference." In *The Ethnic Canon: Histories, Institutions, and Interventions*, ed. David Palumbo-Liu, 153–73. Minneapolis: University of Minnesota, 1995.

————. "Postmodernism and Chicano Literature." *Aztlán* 18.2 (1987): 1–14.

———. *Telling Identities: The California Testimonios*. Minneapolis: University of Minnesota Press, 1995.

Sánchez, Rosaura, and Beatrice Pita. Introduction to *The Squatter and the Don*, ed. Rosaura Sánchez and Beatrice Pita, 5–51. Houston: Arte Público Press, 1992.

Sánchez, Rosaura, and Rosa Martinez Cruz, eds. *Essays on La Mujer*. Los Angeles: Chicano Studies Publications, UCLA, 1977.

Sánchez Korrol, Virginia. *From Colonia to Community: The History of Puerto Ricans in New York City*. 2d ed. Berkeley: University of California Press, 1983.

Sandler, Gregory. "The Affirmative Action Issue; A Policy Designed for Equal Opportunity Is Under Attack and Inspiring Debate." *Hartford Courant*, 29 March 1998, statewide ed., sec. business: 8.

Sandoval, Chela. "Feminism and Racism: A Report on the 1981 National Women's Studies Association Conference." In *Making Face, Making Soul/Haciendo Caras: Creative and Critical Perspectives by Women of Color*, ed. Gloria Anzaldúa, 55–71. San Francisco: Aunt Lute Books, 1990.

———. "U.S. Third World Feminism: The Theory and Method of Oppositional Consciousness in the Postmodern World." *Genders* 10 (Spring 1991): 1–24.

Schlesinger, Arthur M. Jr. *The Disuniting of America*. New York: W. W. Norton, 1992.

Schutte, Ofelia. "Negotiating Latina Identities." In *Hispanics/Latinos in the United States: Ethnicity, Race, and Rights*, ed. Jorge J. E. Gracia and Pablo De Greiff, 61–75. New York: Routledge, 2000.

Scott, Joan. " 'Experience.' " In *Feminists Theorize the Political*, ed. Judith Butler and Joan Scott, 22–40. New York: Routledge, 1992.

Seymour, Gene. "The Great Debate." *Newsday*, 10 October 1990, city ed., part 2: 8.

Singer, Linda. "Feminism and Postmodernism." In *Feminists Theorize the Political*, ed. Judith Butler and Joan Scott, 464–75. New York: Routledge, 1992.

Sleeter, Christine E., and Carl A. Grant. "An Analysis of Multicultural Education in the United States." *Harvard Educational Review* 57.4 (1987): 421–44.

Smith, Barbara Herrnstein. *Belief and Resistance: Dynamics of Contemporary Intellectual Controversy*. Cambridge: Harvard University Press, 1997.

———. *Contingencies of Value: Alternative Perspectives for Critical Theory*. Cambridge: Harvard University Press, 1988.

Smith, Valerie. "Black Feminist Theory and the Representation of the 'Other.'" In *Changing Our Own Words: Essays on Criticism, Theory, and Writing by Black Women*, ed. Cheryl Wall, 38–57. New Brunswick: Rutgers University Press, 1989.

Sollors, Werner. "The Roots of Ethnicity: Etymology and Definitions." In *Harvard Encyclopedia of American Ethnic Groups*, ed. Stephan Thernstrom, 647–65. Cambridge: Harvard University Press, 1980.

Steele, Shelby. *The Content of Our Character: A New Vision of Race in America*. New York: St. Martin's Press, 1990.

Steinbeck, John. *The Grapes of Wrath*. New York: Viking, 1939.

Stone-Mediatore, Shari. "Chandra Mohanty and the Revaluing of 'Experience.' "
   Hypatia 13.2 (1998): 116–33.

Taylor, Charles. "The Politics of Recognition." In *Multiculturalism: Examining
   the Politics of Recognition,* ed. Amy Gutman, 25–73. Princeton: Princeton
   University Press, 1994.

Trujillo, Carla. "Chicana Lesbians: Fear and Loathing in the Chicano Community." In *Chicana Lesbians: The Girls Our Mothers Warned Us About,* ed.
   Carla Trujillo, 186–94. Berkeley: Third Woman Press, 1991.

———, ed. *Living Chicana Theory.* Berkeley: Third Woman Press, 1998.

Ulichny, Polly. "Cultures in Conflict." *Anthropology and Education Quarterly*
   27.3 (1996): 331–64.

Van Hamme, Linda. "American Indian Cultures and the Classroom." *Journal of
   American Indian Education* (Winter 1996): 21–36.

Vidal, Mirta. "New Voice of La Raza: Chicanas Speak Out." In *Chicana Feminist Thought: The Basic Historical Writings,* ed. Alma M. García, 21–24.
   New York: Routledge, 1997.

Villanueva-Collado, Alfredo. "Growing Up Hispanic: Discourse and Ideology in
   Hunger of Memory and *Family Installments." The Americas Review* 16.3–4
   (1988): 75–90.

Viramontes, Helena María. *Under the Feet of Jesus.* New York: Dutton Press,
   1995.

Waugh, Patricia. Introduction to *Postmodernism: A Reader,* ed. Patricia Waugh,
   1–10. London: Edward Arnold, 1992.

Weiss, Kenneth. "Fewer Blacks and Latinos Admitted to Three UC Schools; Education: Irvine, San Diego and Davis Report Declines in First Year after Affirmative Action Was Banned. Two Less Selective Campuses Show Increases."
   Los Angeles Times, 17 March 1998, home ed., sec. A:1.

———, "Mixing Commencement and Culture; Education; UC Regents Debate
   Appropriateness of Ethnic Celebrations." *Los Angeles Times,* 20 June 1998,
   home ed.: A1.

Wells, Amy Stuart, and Irene Serna. "The Politics of Culture: Understanding
   Local Political Resistance to Detracking in Racially Mixed Schools." *Harvard
   Educational Review* 66.1 (1996): 93–118.

Wilkerson, William S. "Is There Something You Need to Tell Me? Coming Out
   and the Ambiguity of Experience." In *Reclaiming Identity: Realist Theory
   and the Predicament of Postmodernism,* ed. Paula M. L. Moya and Michael
   R. Hames-García, 251–78. Berkeley: University of California Press, 2000.

Wills, John S. "Who Needs Multicultural Education? White Students, U.S. History, and the Construction of a Usable Past." *Anthropology and Education
   Quarterly* 27.3 (1996): 365–89.

Wyatt, David. Introduction to *New Essays on "The Grapes of Wrath,"* 1–26.
   New York: Cambridge University Press, 1990.

———, ed. *New Essays on "The Grapes of Wrath."* New York: Cambridge University Press, 1990.

Yarbro-Bejarano, Yvonne. "Gloria Anzaldúa's *Borderlands/La frontera:* Cultural
   Studies, 'Difference,' and the Non-Unitary Subject." *Cultural Critique* 28
   (Fall 1994): 5–28.

Zammito, John H. "Reading 'Experience': The Debate in Intellectual History among Scott, Toews, and LaCapra." In *Reclaiming Identity: Realist Theory and the Predicament of Postmodernism,* ed. Paula M. L. Moya and Michael R. Hames-García, 279–311. Berkeley: University of California Press, 2000.

Zamora, Bernice. "Notes from a Chicana 'Coed.' " *Caracol* 3.9 (1977): 19.

Index

Adams, Natalie, 151, 171
affirmative action, 4; opposition to, 4–5,
101–2, 113, 134, 141–43; University
of California and, 141; University of
Texas and, 141n9
African Americans, 4, 106, 112, 141. *See
also* Carter, Stephen; multicultural education; Steele, Shelby
agency: human, 20–21, 214; literacy
and, 178–79, 204–8; neoconservative
minority view of, 113–14, 133–34;
political struggle and, 12
Alarcón, Norma, 60–61, 66–77; and
Chicanas, 70, 73–74, 77; and discursive contradiction, 67–70, 76–77; and
identity, 69–70, 73; and "subjects-in-
process," 69–74, 75–77
Alcoff, Linda Martín, 9n12, 25, 32n, 58,
99, 187n10; on epistemological denial,
83n25; on strategic essentialism, 15n20
Alexander, Jacqui, 58
Anzaldúa, Gloria, 35n10, 62, 65; and
Borderlands/La Frontera, 78, 88, 95n,
176n2; on *la facultad*, 88; on mestiza
consciousness, 78
Appiah, K. Anthony, 106
Apple, Michael, 166
asimilao, the value of being, 127–28
assimilation, 103n7, 108n11; ethnicity
and, 100–101; multicultural education
and, 154–57, 163–64; neoconservative
minorities and, 102–5, 111–12, 115,
120–21, 127n, 133–34; problems

with, 126–29, 165; value of, 104, 105,
126, 163–64

Babbitt, Susan, 212
Bal, Mieke, 186, 187n, 190, 199n23
Banks, James, 146–47
bias. *See* theoretical mediation
bilingualism, 4, 125–26; education
and, 127n, 136, 142, 145, 148–49,
163–64
Bourdieu, Pierre, 149–50
Boyd, Dwight, 172–73
Boyd, Richard, 12, 15n21, 44, 62
Butler, Judith: and the category of
women, 34; and Cherríe Moraga, 33–
36; and constructivism, 10n, 11n16;
and identity and experience, 10–11,
11n15, 24, 34n, 35–36, 72; and normative judgments, 59; and race, 37n14;
and women of color, 26n

Calhoun, Craig, 6n7, 8n, 16n24
Carter, Stephen: and affirmative action,
113; and meritocracy, 112–13. *See
also* neoconservative minorities
Castellanos, Rosario, 204n
causality: identity formation and, 72–73;
social location and experience and, 50,
86–87. *See also* reference
Chávez, Linda: and American identity,
104; and Hispanic identity, 43n22; and
Out of the Barrio, 114. *See also* neoconservative minorities

Compositor:	BookMatters, Inc.
Text:	10/13 Sabon
Display:	Sabon
Printer and Binder:	Haddon Craftsmen, Inc.